BANKERS IN THE IVORY TOWER

Bankers in the Ivory Tower

The Troubling Rise of Financiers in US Higher Education

CHARLIE EATON

The University of Chicago Press • Chicago & London

The University of Chicago Press, Chicago 60637
The University of Chicago Press, Ltd., London

Published 2022
Printed in the United States of America

31 30 29 28 27 26 25 24 23 22   1 2 3 4 5

ISBN-13: 978-0-226-72042-5 (cloth)
ISBN-13: 978-0-226-72056-2 (e-book)
DOI: https://doi.org/10.7208/chicago/9780226720562.001.0001

Library of Congress Cataloging-in-Publication Data
Names: Eaton, Charlie, author.
Title: Bankers in the ivory tower : the troubling rise of financiers in US higher education / Charlie Eaton.
Description: Chicago : University of Chicago Press, 2022. | Includes bibliographical references and index.
Identifiers: LCCN 2021035850 | ISBN 9780226720425 (cloth) | ISBN 9780226720562 (ebook)
Subjects: LCSH: Education, Higher—United States—Finance. | Education, Higher—Finance—Social aspects—United States. | Education, Higher—Economic aspects—United States. | Capitalists and financiers—United States. | Elite (Social sciences)—United States.
Classification: LCC LB2342 .E19 2022 | DDC 378.1/06—dc23
LC record available at https://lccn.loc.gov/2021035850

♾ This paper meets the requirements of ANSI/NISO Z39.48-1992 (Permanence of Paper).

For all those who have been excluded or exploited by bankers in the ivory tower

CONTENTS

Acknowledgments · *ix*

1. Universities and the Social Circuitry of Finance · *1*
2. Our New Financial Oligarchy · *17*
3. Bankers to the Rescue: The Political Turn to Student Debt · *36*
4. The Top: How Universities Became Hedge Funds · *54*
5. The Bottom: A Wall Street Takeover of For-Profit Colleges · *76*
6. The Middle: A Hidden Squeeze on Public Universities · *98*
7. Reimagining (Higher Education) Finance from Below · *122*

Methodological Appendix: A Comparative, Qualitative, and Quantitative Study of Elites · *145*

Notes · *155*

References · *171*

Index · *189*

ACKNOWLEDGMENTS

As with all new ideas, any original insights in this book came from conversations—literal and figurative—with other thinkers past and present. My role in writing this book resembles what sociologist Marshall Ganz has called a borderland actor. A borderland actor facilitates dialogue between people across different fields so that they can reconcile their different experiences and ideas and, in doing so, create new ideas. In writing this book, I exchanged thoughts and observations with community organizers, union leaders, policy advocates, and academic thinkers of many stripes, including sociologists, political scientists, economists, and organizational scholars. A mostly chronological account will illustrate how many people shaped this book. I am grateful to them all.

Unlike many books by academics, *Bankers in the Ivory Tower* initially sprung from conversations with people outside of the professoriate. Several friends who lead community organizations and labor unions steered my attention to the power of financiers in higher education, including Liz Perlman, Claudia Preparata, and Kathryn Lybarger of the University of California (UC) service workers union AFSCME 3299. I am similarly indebted to early discussions with Amy Schur and Christina Livingston of the Alliance of Californians for Community Empowerment and Jono Shaffer and Stephen Lerner of SEIU.

My academic exchanges for this book started at UC Berkeley with Adam Goldstein, Jacob Habinek, Mukul Kumar, Tamera Lee Stover, Alex Roehrkasse, Jeremy Thompson, Cyrus Dioun, Daniela García Santibáñez Godoy, and Robert Osley-Thomas. I coauthored multiple studies with these colleagues that began to develop the ideas for this book, including the title *Bankers in the Ivory Tower*. Adam and Jacob have provided invaluable feedback on many portions of this book in the years since. Adam recommended that I develop the metaphor of a social circuitry of finance.

My graduate school advisors Margaret Weir, Neil Fligstein, Marion Fourcade, and Henry Brady all provided essential guidance and generous encouragement. From Margaret, I learned how to think about higher education as part of a welfare state that can be warped when private organizations deliver social goods and services. Neil schooled me in how shareholder value institutions and ideologies can empower financiers over subordinate groups like workers, consumers, and students. Marion taught me how to think about student debt and finance as a classification system. Marion also made the critical suggestion that my collaborators and I incorporate an analysis of elite schools with endowments. Henry tutored me in the quantitative methods used in the book while providing a sounding board for how ideas from political science and economics might strengthen my work.

Via Henry, I joined forces with physicist Bob Birgeneau, sociologist Mike Hout, economist Sheisha Kulkarni, sociologist John Stiles, and historian John Douglass to study how public universities have continued to provide a much larger and affordable pathway for social mobility than do private institutions, despite curbs on adequate state funding. The insights and data from our work together were essential for chapters 6 and 7.

While hanging around Henry's office at UC Berkeley's policy school, I talked with economist Constantine Yannelis after he presented his work on student loan defaults. So began a partnership with Constantine and economist Sabrina Howell to link data on private equity ownership of for-profit colleges to a battery of measures for predatory practices and student welfare at those colleges. Chapter 5 would not have been possible without this data and our work together.

I further developed this book in Carol Christ's Gardner Seminar at the UC Berkeley Center for Studies in Higher Education. Seminarian Patrick Lapid taught me new econometric tricks. Ben Gebre-Medhin focused my overarching argument about how public universities have been squeezed by the diversion of financial resources: to the highly endowed strata of private universities and to the bottom strata of predatory for-profit colleges.

I also benefited from a multiyear dialogue with Mitchell Stevens about universities as hubs where people—and, I argue, especially elites—connect across geography and different social domains of industry, media, technology, leisure, and government. Reading and corresponding with Tressie McMillan Cottom similarly helped me expand my thinking about how the role of financiers in higher education is linked to precarity and inequality in what she calls the new economy.

A host of scholars and policy experts helped me hone my analyses in the later stages of writing the book. Sharla Alegria, David Bergeron, Amy Binder, Ken-Hou Lin, Richard Lachmann, Christopher Loss, Megan Neely, Beth Popp Berman, John Skrentny, and Sheila Slaughter all provided generous written comments on chapters. Through the miracle of Twitter, Beth also connected me with Albina Gibadullina, with whom I built the data sets of financiers and other elites used in this book. Hyunsu Oh also provided valuable research assistance on data carpentry. UC Merced librarian extraordinaire Elizabeth Salmon helped secure university board membership records from several recalcitrant institutions that shall remain unnamed.

Through his artful convening, Fred Wherry included me in a new round of exchanges between academics, civic leaders, and policy advocates about student debt. Conversations with Fenaba Addo, Seth Frotman, Alexis Goldstein, Darrick Hamilton, Jason Houle, Tressie, and Fred were especially helpful for chapter 7's account of racial inequalities in student debt and the growing push for debt cancellation and free college. Separate conversations with policy advocates and analysts Debbie Cochrane, Max Espinoza, Bob Shireman, Laura Szabo-Kubitz, Jessica Thompson, and Jeanice Warden-Washington helped me to understand the labyrinthine minutia of state and federal financial aid policy and how they affect students in real life.

This book never would have been possible without mentorship from Paul Almeida, Ed Flores, Ed Walker, and especially Laura Hamilton, who read almost every chapter of the manuscript at least once. Laura and my incredible editor Elizabeth Branch Dyson patiently advised me on how to craft a compelling story that connects the multifarious ways that financiers have transformed higher education. If I have succeeded, it is because of them.

Finally, friends and family kept me from drifting too far out of touch in an ivory tower of my own. Ben, Brandon, Brett, Chelsea, my brother Chris, Dan, Dave, David, Dugan, Justin, Kelsey, Kevin, Leighton, my brother Matt, Sabina, Sean, Seth, Sol, Tom, Thomas, Veva, and, more than anyone, my wife, Emily Jane, sustained me with the joy of their company, music, and the outdoors (tutoring from Emily Jane also helped me improve the software replication packages for the book). These familiars and my parents, who both read much of the manuscript, told me when my ideas were or were not comprehensible to anyone outside of the academic bubble. Hopefully I got a few things right that will pass this test.

1. Universities and the Social Circuitry of Finance

Every fall as students return to college, the United States observes two relatively new rituals. First, higher education watchers and the media gawk at whether Harvard, Yale, or some other elite school added the most cash to its multibillion-dollar endowment in the previous year.[1] Around the same time, and without a trace of irony, commentators debate the potential social consequences of the latest record-breaking growth in student debt.[2]

The rise of wealthy college endowments and student debt have together contributed to increasingly obscene inequality in US higher education and in American society at large. While the most elite private universities typically have grown their endowments tenfold, they also have hoarded this expanding wealth by maintaining undergraduate enrollments close to 1970s levels. As a result, spending on education-related costs by the top ten schools in the US News & World Report rankings grew from an already high $50,000 per student in 1988 to more than $100,000 per student since 2010.[3] This spending has primarily benefited students from privileged backgrounds who dominate admissions to the most elite private universities.[4]

Beyond the Ivy League's islands of wealth, the majority of students now leave college with the burden of student debt. This has not always been the case. In 1975, just one in eight students used student loans to pay for college.[5] Scholars have only begun to unpack the social consequences of these debts. We do know, however, that student debt leaves borrowers at an economic disadvantage relative to wealthier students. This is because most wealthy students, including a supermajority of all students at elite private institutions, leave college debt-free.[6] At Harvard, only 2 percent of undergraduates today take out any federal student loans at all.[7]

Although researchers have begun to study the consequences of rising student debt, few have investigated what caused it.[8] We have even less research to explain the growth of concentrated endowment wealth and its overwhelming use for the benefit of a privileged few. Observers also rarely recognize that these trends are connected. In *Bankers in the Ivory Tower*, I ask why and how these interwoven changes occurred.

The rise of student debt and bulging endowments is not just a story of inequality in higher education. As organizations that confer social rank, social connections, and claims to moral superiority, colleges have become ever more important as sites where people vie for status and resources. Consequently, colleges are microcosms for observing the causes and consequences of rising inequality in America and how they are inextricably tied to the resurgent power of financiers.

Intimate University Ties and the Power of Financiers

Even in comparison to other elites, financiers derive unusual power and profits from colleges and universities. As a result, colleges and financiers have played outsized roles in each other's recent transformations. To explain how the two are linked, I start by tracing who financiers are and what financiers do.

Critically, financiers hold powerful economic roles as middlemen. (They remain overwhelmingly men, especially in high finance.) In myriad varieties of these middleman roles, financiers broker resource transfers between every corner of the economy, including universities and their students. Some key financier roles in higher education include those of commercial bankers who lend to students, hedge fund managers who oversee endowment investments, private equity partners who buy and manage for-profit colleges, and investment bankers who sell university bonds.

Both economists and popular critics have characterized financiers as unusually individualistic, cold, and calculating.[9] As with all good lies, there is some truth in this contention. But financiers also collectively secure their wealth through an unparalleled web of intimate social ties to other elites. Sociologist Viviana Zelizer defines intimate ties as those that convey private information—from feelings we share with only an inner circle to a hedge fund's internal investment plan. In contrast, impersonal ties share only public information, such as the interest rate for a student loan or the price of a stock in a for-profit college.

Scholars of elites have shown that prestigious universities have long been central nodes for financiers' intimate ties. Financiers gain credentials, connections, and social status from their elite university educations more than any other group of US economic elites. Among the four hundred wealthiest billionaires in America, 65 percent of private equity and hedge fund managers have bachelor's degrees from the nation's top thirty private universities.[10] But among technology billionaires, the group with the second most elite degrees, only 36 percent are alumni of the top thirty private schools. This nexus between the Ivy League and high finance has helped maintain the sector's top echelons as the nearly exclusive providence of the well pedigreed.[11]

Compared to other elites, financiers derive more economic benefits from their university ties because financiers of all varieties trade formally and informally in private information. Financiers use private information to assess credit risks, evaluate potential investments, and solicit capital from investors.[12] For example, hedge fund investor Tom Steyer learned from a friend at the 1988 Yale homecoming football game that Yale's endowment manager David Swensen was beginning to make hedge fund investments. Steyer parlayed the tip into raising $300 million, a third of his initial capital, from Yale's endowment.[13] Tales like Steyer's pepper the histories of America's largest private equity and hedge funds.

Financial deregulation since the late 1970s and 1980s gave financiers more freedom to leverage intimate ties and private information for profit. This simultaneously made collegiate ties more valuable and opened new lines of business in the financing of higher education itself. Deregulation let financiers borrow, lend, invest, and trade with fewer restrictions and lower taxes on their profits. As a result, investors could borrow more to make bigger financial bets based on private knowledge. These financiers surpassed in prestige and influence the leaders of other dominant institutions, including government, industrial corporations, and universities. Scholars have referred to this growing power and centrality of financial markets as the *financialization* of society.[14] As the US economy financialized, growing dependence on financiers induced even the leaders of *nonfinancial* institutions to adopt a financial logic: that money should always be allocated where it will yield the highest rate of return. University leaders have been no exception.

These far-reaching financial ideas and financial institutions can be thought of as a social circuitry of finance that connects every member of society, with financiers positioned as the transistors. Imagining a social circuitry helps us see the actions and choices of people that are missing from many abstract accounts of financialization. The circuitry is social because its connective financial ideas and institutions are neither natural nor robotic. In fact, Zelizer and sociologist Frederick Wherry show that the ideas and institutions of social circuits are "incessantly negotiated" through the interactions of people.[15]

Just as transistors connect the varied segments of electronic circuits, financiers and their organizations connect the varied financial relations of billions of people around the world. For example, finance's social circuitry wires the subordinate relationships of student loan borrowers to the investment fund managers that own for-profit colleges. But the circuitry also fuses more equitable interactions between university endowment officers and those same fund managers who invest in for-profit colleges. These complex connections often escape the comprehension of the people involved, including financiers. For proof of this incomprehension, consider that nearly all financiers and financial regulators failed to anticipate the collapse of the mortgage-backed derivative markets that connected homeowners to bond investors.[16]

Financial Deregulation and Higher Education Inequality

In the context of financial deregulation and declining government support for universities, a variety of financiers expanded the social circuitry of finance via three critical interventions in US higher education. First, commercial bankers mobilized to promote radical changes to federal student loan policies. Second, former investment bankers enlisted the endowment managers of their wealthy alma maters to provide some of the earliest and most important capital for their upstart private equity and hedge funds. Third, private equity managers acquired hundreds of for-profit colleges that used federal student loan expansion to prey on millions of working-class and racially marginalized students. Together these interventions drove new and widening inequalities in US higher education.

Financiers' three interventions played out differently across three organizational strata of US universities: elite private colleges at the top, for-profit colleges at the bottom, and less-selective public and private colleges in the middle. At the top, elite private universities hoarded their booming endowments for the benefit of small and mostly well-off student bodies. At the bottom, financial investors' profit model saddled students with greater debt in order to increase tuition revenue. In the middle, public institutions were squeezed by the diversion of government funding to tax cuts and subsidies for financiers and their clients. The diversion of government funding included tens of billions of dollars in annual tax exemptions for university endowments and for public subsidies to for-profit colleges. In response, public universities used student loans to increase tuition revenue. Over the course of this book, I will unpack how these transformations unfolded within each of the three strata.

The results of these transformations are higher education inequalities that both mirror and contribute to expanding wealth and income disparities in America. While the United States was once a leader among wealthy countries in college attainment, growth in US bachelor's degree completion slowed after the 1970s. While the United States continues to compete internationally in rates of college attendance, the nation lags in the share of students who ultimately receive a four-year degree. Just 40 percent of those aged twenty-five to thirty-four held bachelor's degrees in 2019. With this slow growth, the United States fell to eighteenth among the thirty-seven nations tracked by the Organisation for Economic Co-operation and Development (OECD).[17]

The United States has fallen even further when it comes to educational mobility. Americans from the baby boomer generation attained higher degrees than their parents about as often as baby boomers in the median OECD nation. But the US gap in bachelor's degree attainment between young people in the top and bottom quartiles for parental income actually widened from 40 percentage points to 44 percentage points between 1970 and 2015.[18] As a result, the United States now ranks just twenty-fourth among OECD countries for the share of people aged twenty-five to thirty-four who have received higher degrees than their parents.[19]

We can draw relatively straight lines from the financial transformations of US colleges to their persistent roles in social and economic inequality. Behind a veil of meritocracy, finance steers increasing resources to elite private schools where students continue to hail most often from America's white upper class. As of 2017, thirty-eight of the most well-endowed colleges enrolled more students from the top 1 percent of the income spectrum than from the bottom 60 percent combined.[20] Sociologists have shown that this upper-class educational advantage intergenerationally transmits income and wealth, particularly by providing a pathway to the elite MBA, law, and medical degree programs that offer the most valuable intimate ties and credentials.[21]

For-profit colleges also play an outsized role in low educational and income mobility among those whose parents did not complete college. The United States is unique among OECD countries for its large for-profit college system that overwhelmingly enrolls low-income and racially subordinated students. These colleges enrolled 12 percent of all US undergraduates at their peak and have been definitively shown to have provided almost no discernible educational or economic benefit to students.[22]

But financiers' impact on higher education inequalities and economic disparities is most glaring in the highly unequal explosion of student debt. The United States is again unique among wealthy nations for the amount of nondischargeable student debt that it foists on middle-class and lower-income students.[23] Educational debt places these students at further economic disadvantage compared to wealthy students, who overwhelmingly leave college debt-free.

The leg up that wealthy students receive by leaving college debt-free is substantial. Because graduation rates have been suppressed by inadequate instructional funding, a majority of students leaving public institutions with debt do not enjoy the substantial earnings boost that typically comes with a bachelor's degree. Average income boosts from degrees are also far from universal. As a result, 46 percent of all borrowers have missed payments on federal student loans even since the 2008 recession subsided.[24] More than one million federal student loan borrowers have defaulted annually since the 2008 financial crisis, including 47 percent of borrowers at for-profits, 38 percent of borrowers at community colleges, and 27 percent of students at nonselective four-year public and private colleges.[25]

Because of the racial wealth gap and persistent labor market inequalities, student debt outcomes are even worse for Black borrowers. Among students who began college in 2003–2004, Black borrowers still owed 113 percent of their original loan after twelve years due to compounding interest—compared to 83 percent for Latinx students and 65 percent for white students.[26] The prospects for repaying these educational debts only worsened during the severe economic downturn triggered by the COVID-19 pandemic.

These disparities in student debt are exacerbated by the divergent ways that financiers have transformed the three strata of US universities. With booming endowments and wealthy students, elite private institutions have become the last bastion of debt-free college in America. Throughout the rest of the higher education system, student borrowing has grown relentlessly. This unequal expansion of student debt was fastest in the 1990s but has continued since 2000, when it became possible to break out borrowing data between the different strata of colleges.

Figure 1.1 shows the percentage of first-year students with zero student loan debt by strata.[27] The figure breaks out the thirty top-ranked private universities and thirty top-ranked public universities in the 2016 Times Higher Education (THE) rankings. Among the top privates, students with zero educational debt actually increased from 55 percent of first-years in 2001 to 72 percent in 2016. At the bottom, students with zero debt at for-profit colleges declined from 39 percent in 2001 to just 22 percent in 2016. In the middle, the percentage of students with zero debt declined more gradually but fell below 50 percent at less prestigious public universities and private colleges.

Financier-abetted higher education failures have bigger consequences

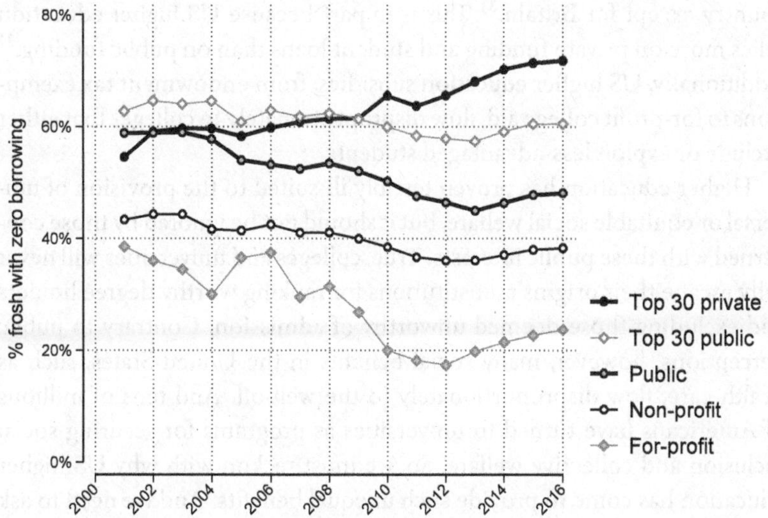

FIGURE 1.1 Percentage frosh with zero student debt by higher education strata

NOTE: Top thirty private and top thirty public universities are based on 2016 Times Higher Education rankings. Student loan borrowing are from the Integrated Postsecondary Education Data System. See Methodological Appendix for a list and further details. Data and code: https://github.com/HigherEdData/bankersintheivorytower.

today because students have fewer noncollege paths to civic and economic empowerment than in other countries or in our past. US labor unions have declined, and welfare-state development has stalled. Financiers also played a leading role in these shifts.[28] As sociologist Tressie McMillan Cottom has written, poor and, especially, Black students turned to for-profit colleges and student loans because of these failures of the new economy and because of their long-standing exclusion from adequately funded public and private institutions.[29] Colleges under the sway of financiers thus exploited and widened the racial inequalities that continue to define American society.

Lacking alternatives, a growing number of Americans have turned to the US higher education system as one of the nation's largest social welfare programs for adults. The nation spends more than $600 billion annually on higher education from public and private sources, the second highest share of all economic activity in the OECD.[30] Government spending and tax subsidies for students and universities are arguably the nation's largest paid job training program—far larger than the $11 billion annual budget for the entire federal Department of Labor. Yet even US public universities charge students more in tuition than public institutions in every OECD country except for Britain.[31] This is in part because US higher education relies more on private funding and student loans than on public funding.[32] Additionally, US higher education subsidies, from endowment tax exemptions to for-profit college aid, flow disproportionately to colleges that either exclude or exploit less-advantaged students.

Higher education has proven terribly ill-suited to the provision of universal or equitable social welfare, but it should not be ignored by those concerned with these public interests. True, colleges and universities will never fully escape their origins as institutions for ranking worthy degree holders and excluding those deemed unworthy of admission. Contrary to public perceptions, however, many social benefits in the United States, such as health care, flow disproportionately to the well-off. And tens of millions of Americans have turned to universities as programs for securing social inclusion and collective welfare. So, we must reckon with why US higher education has come to provide such unequal benefits. And we need to ask how the playing field might be leveled.

The pages ahead will further detail how financiers drove US higher education toward greater inequality. But ivory tower bankers found willing accomplices in both lawmakers and university leaders. Together, they reshaped colleges in varied ways that fit with long-standing organizational differences between the three strata of colleges and universities. To show how these different financial transformations were connected, it will help to first recount how the different strata diverged before the new march of finance.

Universities as Stratified Welfare Providers

As financiers transformed US higher education, they did not start from scratch. They inherited a heterogeneous system that I conceptualize as an organizational ecology of stratified welfare providers.[33] Between the three strata of higher education, colleges have organizational differences in who governs them, whose welfare they primarily serve, and the source and scope of their financial resources. These variations provided financiers with multiple opportunities to advance their status projects and to profit as middlemen in the 1980s when American lawmakers slammed the breaks on taxpayer funding for higher education.

People typically think of welfare systems as distributing social goods such as health care, subsidized housing, and unemployment insurance. The sociologist T. H. Marshall theorized access to these goods as a social right that all persons need in order to participate fully in a society and polity.[34] Few today think of education as Marshall did, as one of the most important social goods provided by the welfare state.[35]

Unlike Social Security or other benefits that entail only a check in the mail, higher education is not a one-size-fits-all social good.[36] Organizational heterogeneity among the three higher education strata reflects the highly varied demands and values associated with different types of specialized knowledge in contemporary societies' complex division of labor. Even the subarea of undergraduate education, which is the focus of this book, ranges from four-year liberal arts programs to community college and for-profit vocational programs that lead to a certificate or license in a matter of months.[37]

To understand US higher education, it also helps to consider another insight from scholars of the welfare state: that social provision in the United States is particularly decentralized because of the federalist institutions of US politics.[38] Federalism historically has favored the delivery of social benefits—from Medicaid to Head Start—through state governments, local agencies, and a mix of for-profit and nonprofit organizations such as private hospitals.[39] Policy choices to support higher education expansion through decentralized federal funding of public and private institutions similarly expanded a heterogeneous multiplicity of colleges within the three organizational strata of higher education.

Policy makers made several attempts during the twentieth century to narrow inequalities between the three strata by using federal spending as a carrot for expanding access to the most elite private colleges. Yet, they encountered resistance from elite universities. For example, several top private university leaders resisted the 1945 GI Bill, viewing it as one of US lawmakers' first major initiatives to pry open their doors for students beyond the children of elite alumni.[40] University of Chicago President Robert M. Hutchins wrote that the bill was a "threat to American education" that would turn universities into "hobo jungles."[41] Ultimately, the GI Bill did spur even private colleges to enroll World War II veterans from a variety of class backgrounds.[42] The GI Bill did so by providing veterans with grants adequate to afford tuition, room, and board at almost any school that would admit them.

Policy makers continued their push to expand higher education access and equity in 1965 in conjunction with President Johnson's establishment of an array of social programs including Medicare, Medicaid, Head Start, and food stamps—all parts of Johnson's Great Society and war on poverty agenda. Through the 1965 Higher Education Act, Congress created what would become the federal Pell Grant program.[43] Ominously, however, lawmakers never assigned Pell Grants full entitlement status. In contrast, Great Society legislation made Medicaid, Medicare, and Social Security full entitlements, which commits adequate funding in future years to cover all the costs of qualifying beneficiaries.

Despite the failure to give Pell Grants full entitlement status, tax-funded government support for higher education gave lawmakers and their constituents more say in the governance of universities and the postsecondary ecology as a whole. State governments built on the GI Bill and Pell Grants by passing laws and allocating funds to push rapid enrollment growth at public universities and community colleges.[44] Voters and their elected representatives also gained authority to elect or appoint the governing boards of rapidly growing state universities and community colleges. To receive funds from the massive expansion of federal financial support under the 1965 Higher Education Act, all colleges and universities also had to comply with new protections for women's rights and civil rights.[45]

As voters and elected representatives gained power in university governance, the taxpayer-funded growth of undergraduate education expanded the middle and bottom strata of US higher education, complicating the metaphor of the university as an ivory tower apart from society. Postsecondary enrollment doubled from five million in 1964 to nearly eleven million in 1975. Most enrollment growth occurred at public universities and community colleges. For-profit colleges also grew by disproportionately enrolling Pell Grant recipients in vocational education niches such as graphic arts and cosmetology. By 1981, 32 percent of US residents over the age of twenty-five had attended at least some college. That share has continued to rise, surpassing 50 percent in 2000 and reaching 61 percent in 2017.[46]

Even before cuts to government funding, however, equity in higher education remained hobbled by a persistent organizational stratification of resources and status between colleges.[47] First, the smaller student bodies at elite private schools continued to hail from wealthier and more educated backgrounds.[48] The expansion of undergraduate education to underrepresented racial and ethnic groups was also incomplete at both elite private schools and more selective public universities.[49] Even at the peak of government funding for undergraduate education in 1975, spending on educational support at institutions serving the most disadvantaged students fell far short of spending at the most elite colleges.[50]

At the end of the 1970s, the rise of a new political coalition between business and the conservative movement effectively ended the incomplete expansion of taxpayer-funded undergraduate education. Later, I document in detail how the combined state and federal funding per student for postsecondary education declined steadily by 28 percentage points from its high of $7,114 in 1976 to just $5,129 in 1994, its lowest level since 1969 (2016 constant dollars). It was during this underappreciated retrenchment of state support that colleges and universities pivoted decisively to financial markets and financial middlemen.

Financial Dependence and Finance Control

It is a maxim of organizational theory that organizations are governed by whoever controls the purse strings. Just as lawmakers and citizens gained more say over universities as they increased government funding, financiers won increasing sway as colleges turned toward financial markets for resources. The increasing power of financiers accordingly eroded newfound popular and democratic influence over who can gain a degree and who will pay for it. This shift parallels a broader decoupling of governance in US industrial corporations from people and concerns that do not align with profit maximization.[51] But university leaders turned to finance in different ways that depended on their position in the tripartite hierarchy of US colleges and universities. Universities' new dependency on financiers thus had divergent impacts on their beneficiaries, with marginalized students at for-profit and less-selective institutions paying the highest prices.

All three strata were reshaped, albeit in different ways, by a massive expansion of federal loan programs in the 1990s. At the top, elite private university leaders could use their baseline endowment wealth and prestige to pocket student loan–financed revenue as gravy for their bounty of investment returns. This worked mostly to the benefit of their privileged students.

At the bottom, investors bought and expanded low-status for-profit colleges to use federal student loan programs for enrolling millions of additional students from low-income households and communities of color. This dependency on student loans left countless students worse off, with unpayable debt and nothing to show for it.

In the middle, less-selective colleges lost taxpayer funding to tax subsidies for elite endowments and federal student aid subsidies to for-profit colleges.[52] Squeezed for resources, these schools also turned to student loan–financed tuition for revenue. To expand and update campuses for increasing enrollments, public university leaders also increased their borrowing from bond markets for capital projects.[53] But popular control and educational mobility have endured most at public universities. Even as they became more dependent on financial markets, state governments and public governing boards placed limits on increases to tuition and student debt. Pushed by demands for increased access from constituents, students, and unionized university employees, public universities also continued to increase enrollments.

Today, public universities remain the massive middle of the US higher education system, enrolling 65 percent of the nation's ten million bachelor's degree seekers.[54] The universities with the largest portions of students who move from the bottom 40 percent of the US income spectrum to the top 40 percent, moreover, were almost uniformly less-selective public universities in the City University of New York, California State University, and University of Texas systems.[55] And the organized constituencies of public universities, we shall see, are playing central roles in a new push to free US universities and students from their dependence on financiers.

The Evidence

At one level, this book is a case study of financiers in US higher education since the 1980s. Viewed through this lens, private university leaders, federal student loan policy makers, hedge fund managers, for-profit college investors, public university officials, and students of different social stations are all part of the same stratifying system. But I also make sense of the system by comparing its private, for-profit, and public strata.[56]

To study this system, I spent seven years gathering a range of data for this book. I gathered archival data and conducted interviews with people in different parts of finance and higher education to gain a multidimensional perspective of the system over time. I also gathered statistical data to analyze particular large-scale dynamics of the system. Sociologists sometimes use the term *triangulation* for this method of gathering, analyzing, and integrating both qualitative and quantitative data. W. E. B. Du Bois provided some of the first blueprints for triangulation in his early twentieth-century studies showing the relationship between schools, racial exploitation, and struggles for racial equality in the US.[57]

My quantitative data gathering and analyses were guided by primary and secondary sources of qualitative data gathered according to what sociologists Theda Skocpol and Sarah Quinn have called the targeted primary methodology.[58] This approach uses theories and evidence from existing journalistic and scholarly studies and supplements them with new data to fill in gaps. The targeted primary approach is especially promising for studying elites like financiers because they are relatively small in number and unusually motivated to protect their privacy from public examination.[59]

In research for this book, I particularly drew on ethnographic and interview evidence from scholarly studies by Tressie McMillan Cottom, Megan Neely, Lauren Rivera, Hannah Appel, Caitlin Zaloom, Karen Ho, Amy Binder, Andrea Abel, Daniel Davis, Nick Bloom, Laura Hamilton, and Kelly Nielsen.[60] I draw similar evidence from financier interviews in major newspapers and in books by journalists like Michael Lewis, Sebastian Mallaby, and Steven Waldman.[61] I cite each of these authors when using evidence from their studies in the book. Their combined observations of hundreds of elite university students, financial-sector elites, and for-profit college managers provide indispensable data for my analyses. These data helped me begin to see how financiers used higher education social ties to amass their fortunes, and to identify where I needed more data.

To fill in gaps in existing secondary data, I gathered two forms of original qualitative data for the book. First, I conducted nineteen in-depth interviews with people in key parts of finance and the higher education system at transformative moments in time. One purpose of these interviews was to consult "people who were there" to make sure that I was not missing something in my reading of secondary sources regarding how financiers, university leaders, or others understood the meanings of their actions. Second, I collected congressional hearing transcripts, university board minutes, and other original historical documents for my analyses. I include a methodological appendix at the end of the book with further details about all quantitative and qualitative data in the book. I also provide additional details when presenting particular data in each chapter. Finally, I have published an online repository of replication code for all the data analyses and visualizations in the book.[62] Where it is permitted by the source of the particular data I analyze, the repository also includes data files for the analyses.

The quantitative analyses of the book use a unique new database I built to harmonize school-level time-series data for dozens of variables measuring aspects of universities' governing boards, finances, personnel, students, and prestige. I partnered with Albina Gibadullina to also link data on the economic affiliations, alumni ties, and university board memberships of the four hundred wealthiest Americans in the United States in 1989, 2003, and 2017.[63] The data set encompasses all 14,759 schools that were eligible to enroll students with federal student loans at any time since 1981. This data set makes it possible, for the first time, to observe how financiers contributed to far-reaching transformations across the entire US higher education system—including under studied parts of the higher education ecology such as for-profit colleges and less-selective public universities.

Organization of the Book

Each of the following chapters will link the experiences of individual financiers, university leaders, and students to statistical analyses of the financialization of US higher education. Chapter 2, "Our New Financial Oligarchy," begins by expanding on financiers' intimate ties to other elites that run through their prestigious and private alma maters. I show that financiers received undergraduate degrees from the most selective private schools at much higher rates than others among the four hundred wealthiest Americans. The chapter explains how financiers like Yale alumnus and billionaire Tom Steyer drew on their college ties to create the lucrative new business models of private equity funds, hedge funds, and consolidated financial service corporations. Chapter 2 also uses data on the financial ties of college governing board members to show a subsequent doubling in the share of private university board slots going to these new financial oligarchs. The chapter theorizes the ascent of financiers on these governing boards as occurring through a mobilization of intimate social ties that confer mutual benefits of social status and economic advantage to top private schools and financiers.

Chapter 3, "Bankers to the Rescue," shows how Sallie Mae CEO Larry Hough and other commercial banking leaders used their social ties to push a radical expansion of federal student loan programs at the beginning of the 1990s. Using congressional hearing minutes and interviews with industry representatives, chapter 3 documents the importance of intimate ties between financiers, university leaders, financial aid officers, and politicians in the construction of a political coalition for expanding federal loan programs. The expanded federal student loan programs became a fulcrum for the turn to finance across the three major strata of US higher education.

Chapters 4, 5, and 6 then turn to how financiers used their elite ties and the expanded federal loan programs to establish new financial dependencies in each of the three major strata. First, chapter 4, "The Top: How Universities Became Hedge Funds," documents how private universities used an endowment boom mostly for the benefit of their well-off students. Chapter 4 then uses data on university board membership, endowment rates of return, and charitable donations to show how financier ties facilitated this endowment boom and hoarding.

Chapter 5, "The Bottom: A Wall Street Takeover of For-Profit Colleges," narrates how the New England Institute of Art (NEIA) exploited the educational dreams of students like Kim Tran. NEIA recruiters enrolled Tran two years after their parent company was acquired for $3.4 billion by private equity investor and Brown University board member Jonathan Nelson. Tran and Nelson lived just fifteen minutes from each other, but their lives would have remained disconnected were it not for a mix of intimate and impersonal financial ties employed in the private equity buyout of Tran's school. The transaction ended in disaster for Tran and tens of thousands of other low-income students who ended up with unpayable debts. Yet, Nelson remains Rhode Island's only billionaire. I expand on Tran and Nelson's story to document the mechanisms and consequences of how private equity investors have spread a "shareholder value" logic to sectors like higher education, where publicly traded corporations were once rare.

Chapter 6, "The Middle: A Hidden Squeeze on Public Universities," uses a case study of the University of California (UC) to show how financier tax avoidance and subsidy capture have squeezed funding for public institutions. Private equity financier Dick Blum was appointed to the UC Board of Regents in 2002 when state funding cuts began to intensify. As board chair, Blum and other UC finance leaders lamented state funding cuts but initially declined to support state tax increases to restore revenue lost to financier tax avoidance. Instead, they increased the university's dependence on student loans and municipal bond borrowing to offset declining state support. But public universities create more universal social identities and networks that connect even financier alumni like Blum to nonelites in ways that are rare at private universities. These ties made UC more attentive to low-income students. UC enrolled low-income students at twice the rate of elite private schools in part by using tuition to maintain mass enrollments. UC also used grant aid to actually reduce loan borrowing by low-income students.

The book concludes with chapter 7, "Reimagining (Higher Education) Finance from Below." This task gained urgency amid the social and economic catastrophes associated with COVID-19. With an eye to the crisis, I ask how we might imagine more inclusive and equitable financial systems in higher education and beyond.

Financiers did not remake higher education finance from scratch and neither will those who imagine its next iteration. Accordingly, chapter 7 shows how overlapping coalitions have developed two complementary strategies for mobilizing the higher education ties of today to win a better tomorrow. I theorize one strategy as a more gradual *bargaining with bankers* and another as a *big bang* of student debt cancellation. The coalitions behind these strategies paradoxically mirror financiers by mobilizing shared identities and social ties created by undergraduate education and the experience of student debt. But unlike the elite university ties of ivory tower bankers, both insurgent social groups and elites are connected by the higher education ties of these coalitions. They unite associations of students, education workers, communities of color, and service employees with legal advocates, policy experts, liberal politicians, and even the occasional financier. I assess how their respective reform proposals might relocate higher education financing decisions from the intimate networks of financiers to both public and intimate deliberations by nonelites.

By explaining the relationship between financier power and higher education inequality—and their alternatives—I also provide insights about the role of financiers in other economic and social domains. Universities were the first chartered corporations in North America. Ideals of scientific discovery, critical reexamination, and educational mobility have sustained them. Democratic participation and governance have remained much more core to their organizational form than for other corporate organizations. There is no better site to study what finance is and what it might be. I begin this task by looking back at the ties between financiers and elite private universities throughout the twentieth and twenty-first centuries.

2. Our New Financial Oligarchy

In 1913, future US Supreme Court justice Louis Brandeis published a series of articles under the title *Other People's Money and How the Bankers Use It.* Later published as a book, Brandeis's opus documented the rise of what he called "our financial oligarchy." J. P. Morgan and a cartel of US banks had formed a money monopoly as the exclusive gatekeepers to capital markets. Through their monopoly, the bankers effectively controlled the largest corporations in key sectors from railroads to steel. This facilitated industrial collusion and the extraction of profits above what more competitive markets would have yielded. Morgan and his collaborators further parlayed this economic domination into political power.[1] Their financial oligarchy only declined after New Deal reforms curtailed the power of the banks in response to their role in the onset of the Great Depression.

More than one hundred years later, financiers have regained levels of wealth that rival or even surpass those of Brandeis's day. But they have done so without restoring the sorts of banking cartels that Morgan built. Some economic sociologists have even argued that financial elites and financial organizations are more fragmented today than they were in the 1950s.[2] But it takes large-scale social coordination for any group of people to accumulate a financial fortune. How then have today's financiers amassed such vast wealth?

The answer is that our new financial oligarchs—and perhaps their predecessors as well—are connected by the elite social life and culture I call the social circuitry of finance. These social ties permeate their investment firms. But elites also weave these connections via social organizations and institutions that parallel the economy, from country clubs to opera societies. And as centuries-old finishing schools for American elites, there are no more important organizations for constructing the networks, culture, and status of financiers than the nation's most selective private colleges and universities.[3]

Even as the power of banks waned in the middle of the twentieth century, sociologist C. Wright Mills observed in *The Power Elite* that private university ties had helped the nation's leading financiers to preserve their position atop a power triangle of corporate executives, politicians, and military leaders.[4] He noted that the ten top financiers of 1905 had sent twelve of their fifteen sons who lived to adulthood to Harvard or Yale. The other three went to Amherst, Brown, and Columbia.[5]

Today, a new generation of researchers and thinkers is showing how financiers and elite university leaders have partnered to increase each other's status and wealth. Through ethnographies and in-depth interviews, these researchers have found that the highest-status investment bank and hedge fund managers mostly hire and promote new entrants who share their elite private university experiences, cultures, and identities.[6] A separate group of economic sociologists has shown that deregulation, beginning in the late 1970s, helped these financiers to position themselves as gatekeepers between expanded financial markets and an enlarged customer base for capital. The resulting rise in financiers' wealth and income has been a primary driver of growing inequality in America.[7] University leaders have, in turn, bolstered their reputations, and their endowments, through their associations with ascendant financial organizations from the Sallie Mae student loan corporation to the hedge fund division of JPMorgan, the financial corporation that still bears the name of its founding oligarch.[8]

While academics have documented qualitatively the ties between prestigious universities and careers in finance, few have studied these relationships on a large scale. Researchers have also devoted little attention to comparing whether financiers are more likely to have Ivy League pedigrees than are wealthy Americans who obtained their riches in other sectors. Legal scholar Gary Jenkins has shown that financiers have held a disproportionate and increasing share of board seats at elite private colleges and universities since at least the late 1980s. Jenkins's study, however, lacked comparisons with other types of schools and did not account for the substantial differences in social status and income between different types of financiers.

In this chapter, I use data on the four hundred wealthiest Americans and the members of both public and private university boards over time to show that a new financial oligarchy indeed has many more ties involving prestigious private schools than do other elites. The data reflect how financiers use university ties to position themselves as the transistors of the social circuitry of finance. These intimate social ties are conduits of capital and private information that private equity and hedge fund managers tapped to become the wealthiest grouping in America's elite.

The hierarchy of finance's social circuitry adds a dimension to a related theory that economic transactions are embedded in social ties.[9] Researchers have tended to measure embeddedness in the duration and multiplexity of economic ties, such as the consistent patronage of a commercial bank for all one's banking. But ties from parallel social organizations also facilitate economic activity. From institutions like universities and recreational sports leagues to neighborhood groups and parent teacher associations, contemporary social structures facilitate trust and reciprocity as essential ingredients for doing business. Through participation in these formations, people develop mutual identities, cultural understandings, and dependencies on others with whom they must maintain a good reputation in order to preserve their social status.[10] Sociologist Viviana Zelizer has shown that members of these networks also exchange valuable private information.

But parallel social organizations are highly stratified. Most people do not live in high-end neighborhoods, frequent country clubs, or study at the most selective colleges. As a result, elites tend to monopolize the economic advantages of trust and reciprocity with other elites who possess capital, power in government, and private information of economic value. By extension, the economic organizations of elites also benefit from their exclusive social ties. JPMorgan in its current incarnation is maintained in part as a trusted brand and high-status employer via the connectedness of its top investment managers to other elites.

Elite social ties are especially valuable for financiers because they transact in private information and because they intermediate the economic activities of other elites. Private equity and hedge fund managers benefit even more than other financiers because of the particular importance of trust and private information in their high-risk investment strategies. As a result, these financiers have by far the highest rate of elite university degree holding among the four hundred richest Americans. Elite private university leaders also added more of these financiers to their boards than did other schools. Our new financial oligarchs, in turn, drew on these ties as they transformed the entire US higher education system via student loans, for-profit colleges, and more.

Financiers and the Power Elite

"They are all that we are not," wrote C. Wright Mills in the opening paragraphs of his 1956 book *The Power Elite*. To Mills, the 1950s American elite were set aside from the rest of society by their wealth, their control of organizations, and their prestige.[11] They occupied positions of authority atop a triangle of corporations, political institutions, and the military. Elite theorists in subsequent decades have shown a primacy of corporate elites in this power triangle. Few have appreciated, however, the extent to which Mills, like Brandeis before him, found a central position for financiers among the corporate elites of the 1950s. Nor have recent scholars recalled the important role that Mills saw for private universities in the production of the power elite. In fact, we can use Mills's profiles of twentieth-century financiers to see how they compare with today's financial elite in terms of educational origins and social power.

From Morgan and Carnegie to Buffet and Icahn, financial elites have occupied a premier position among America's very rich throughout the twentieth and twenty-first centuries. This flows from financiers' position as middlemen between those in need of capital and "other people's money." In 1950s America, high tax rates on top earners, strong labor unions, and the postwar social contract had reduced the gap in wealth and incomes between the very rich and the rest. Still, Mills observed that finance occupied a central position among the ninety richest Americans at the time. Critiquing the Austrian political economist Joseph Schumpeter, Mills wrote,

> It is, as a matter of fact, not the far-seeing inventor or the captain of industry but the general of finance who becomes one of the very rich. . . . The accumulation of advantages has usually required the merging of other businesses with the first one founded—a financial operation—until a large "trust" is formed. The manipulation of securities and fast legal footwork are the major keys to the success of such higher entrepreneurs.[12]

These generals of finance commonly invoked social ties in their financial manipulations, Mills added. For example, Harvard alumnus Charles Copeland married Luisa D'Anbelot du Pont as he brokered a merger of the two largest weapons and chemical manufacturers into the Dupont Corporation during World War II.[13]

Mills also recorded the importance of universities in the social ties of the very wealthy. Half of the ninety richest Americans at the time who had ever attended college had gone to the Ivy League, with almost a third having gone to Harvard or Yale. Another 10 percent had attended "other famous eastern colleges, such as Amherst, Brown, Lafayette, Williams, Bowdoin."[14] As was noted earlier, the same was true of the children of early twentieth-century financiers.[15]

The share of income and wealth going to finance was nevertheless substantially lower in 1950s America than it is today. At an industry level, sociologist Greta Krippner has shown that the share of profits going to finance in the US economy increased from just over 10 percent in 1950 to more than 40 percent in the mid-2000s.[16]

Increased profits in the financial sector have, in turn, increased the share of US income going to the owners of financial institutions. Elite financial workers have also increased their share of US income. Before 1980, per-employee earnings in the financial sector were equivalent to the national average in earnings per employee. By 2000, earnings per employee in the financial sector were 60 percent higher than the national average.[17] During the same period, nonfinancial corporations also increasingly engaged in financial activities from consumer and commercial lending to derivative trading. This fueled greater inequality in earnings between the highest- and lowest-paid workers in nonfinancial industries.[18]

How is it that financiers were able to attain an even more dominant economic position among US elites? Scholars have argued that broader shifts in economic ideas, technology, and politics enabled financial professions and financial organizations to strengthen their position as intermediaries between expanded capital markets and the rest of the economy.[19] Elite higher education played a part in each of these transformations.

In the years following World War II, US corporations maintained relatively larger internal supplies of capital, making them less dependent on financial markets for capital.[20] By the 1970s, stagflation and declining corporate profits had reduced corporations' internal capital reserves.[21] At the same time, the rise of pensions, mutual funds, and *college endowments* offered potential new sources of wealth that could be invested in capital-starved corporations.[22] Computerization and new ideas from academic economists simultaneously enabled financial technicians to assess credit risks for corporate and individual borrowers and investors at a radically increased scale[23]—and to conduct daily trades in stocks and corporate debt instruments numbering in the billions rather than the millions.[24]

At the end of the 1970s, a new political coalition was forged between big business, the old financial elite, and a rising conservative movement. The coalition would push the US government to deregulate financial activities and cut taxes in crucial ways for the resurgence of financier wealth and power. Charls Walker, a graduate of Penn's Wharton School and onetime executive head of the American Bankers Association, played a central role in forging and formally leading this new coalition.[25] With an Ivy League pedigree and ties to finance and the conservative movement, Walker is what sociologists call a borderlands actor who can draw on social ties across multiple fields to mobilize the resources necessary to change entrenched social structures.[26] In chapter 3, I will detail how a group of borderland financiers particularly used their university ties to promote a massive expansion of federal subsidies for private student lenders in 1992.

Under pressure from Walker's new conservative-business-finance coalition in the late 1970s, Republicans and Democrats alike voted in Congress to cut top income tax rates and capital gains taxes.[27] The tax cuts ratcheted up incentives to increase profits at the expense of workers and pass those profits on to investors and financial intermediaries.[28] On top of tax cuts, policy makers piled deregulations such as a repeal of interest rate caps to allow financial institutions to expand both the scale and profitability of financial transactions.[29] Deregulation also allowed the combination of previously firewalled financial activities, and policy makers opted to not regulate complex new financial products such as derivatives.[30]

To amass new fortunes from these structural opportunities, however, financiers would first have to reconfigure the organizations that intermediate financial markets. These new organizational forms have linked financiers in new ways, both impersonally and intimately, to US universities and students.

The New Financial Elite

Since the 1980s, financial-sector operatives built two key types of financial organizations for the transformation of US higher education. First, bankers fashioned consolidated financial service corporations from the combination of commercial and investment banking. Second, a new class of high financiers created private equity and hedge funds around new strategies for investing on behalf of wealthy individuals, college endowments, and eventually pension funds. The rise of these organizations has driven the spectacular growth in wealth and incomes for the top 1 percent of Americans since the 1980s.[31] In the process, the leaders of private equity and hedge funds particularly gained outsized representation on the boards of America's most prestigious universities.

Consolidated financial corporations and the new funds of haute finance have played distinct but complementary roles in the turn to private capital by US higher education. In chapter 3, we shall see that consolidated financial service corporations captured federal subsidies to expand the federal student loan system. Chapter 4 will detail how private equity and hedge funds oversaw fast-growing investment portfolios for the endowments of the wealthiest universities—and generously donated to those same endowments. Chapter 5 explains how private equity and hedge funds also capitalized and extracted massive profits from the expansion of for-profit colleges. In chapter 6, we will see how tax avoidance and subsidy capture by private equity and hedge funds diverted resources from public universities.

I provide a primer here on the two new types of financial organizations that have transformed US higher education. I then detail how the fortunes amassed by private equity and hedge fund managers doubled the number of financiers among the wealthiest Americans between 1989 and 2017. Table 2.1 summarizes key organizational characteristics and higher

TABLE 2.1 Organizational forms of financial intermediation in US higher education

	Consolidated financial service corporations	*Private equity (including venture capital) and hedge funds*
Primary sources of capital	• Deposits (commercial banking) • Equity buyers, security buyers (investment banking) • Corporate and individual investors (asset management)	• Wealthy individuals • Pension funds • College endowments • Junk bonds • Margin loans • Derivatives
Organizational form	• Publicly traded • 200,000 employees of large firms on average • Dividends and capital gains for shareholders • Salaries and bonuses for managing partners in investment banking	• Private partnership • Several hundred employees for large firms • 20 percent share of profits for general partners in the form of carried interest
Intermediary roles in higher education	• Federal student loan origination prior to 2010 • Federal student loan servicing • Municipal bond underwriting for university capital projects • Endowment investing in conventional assets	• Endowment investments with funds • Private equity–leveraged buyouts of for-profit colleges • Hedge fund investments in for-profit college stocks, debts, and derivatives
Types of colleges involved	• All types (student loans) • Public and private nonprofit (municipal bonds) • All types (endowment investment management)	• Elite private institutions and large public universities • For-profit college buyout targets
Largest firms	• Sallie Mae (student loans) • Bank of America Merrill Lynch (municipal bonds and student loans) • Fidelity (asset management)	• The Blackstone Group • Kohlberg Kravis Roberts • Bridgewater Associates • AQR Capital Management
Market concentration	• 69 percent market share for top ten FFEL loan originators in 2008 • 92 percent market share for four top student loan servicers in 2018 • 72 percent market share for ten top municipal bond underwriters • 60 percent market share for ten largest asset managers	• 22 percent market share for top ten private equity firms • 20 percent market share for top ten hedge funds

education roles of the two types of new financial organizations. I elaborate on the contents of the table by first explaining how financiers created consolidated financial service organizations from the merger of commercial banks, investment banks, and asset management companies. I then explain how private equity and hedge funds developed new financing techniques around the idea that corporations should be managed to maximize shareholder value for investors.

Consolidated Financial Service Corporations

Financial deregulation in the 1980s and 1990s allowed for a wave of mergers to create consolidated financial service corporations. New financial behemoths such as the Big Four of Bank of America, Citigroup, JPMorgan Chase, and Wells Fargo arose to encompass commercial banking, investment banking, insurance, and eventually even private equity and hedge fund activities. Stockholders in these massive new banking corporations have received the lion's share of the financial sector's increasing share of overall US profits since 1980.[32]

Crucially for US higher education, consolidated financial service corporations used new forms of securitization to capitalize a massive expansion of consumer credit, including student loans and home mortgages. Securitization is the practice of pooling together loans and selling the future payments on those loans to investors, much like a corporation or government would sell a bond. Ironically, the securitization of consumer loans was originally pioneered as a way for government-sponsored enterprises to raise capital for making consumer loans. The federal government founded the Student Loan Marketing Association (Sallie Mae) for this purpose in the case of student loans and founded Fannie Mae for the purpose of home loans.[33] As is detailed in chapter 3, Sallie Mae became one of the nation's largest consolidated financial service corporations and was eventually privatized, making money both by administering and servicing federal student loans and by selling securities backed by those student loans. Aided by federal subsidies, each of the Big Four consolidated financial services organizations followed Sallie Mae into the federal student loan business.

The Big Four and other consolidated financial service organizations also underwrite municipal bonds, which colleges and universities have increasingly used to finance capital projects investments.[34] Finally, consolidated financial service corporations such as the Big Four, Fidelity, and BlackRock provide asset management services for investors such as college endowments. These activities encompass mutual funds and index funds as structures for conventional investing in stocks and bonds but have also grown to encompass hedge funds and private equity funds, about which we will learn more shortly.

Scholars have argued that an oligarchic lack of market competition has helped consolidated financial service corporations to extract a growing and disproportionate share of profits in the US economy. Before the elimination of private-sector financing of federal student loans, the top ten lenders held a 69 percent market share.[35] While barred since 2010 from the financing of federal student loans, financial service corporations still contract with the US Department of Education to collect payments on federal student loans, with just four corporations controlling 92 percent of the market.[36] Similarly, the top ten municipal bond underwriters have a 72 percent market share.[37] The top ten asset managers have a 60 percent market share.[38] For comparison, only the utilities industry has comparable market concentration. In transportation and warehousing, the industry with the next highest market concentration, the largest fifty firms receive only 42 percent of all industry revenue.[39] Leading researchers have argued that even that level of market concentration has contributed to rising income inequality and excessive costs for consumers.[40]

Consolidated financial service corporations tend to be publicly traded corporations. Unlike stand-alone private equity and hedge funds, they therefore pass on a large share of their profits to shareholders who are passive in the management of their companies. Nevertheless, CEOs of these financial corporations typically receive tens of millions of dollars in compensation annually. JPMorgan Chase CEO Jamie Dimon, a Harvard alumnus, is the wealthiest among them with a net worth of more than $1 billion since 2015.[41] With each of the Big Four employing an average of two hundred thousand employees and thousands of managing directors, consolidated financial services also employ more millionaires than all other US industries combined. Two leading economists conservatively estimated that 6,900 investment bankers in financial service corporations had earnings in the top 0.1 percent of all US incomes in 2004 ($1.4 million annually and higher), making up 30 percent of all earners in the top 0.1 percent. This constituted a larger share than the combined share of all top celebrities, law partners, and top-five executives at all publicly traded nonfinancial corporations.[42]

Private Equity and Hedge Funds

While managing directors of consolidated financial service corporations dominate the US millionaire class, private equity and hedge fund managers are the core of the nation's expanding billionaire class. I group private equity and hedge fund managers together because they are both extremely reliant on private information and high-risk debt leveraging. This makes elite social ties comparably valuable to both. Reflecting this value of intimate ties, private equity and hedge fund managers have greater alumni and governing board links to prestigious private schools.

Private equity and hedge fund managers rose to wealth by pioneering new investment strategies that explicitly relied on social ties to exploit opportunities from financial deregulation. These strategies applied a new idea known as shareholder value. These strategies would also help to transform US higher education by earning previously unseen returns for the elite private colleges and universities that have invested in private equity and hedge funds.

Financial economists had argued in the 1970s that executives of publicly traded companies often prospered happily while failing to maximize share values in the company because top managers enjoyed too much autonomy from investor-owners.[43] Private equity investors such as Princeton alumnus Carl Icahn sought to exploit such situations by raising large amounts of capital to buy controlling shares of stocks in hostile takeovers of undervalued publicly traded companies like the now defunct Trans World Airlines.[44] This strategy had become possible because financial deregulation enabled private equity firms to borrow large sums of capital through high-interest and high-risk vehicles known as junk bonds.

Following hostile takeovers, private equity owners take companies private and implement new practices to increase the shareholder value of the company. These practices, including streamlining, cost-cutting, outsourcing, and union busting, tend to come at the expense of workers and communities.[45] If these techniques failed, the private equity financiers could still discharge their dangerously large amounts of borrowing by shifting the debt onto the corporation they had acquired. If successful, the private equity investors would later sell off parts of the company to other investors or sell the company in a new public offering of stock, but for a substantially higher price than they paid during the hostile takeover. And because the investment had been financed with heavy debt leveraging, private equity financiers could net unprecedented returns not just on their own capital but also on the borrowed capital. In chapter 5, we shall see how private equity used these tactics to rake in billions from for-profit colleges at the expense of students and taxpayers in recent decades.

Private equity overlaps substantially with the smaller venture capital sector, with the same firms sometimes operating both leveraged buyout funds and venture funds. The analyses ahead therefore analyze both private equity and venture capital together as a single private equity sector. Venture capital differs from private equity primarily in that venture capital firms tend to purchase noncontrolling minority stakes in start-up firms, often in technology-related sectors.[46]

Just like in private equity, hedge fund managers also use heavy debt leveraging to make massive calculated bets that can amplify their potential returns. Hedge funds differ from private equity, however, in that they tend to invest in stocks and various types of derivatives rather than purchasing entire companies.[47] This makes hedge fund investments more liquid. The term *hedge fund* is connected to hedge fund managers' use of derivatives to take "short positions" that "hedge" against overall declines in financial asset values. For example, a hedge fund manager can bet that a stock will decline by buying a put option that obliges the writer of the option to buy the stock at a set price in the future. If the stock then declines in value, the hedge fund manager can buy the stock at its lower price in order to sell it to the option writer at a profit for the higher price required by the put option. Hedge funds can hedge against the risk of a broader market downturn by balancing their investments between assets they expect to increase in value and derivative bets (like put options) against assets that they expect will decrease in value. Hedge funds can also effectively use options, futures, and swaps to borrow large sums of capital from investors in these derivative markets.[48] This borrowing typically takes the form of financial assets that hedge funds will be required to return or pay for in the future. Like private equity funds, hedge fund trading activities also promote the idea of shareholder value by punishing companies that fail to maximize short-term share values for investors and rewarding those who do.

Except in cases where consolidated financial service corporations have created their own funds, even the largest private equity and hedge funds tend to be private partnerships that employ several hundred employees. Private equity and hedge fund partners therefore do not have to pass on profits to shareholders. Instead, they retain profits for themselves in the form of a standard 20 percent share of all profits earned for investor clients, such as college endowments.[49] This high compensation rate was established in the early 1980s when just a few private equity firms dominated the entire market. The market concentration of private equity and hedge funds has since declined to levels below that of consolidated financial service corporations. Nevertheless, the top ten US private equity firms still control a 22 percent market share, and the top ten hedge funds still control a 20 percent market share. These market concentrations are well above nearly all the most uncompetitive nonfinancial industries.[50]

With high market concentration and most firm profits going to managing partners, the new fund managers went from a virtually nonexistent profession in the 1970s to the most common source of wealth for the wealthiest

Americans. In 2004, 6,360 individuals working at private equity and hedge funds were conservatively estimated to have earnings in the top 0.1 percent at over $1.4 million annually, over 27 percent of the study's sample for that earning category (together with investment bankers, the new fund managers made up 57 percent of people in this income category).[51] The new fund managers made up an even larger 32 percent of people with incomes in the top 0.001 percent (greater than $31 million) and 82 percent of all people with incomes in the top 0.0001 (greater than $100 million annually).

High incomes in private equity and hedge funds elevated finance as the largest industry grouping among the Forbes 400 list of the four hundred wealthiest Americans.[52] Albina Gibadullina and I have shown elsewhere that in 1989, all financiers combined made up just 12.5 percent of the Forbes 400.[53] Just 5.25 percent of those wealthiest Americans came from private equity and hedge funds with the remainder working in other forms of finance that have come to be encompassed by consolidated financial service corporations. In 2017, private equity and hedge fund managers alone made up 16.25 percent of the Forbes 400.[54] This boosted finance's overall share of these wealthiest Americans to 25 percent. Nonfinanciers with technology company affiliations were the next largest group in 2017, making up 13.75 percent of the Forbes 400.

Ivory Tower Social Ties

To amass their new fortunes, private equity and hedge fund managers explicitly drew on social ties to obtain private information and maintain trust with investment clients. Trust from social ties was important because of the high risks and volatile returns of their previously untested strategies. In this way, elite social ties were even more valuable to private equity and hedge funds than to other types of financial organizations. Few institutions foster elite social ties at a scale or intensity comparable to those forged by the nation's most prestigious private colleges and universities. Elite college endowments also offered a critical source of early capital for private equity and hedge funds. In this context, we shall see that Ivy League alumni came to make up a much larger share of private equity and hedge fund managers than among the richest groups of Americans from other industries.

Intimate Ties in the Ivory Tower

Scholars have given little attention to the importance of economic actors' social ties that are superficially more distant from economic activity. Perhaps because suitable measures are difficult to come by, economic activity is mostly studied as independent from a range of social structures, such as residential neighborhoods, K–12 education, sports, popular culture, and other forms of leisure—or the colleges and universities through which all these social structures intersect. Instead, researchers have tended to measure embeddedness in the duration and multiplexity of economic ties. Long-standing and multifaceted economic ties—such as the consistent patronage of a commercial bank for all one's banking needs—have been shown to particularly build trust and social reciprocity over time.[55]

Top colleges and universities provide a parallel social circuitry for economic action. But university social ties are highly stratified. Social homophily, the tendency of people to gravitate toward others with similar cultures and identities, leads elite institutions to exclude most people with less privileged backgrounds.[56] As Mills wrote of the elite, "They belong to the same associations at the same set of Ivy League colleges, and they remain in social and business touch by means of the big-city network of metropolitan clubs. In each of the nation's leading cities, they recognize one another, if not strictly as peers, as people with much in common."[57]

Today, formal admissions advantages for elites at top private schools remain intact through the system of "legacy" admissions for the children of alumni. Under this admissions regime, African American and Latinx students have become even more underrepresented in the Ivy League and other elite schools than they were in 1980.[58] Meanwhile, thirty-eight top private colleges today enroll more students from households in the top 1 percent for income than from the bottom 60 percent combined.[59] These trends have deep historical and institutional roots.[60] For example, Yale and Harvard both ranked their students into the 1700s in part according to their father's wealth and social position in society.[61]

Once students graduate from an elite institution, they are stamped with a prestigious social status that can be displayed on their social media profiles, exercise clothes, and even car bumpers. This social status and access to elite networks helps them move into a well-compensated adulthood, perhaps even in finance.[62] As a result, it remains true, as Mills wrote, that in the construction of elite social status, "that top level is always being renovated."[63] But the deep ties between elite higher education and finance have severely restricted the pool of those who might move into the renovated top level of the very richest Americans. It is chiefly those from about the top 1 percent that higher education and finance together elevate into the top 0.001 percent and the rarified club of the Forbes 400.

Ivy League Ties in Action

Private equity and hedge fund investors gain an unusually high premium from the elite ties fostered by Ivy League educations. First, they use private information to make investments involving assets that they think are undervalued or overvalued. These information asymmetries can arise because of a lack of public information or because of misinterpretations by market investors.[64] Social ties are major conduits of private information, and this makes connections to other economic elites especially valuable to private equity investors. For example, Yale and Harvard alumnus Wilbur Ross tapped insider knowledge of planned steel tariffs by fellow Yalie President George W. Bush in 2002.[65] Ross acquired LTV Steel in February of that year. One month later, President Bush imposed a 30 percent tariff on Chinese steel, bolstering US steel companies. Ross then sold his steel holdings for earnings of $4.5 billion.

Journalists and scholars have further documented that hedge funds explicitly seek out private information through social ties to economic and political elites.[66] For example, Michael Lewis has traced how an array of hedge fund investors such as Harvard alumnus and megadonor John Paulson decided to bet against mortgage-backed securities after learning through his social networks that mortgage-backed securities were based on gross misestimations of mortgage default risk.[67]

Elite university ties were also crucial for raising capital in the early days of private equity and hedge funds. For one, private university endowments were the largest potential institutional investors in fledgling private equity and hedge funds prior to shifts in pension fund regulations and practices.[68] Social ties via a shared alma mater, moreover, can facilitate trust, which was particularly important in the 1980s when high-risk private equity and hedge fund investment strategies remained little understood and untested. As a result, sociologist Megan Neely has documented that investment managers draw heavily on social ties, including those formed via prestigious colleges' alumni networks, to raise capital for their investments.[69] Investment managers told Neely that the trust and loyalty involved in social relationships help to overcome the uncertainty of investment strategies for which returns can be highly volatile from one year to the next. For this same reason, Neely found that hedge funds recruit overwhelmingly from their elite college alumni networks. Sociologist Lauren Rivera found similar practices in the investment banking divisions of consolidated financial service corporations—organizations where many investors worked prior to founding the first private equity and hedge funds.[70]

Consistent with Neely's account, it took a Yale economics PhD, David Swensen, who had worked on Wall Street, to steer the biggest college endowments past their early ambivalence about the risks of private equity investment. After earning his PhD in 1980, Swensen worked for Lehman Brothers and Solomon Brothers when the firms provided some of the earliest financing for leveraged buyouts and currency derivatives.[71] Following his appointment to lead Yale's endowment in 1985, Swensen turned Yale into a leader in such investments. Following Swenson's lead, college endowments became the largest institutional investors for the sector prior to shifts in pension fund investing.[72]

Yale alumnus and hedge fund billionaire Tom Steyer relatedly began courting Yale to invest in his hedge fund after learning of Swensen's appointment to lead the school's endowment at a 1988 homecoming football game.[73] Two years later, Swensen provided Steyer's Farallon Capital with $300 million, a third of its total investment capital.

Consistent with the benefits of prestigious private university networks described here, private equity and hedge fund managers in the Forbes 400 list have elite private university backgrounds at much higher rates than do billionaires from other economic sectors. Figure 2.1 shows that just 26 percent of nontechnology and nonfinance members of the Forbes 400 had bachelor's degrees from the top thirty private universities in 1989.[74] That

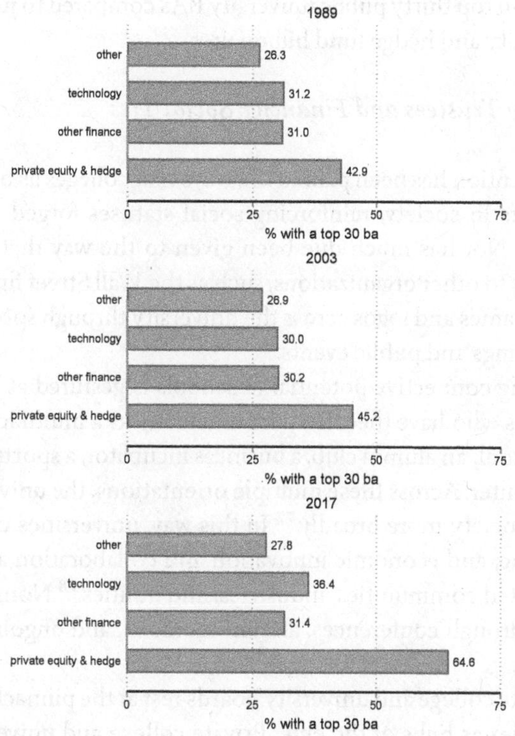

FIGURE 2.1 Shares of Forbes 400 billionaires with top thirty private university BAs

NOTE: Data from the Forbes 400 list of the wealthiest US residents and author-gathered data on economic affiliations and degree holding.

year, 43 percent of the private equity and hedge fund managers in the Forbes 400 had bachelor's degrees from those schools, rising to 65 percent in 2017.

For comparison, figure 2.1 also breaks out degree holding for Forbes 400 members who were technology-sector entrepreneurs. Economists have suggested that financiers and technology executives might particularly reap economic rewards from elite higher education because their businesses require more difficult skills.[75] Elite private educations might both impart and validate those skills. But the share of technology-sector members of the Forbes 400 with elite bachelor's degrees remained persistently lower than for haute financiers, increasing from 31 percent in 1989 to 36 percent in 2017.

A comparison with public university degree holding gives another indication that financiers gain more from social ties than from skills acquired or indicated by elite private school admission. Gibadullina and I show in a prior study that Forbes 400 members from nonfinancial sectors have consistently matched or exceeded private equity and hedge fund managers in top thirty public university degree holding.[76] Among Forbes 400 members in 2017, 16 percent of technology-sector billionaires and 12 percent of other billionaires had top thirty public university BAs compared to just 11 percent of private equity and hedge fund billionaires.

University Trustees and Financier Social Ties

Much less attention has been paid to the ways that colleges as organizations connect adults in society, reinforcing social statuses forged during their college years. Nor has much due been given to the way that universities provide status to other organizations, such as the Wall Street firms who emblazon their names and logos across the university through sponsorships of campus buildings and public events.

The lifelong connective potential of schools is gestured at by organizational scholars who have theorized the university as a multifaceted organization—a school, an alumni club, a business incubator, a sports franchise, a conference center. Across these multiple orientations, the university serves as a hub for society more broadly.[77] In this way, universities can foster intellectual, civic, and economic innovation and collaboration across otherwise fragmented communities, industries, and polities.[78] Nonstudents can be engaged through conferences, alumni reunions, and ongoing consortia with industry.

Elite private college and university boards rest at the pinnacle of colleges and universities as hubs of the elite. Private college and university boards are deliberately populated by the largest donors and fundraisers for the institution. Board members are also overwhelmingly drawn from the alumni who tend to donate most generously to their own alma mater.[79] With the most alumni among wealthy private equity and hedge fund managers, the most prestigious colleges and universities have a larger pool from which to recruit these financiers to their boards. The most prestigious universities, moreover, can leverage their higher social status to recruit private equity and hedge fund financiers at higher rates.

Consistent with these advantages, elite private universities dramatically increased private equity and hedge fund representation on their boards in recent decades. Public universities made no comparable additions of private equity or public university financiers to their boards. Figure 2.2 presents the share of board members from finance for the top thirty private universities. Data for 1989 only covers the top twenty-two private universities for which Jenkins collected data.[80] This shows that the share of board members from all of finance for these schools increased from 17 percent in 1989 to 29 percent in 2003, plateauing at 35 percent since 2014. Roughly half of this increase came from growth in private equity and hedge fund manager board membership, which increased from 3 percent in 1989 to 9 percent in 2003 and to 18 percent since 2013.

Gibadullina and I also have shown that Forbes 400 members from private equity and finance also serve on top thirty private university boards at

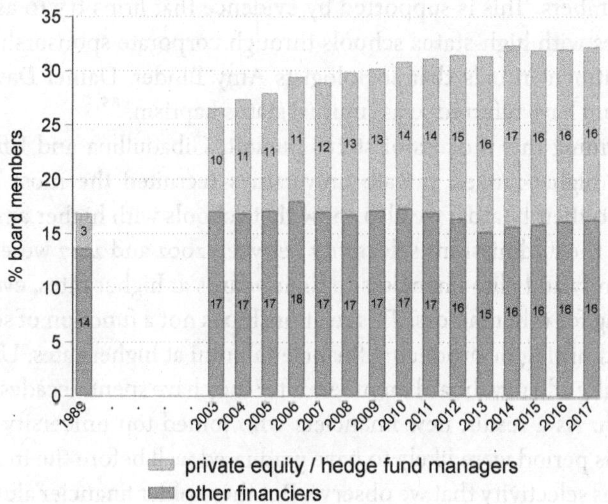

FIGURE 2.2 Mean percentage of board members from finance

NOTE: Data for 2003 to 2017 from authors' original database of board members for top thirty public and top thirty private universities. Data for 1989 for the top twenty-two private universities is from the Jenkins study (2015). Data and code: https://github.com/HigherEdData/bankersintheivorytower.

much higher rates than do other billionaires.[81] In 2017, 29 percent of private equity and hedge fund Forbes 400 members sat on the board of at least one top thirty private university. For other financiers in the Forbes 400, 20 percent sat on a top thirty private board. For technology-sector Forbes 400 members, just 13 percent served on such boards. Just 11 percent of other Forbes 400 billionaires served on such boards. Regression models that control for wealth and inheritance show that private equity and hedge fund managers are more than three times as likely to serve on top thirty private boards.[82] About half of this relationship is due to greater levels of top thirty private school alumni status. But even among billionaire alumni of top thirty private schools, private equity and hedge fund managers are 1.7 times more likely than other billionaires to serve on these boards. Zero Forbes 400 billionaires served on a top thirty public university board.

The Payoffs of Prestige

Gibadullina and I have shown elsewhere that higher levels of university prestige attract private equity and hedge fund managers to serve on college boards at higher rates.[83] Contention for board seats by financial elites matches research showing the importance of philanthropy for securing social status among elites.[84] Board seats also lend status to the businesses of board members. This is supported by evidence that firms try to associate themselves with high-status schools through corporate sponsorships and job recruitment rituals that sociologists Amy Binder, Daniel Davis, and Nick Bloom have referred to as "mutual status baptism."[85]

Confirming this process of status pursuit, Gibadullina and I find not only that higher-ranked private universities recruited the most elite financiers to their boards; we also show that schools with higher annual increases in their admissions selectivity between 2002 and 2017 were able to subsequently add elite financiers to their boards at higher rates, even after controlling for other factors. This relationship is not a function of selective schools admitting or producing financier alumni at higher rates. Universities typically add new board members after they have spent decades amassing wealth. As a result, new financiers who joined top university boards during this period were likely to have graduated well before the increasing admissions selectivity that we observe. But these older financier alumni become more attracted to serving on the board of their alma mater as it gains prestige from increasingly selective admissions.

As governing board members, financial elites have special power to maintain the kinds of academic and extracurricular structures that helped give them their own pedigree. By preserving these structures, financiers help produce new cohorts of high-status graduates for their recruiters.[86] In his 1980s indictment of Wall Street, Michael Lewis noted that 40 percent of Yale's graduating class of 1986 applied to work at a single investment bank, First Boston. This tradition remains alive and well in the Ivy League, with 70 percent of Harvard graduates typically applying to work for a top investment bank or consulting firm.[87] Top financial firms, in turn, advertise that many of their employees hold degrees from Ivy League institutions. Top fund managers also eagerly list in their biographies that they sit on the boards of the most prestigious schools. Through these signals, financiers celebrate that finance elevates those with Ivy League educations into America's wealthiest inner circle at higher rates than do other industries.

The aura of prestige cultivated by these links to the ivory tower then provides financial firms with social status for influencing public policy, retaining clients, and raising investment capital—including from college endowments. In this way, intimate ties created at prestigious schools helped financiers to extend their power and reach into far-flung corners of America's economy, society, and higher education system.

The pages ahead will elaborate on how the financial organizations introduced here carried out particular business projects that made the different strata of higher education more dependent on private capital markets. We begin with the expansion of federal student loan programs at the beginning of the 1990s. In this drama, the protagonists are the new consolidated financial service corporations that used securitization to radically expand the availability of capital for consumer loans. As with each financial transformation of US higher education since the 1980s, the elite university ties of these new financiers would prove an invaluable asset.

3.

Bankers to the Rescue

The Political Turn to Student Debt

In the first quarter of 2017, the US Department of Education effectively became the largest commercial bank in America, holding $971 billion in outstanding debt.[1] This milestone marked a revolution that has transformed US higher education since the 1970s, when only a small fraction of US students used loans to pay for college. In the broader economy, commercial banks had long been the largest holders of commercial debt via products like mortgages, credit cards, and business loans.[2] Through the rise of student loans, however, the US federal government had overtaken all the biggest lenders.

How and why did the US government make this radical turn to student loans as its primary tool for funding higher education? Scholars have made surprisingly few efforts to explain this policy shift. Some have argued implicitly that colleges sought the expansion of federal student loan programs as a way to net greater tuition revenue for overcompensated and inefficient faculty and staff.[3] This deserves consideration, but so do other possibilities.

We can find other explanations for the rise of student debt in research on the origins of tax cuts, financial deregulation, and mortgage industry expansion since the late 1970s. A number of academics have argued that government officials adopted these measures as solutions for distributional conflicts between economic classes and social groups.[4] In the late 1960s and 1970s, workers and communities of color increasingly took to the streets and the picket line to demand higher wages, educational programs, and social benefits.[5] Rather than meet these distributional demands through higher taxes on the better-off or other measures that might cut into corporate profits, as the argument goes, policy makers opted to use tax cuts, financial deregulation, and consumer credit to stimulate the economy and satisfy social demands without picking obvious winners and losers.[6] Others, like Jacob Hacker and Paul Pierson, have argued that a new political coalition of business leaders and conservative activists since the 1970s pushed through financial deregulation and tax cuts for corporations and the wealthy, especially in the financial sector.[7] Hacker and Pierson refer to the coordinated policy development, lobbying, and political campaign spending by this coalition as a thirty-year war (now forty years).

In the specific case of educational loans, Congress passed major changes to the US Higher Education Act in 1992 that transformed student debt. New loan policies in the act triggered a radical spike after more than a decade of flat trends in borrowing. The spike in student loan borrowing is illustrated in figure 3.1. Annual federal student loan borrowing held flat at $20 billion in the decade prior to 1992. With the implementation of the 1992 reforms from 1994 onward, borrowing grew sixfold to $120 billion at its peak in 2011.[8] Borrowing per full-time equivalent student increased more than threefold from a little less than $2,000 per student in the 1980s to over $7,000 in 2011. Yet the origins of the policies behind this spike in borrowing have received almost no attention from researchers.

By looking at the historical record, we will see that financiers were able to push through the 1992 student loan amendments because of earlier victories in the thirty-year war. More Americans than ever wanted to go to college after business leaders had undermined blue-collar wages by breaking

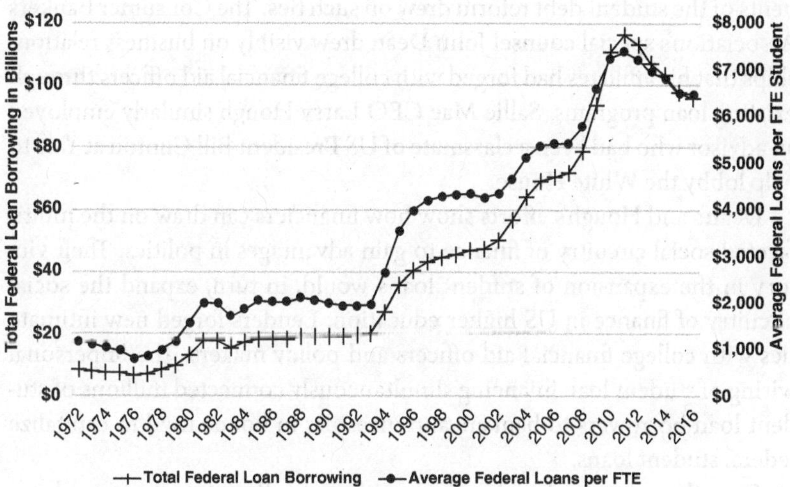

FIGURE 3.1 Annual federal student loan borrowing

NOTE: Data from table 2 of College Board *Trends in Student Aid*. Amounts in 2016 constant dollars.

unions and relocating factories.[9] But tax and spending cuts provided less funding to pay for lower-income students to go to college.[10] These twin pressures squeezed US colleges and universities.

Financiers responded to the squeeze on universities with proposals for increasing subsidies to themselves to expand federal student loans. They lobbied Congress for the proposals. They also partnered with complicit university leaders to advance their proposals, drawing on both alumni ties and client relationships with schools for whom they already had managed student lending at a smaller scale. In this mobilization, bankers presented themselves as coming to the rescue of colleges and students who were failed by a "centralized, federally administered program."[11] Through this intervention, bankers employed a political mobilization to offer financial markets and themselves as an alternative to tax-and-spend solutions for the distributional pressures that had beset US higher education. But in seeking federal subsidies for themselves, the bankers also confirmed that financial markets and their enterprises are not an unfettered private domain but rather one that almost always requires regulation and even direct government support.[12]

Contrary to the idea that schools sought the loan expansion, only a segment of college leaders came on board, and they did so mostly after bankers presented themselves as an alternative to government funding. At the same time, both intimate and impersonal ties helped financiers to enlist the support of colleges and elected officials.[13] Two of the most important proponents of the student debt reform drew on such ties. The Consumer Bankers Association's special counsel John Dean drew visibly on business relationships that his affiliates had forged with college financial aid officers through existing loan programs. Sallie Mae CEO Larry Hough similarly employed an advisor who had been a classmate of US President Bill Clinton at Yale to help lobby the White House.

Dean's and Hough's efforts show how financiers can draw on the multifaceted social circuitry of finance to gain advantages in politics. Their victory in the expansion of student loans would, in turn, expand the social circuitry of finance in US higher education. Lenders forged new intimate ties with college financial aid officers and policy makers. The impersonal wiring of student loan financing simultaneously connected millions of student loan borrowers to bankers and investors in bonds used to capitalize federal student loans.

Over the next two decades, the rewiring of college finance around student loans would transform the entire US higher education system. The loan expansion quickly fueled the rise of predatory for-profit colleges and gradually left student loan borrowers at a growing disadvantage relative to wealthy students who could attain a degree without any borrowing. In this way, the mobilization to expand student loans shows how the social power of financiers, if unchecked, can empower them to win policies that exploit distributional conflicts rather than resolve them.

Tax Cuts and the End of Loan-Free Higher Education

US policy makers originally intended for student loans to play only a small role when they created policies for financing the mass enrollment of the 1960s and 1970s.[14] Both government and college officials were mostly united in their preference for tax-financed government spending as the primary revenue source of undergraduate education. Loan-free higher education remained especially vulnerable to future distributional pressures, however, because initial federal policies to expand higher education in the 1960s did not create the new benefits as full entitlements with mandatory funding by Congress. Faced with competing demands for tax cuts and social spending increases in the late 1970s, it was easier for policy makers to freeze funding for loan-free education programs than for other full entitlement programs such as Social Security and Medicare.

Federal policy makers established the foundation for college financing with the 1965 Higher Education Act (HEA) as part of President Johnson's Great Society initiatives. In a 1974 congressional hearing, Senator Claiborne Pell said of the original HEA,

> It was the original intent of the Congress that [grants and work-study] would be of primary importance and the then-new loan program would be a supplemental standby mechanism . . . a floor, not necessarily paying for Yale or some other high-cost place, but a floor of education just like they have for 12 years at high school.[15]

Consistent with federal policy makers' original emphasis on nonloan-based support, both federal and state spending on higher education increased dramatically from 1964 until the end of the 1970s. Figure 3.2 plots higher education spending from 1964 until 2016. The figure uses three-year rolling averages to account for recessionary swings in higher education demand and government appropriations.[16] Congress tripled federal spending per college student on grant aid and work study from $630 in 1964 to a high of $1,976 in 1977 under that year's renewal of the HEA (2016 constant dollars). The 1976 renewal went so far as to fund Pell Grants to serve as a middle-class entitlement, available to most students from families making the equivalent of $90,000 or less in 2016 constant dollars.[17] State govern-

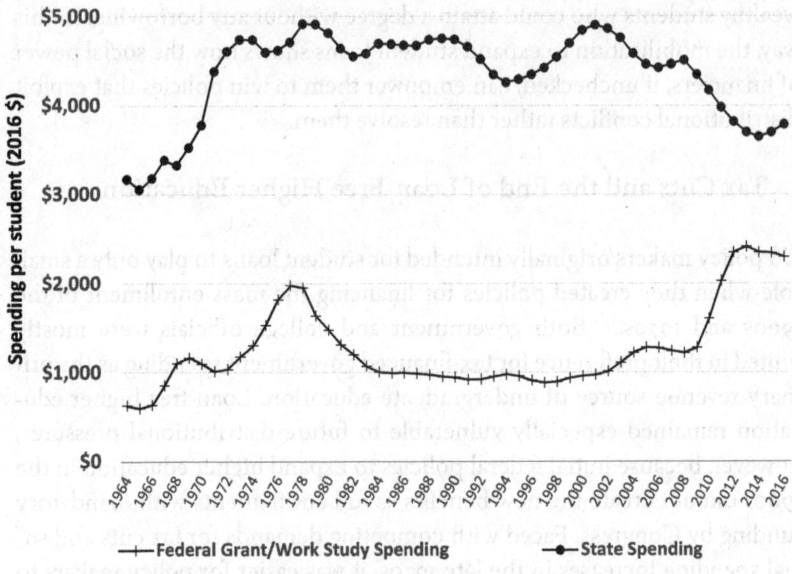

FIGURE 3.2 State and federal spending per student

NOTE: See note 16 for details on data sources.

ment spending on higher education per student also nearly doubled from $3,171 in 1964 to a high of $4,915 in 1978. These spending levels are on a per-student basis for all students at all types of colleges, including private colleges, in order to reflect overall college demand. The large increases in per-student spending are all the more striking because total college enrollment more than doubled during this period, from five million to nearly twelve million.

Contrary to the argument that university demands for tuition revenue led to the expansion of student debt, public university officials still preferred an expansion of nonloan aid in the 1980 reauthorization of the HEA. Representatives in Washington for private nonprofit and public universities all took a unified position for expanding Pell Grants further through their common federation, the American Council on Education (ACE). Georgetown University's president, Father Timothy Healy, told a US Senate hearing on the bill that grant awards should be increased from covering 50 percent of college costs to covering 75 percent of college costs at lower-cost public institutions.[18]

ACE meanwhile opposed a significant expansion of federal student loans in 1980 because they said it might undermine support for Pell Grant funding and for state appropriations for higher education. Father Healy told the Senate in testimony,

> Other questions arise in considering any "entitlement" program designed to assure the availability of loans: could the guaranteed availability of student loans serve to undermine funding of federal grant programs, or reduce state efforts in support of higher education? What would be the impact of increased loan availability on college costs?[19]

Congress acted accordingly to maintain only limited availability of federal student loans for low- and middle-income students in its 1980 and 1986 renewals of the HEA.

The new business and conservative coalition, however, created new distributional pressures at the end of the 1970s. Hacker and Pierson have focused on the impact of this coalition's thirty-year war on workers' wages and on rising incomes for the rich.[20] Few have appreciated, however, that Pell Grants and state funding for higher education were two of the earliest casualties of the thirty-year war because neither were ever enshrined as full entitlements like Medicare or Social Security. In what others have called America's delegated welfare state, entitlements establish a permanent funding obligation for social programs by both state and federal governments.[21] Federal Medicaid legislation required states to use state tax dollars to receive federal Medicaid funding. At the same time, federal Medicaid legislation required the federal government to increase funding to provide a minimum level of benefit to all persons eligible for Medicaid.

In contrast to legislation for full entitlements like Medicaid, Pell Grant legislation also required the Department of Education to only award Pell Grants to as many students as could be funded by congressional appropriations to the program. So, Pell Grant spending per student began to decline at the end of the 1970s and into the 1980s as Congress struggled to increase spending to keep up with inflation and the rise in the number of eligible students. Congress also significantly cut middle-class eligibility for Pell Grants in 1986.[22] As a result, we can see in figure 3.2 that per-student federal spending on Pell Grants and work study fell from its high of $1,976 in 1976 to less than $1,000 from 1985 until 2002. Looking back during the 1992 reauthorization hearings, Towson State University President and ACE Vice Chair Hoke Smith said, "The pressure to cut the federal deficit caused no increase in the maximum [Pell] award for seven out of twelve years."[23]

Figure 3.2 also shows that state higher education funding per student began falling in 1980 and has never recovered. The thirty-year war on state and federal taxes eroded the funding base for state spending.[24] At the same time, it was easier for states to cut higher education spending than to cut spending on other programs, like Medicaid, that had entitlement protections. Unlike federal requirements for states to receive federal Medicaid funds, Pell Grants required no spending by state governments. Longtime ACE lobbyist Becky Timmons explained to me in an interview,

> The expansion of Medicaid and the fact that the states are on the hook for so much of that entitlement system has caused them to radically reduce their funding for higher education. . . . It's always the first to go, the first to be cut.

Did financiers play a particularly important role in pushing the tax cuts that ratcheted up pressures against funding for higher education? Sociologist Mark Mizruchi has argued that commercial bankers played a preeminent role in forging a political consensus among corporate executives during this period. According to Mizruchi, commercial bankers played this role by serving on the boards of multiple nonfinancial corporations, thereby providing a connection between corporations known as a board interlock.[25] Firms connected by these banker board ties, in turn, are disproportionately likely to take the same political positions and make the same political contributions.[26]

Consistent with Mizruchi's theory, financiers were at the leading edge of the mobilizations to cut taxes that ratcheted up pressures to constrain federal spending on higher education. For example, Mizruchi, Hacker, and Pierson all single out Charls Walker as a key leader of the tax-cut movement. Walker cofounded the Business Roundtable, the American Council on Capital Formation, and Carleton Group, which spearheaded the successful efforts to cut capital gains taxes in 1978 and corporate taxes in 1981.[27] Having earned a PhD in finance at University of Pennsylvania's Wharton School of Business, Walker had emerged from the nexus of academic finance and Wall Street that elevated the free-market ideologies that animated the emergent tax-cut movement of the 1970s.[28] More broadly, researchers have similarly found that financial professionals tend to support tax cuts at much higher rates than do other well-compensated professionals, such as doctors and lawyers.[29]

Beyond Walker's leadership, financiers have wielded more clout in politics in recent decades in ways that are intrinsically social. Financiers' high rates of elite university social ties are a potentially valuable asset for political action. Simon Johnson and James Kwak have shown that bankers are more politically influential because of a long-standing revolving door between Wall Street and government.[30] Members of the financial sector also consistently spend more on campaign contributions and lobbying than do groups from any other part of the economy.[31] The elite centrality of financiers helps them to fundraise and bundle campaign contributions to antitax organizations and candidates. In sum, financiers' university social ties made them power players in pushing financial deregulation and the tax cuts that helped push down government higher education spending per student. These ties would also serve bankers well once the time was ripe to propose increased federal subsidies to student lenders.

Shareholder Value and Increasing College Demand

The thirty-year war blocked adequate fiscal support for loan-free higher education and decimated good jobs that required no college degree. Parallel to their efforts on tax cuts, the conservative-business coalition and their allies in the Reagan administration eviscerated regulations to protect worker and union rights.[32] Financiers simultaneously sought and won a series of financial deregulations that enabled the rise of private equity investors and the hostile takeover movement discussed in chapter 2.[33] After takeovers, investors would then use layoffs, plant closures, offshoring, automation, and union busting to extract profits from major corporations.[34] To avert hostile takeovers and satisfy investors, even more corporate executives adopted private equity's playbook to increase profits within their own companies. Increases in corporate profits by executives increased dividends and the market price of stocks for their shareholders—something that financial economists refer to as *shareholder value*.[35] The rise of shareholder value also contributed to deindustrialization more broadly. As a result, low-wage service-sector jobs replaced many high-wage industrial jobs for workers without a college degree.[36]

The decline of good jobs for those without college degrees added to distributional pressures in US higher education. With good jobs disappearing for those without college degrees, sociologist Tressie McMillan Cottom has argued that students from less-advantaged backgrounds embraced an *education gospel* that college is the best path to economic success and security.[37] As a growing share of students followed the education gospel, policy makers had to confront how to pay for increased enrollments and the financial aid for which low-income students were eligible.

During the hearings for the 1992 reauthorization of the HEA, policy makers and colleges expressed a new urgency for expanding higher education because of the decline in blue-collar jobs. While the number of students in college held relatively steady in the 1980s, the displacement of blue-collar workers contributed to an increase in older and financially needy students. In his testimony for ACE, Hoke Williams explained,

> There was a large increase in the number of older, independent [Pell Grant] recipients whose incomes were so low they were entitled to large awards.

> These students are most often enrolled in short-term training programs. The number of recipients with no Expected Family Contribution rose from 972,000 in 1979 to 1.7 million in 1988.[38]

Williams went on to lament that increased spending on Pell Grants for displaced older workers led to a decline in spending on younger middle-class students who remained dependent on their parents:

> These events contributed to a significant decline in the number of dependent students receiving Pell Grants between 1979 and 1988. The number of recipients 19 years old or younger declined 15 percent during this period. In contrast, the number of recipients 24 years or older nearly tripled, from 588,000 to 1.5 million, or 48 percent of all Pell recipients.

Pressures from the growth of older, working-class enrollment are also noted in testimony on behalf of community colleges[39] and student organizations.[40]

Democratic policy makers and the college associations continually pushed for more funding for Pell Grants and middle-class student assistance during the 1980s but to no avail. Former ACE and Pitzer College president Bob Atwell told me in an interview of the time, "We were always making a pitch for Pell Grants and for the other grant programs and were always losing a lot of those battles."[41] The Democratic Senate Subcommittee on Education, Arts, and Humanities chair Claiborne Pell said during a 1991 hearing that middle-income student assistance "dwindled away rapidly under the Reagan administration so that it is nonexistent at this point."[42] Unable to secure adequate direct grant funding for students, universities and lawmakers would need to secure new resources elsewhere.

Financiers Mobilize for Student Loan Expansion

With colleges squeezed by the distributional pressures of tax cuts and rising college demand, commercial banks and other lenders seized the opportunity to promote an expansion of federal student loans as a solution to the distributional dilemma. Earlier federal policies had brought commercial banks into the market and even created some of the lenders. Under the original policies the overall scope for student loans was limited. Private lenders, however, stood to reap windfall profits if they were tapped to provide financing that would replace federal grant aid and state appropriations for a growing higher education system. Accordingly, financiers proposed and aggressively mobilized for policies that would not only use loans to expand higher education but also provide billions of dollars in subsidies to private lenders.

Building on GI Bill programs, federal student loan programs were established in the 1960s and 1970s primarily to help upper-middle-class students attend higher-tuition private colleges. Government budget rules made it difficult for the federal government to lend directly to students without having to report the loans as adding to the deficit.[43] Congress took a series of steps to subsidize and incentivize the provision of federal loans by private lenders.[44] First, the Department of Education provided guarantees to private lenders that the federal government would cover their losses if students failed to repay loans. Second, the federal government created the Student Loan Marketing Association, commonly known as Sallie Mae, in 1973. Sallie Mae began as a for-profit government-sponsored enterprise. Sallie Mae raised capital to buy and offer student loans by securitizing loans and selling those securities to investors.

Sociologists Elizabeth Popp Berman and Abby Stivers portray Sallie Mae and private lenders as reluctant participants in the market until the 1992 HEA reauthorization. Sallie Mae had only been founded in 1973, and there were suggestions that banks did not see student loans as profitable. "The banks had threatened to walk away from the program whenever lawmakers tried to change it."[45] But threats by the banks to walk away may have been tactical. "By the mid-1980s however, the banking industry had the most active lobbyists around the GSL [guaranteed student loan] program."[46]

During the 1992 reauthorization, a coalition of lenders led by Larry Hough and John Dean advanced three critical proposals that would drive a massive expansion of borrowing over the next twenty years. Hough's Sallie Mae and Dean's Commercial Bankers Association were two of the most powerful members of the National Council of Higher Education Loan Program (NCHELP) trade association. All three of the proposals by NCHELP involved an expansion of federal student loans that would be financed and administered by private lenders. The US Department of Education, however, would "guarantee" these loans by paying the private lenders whenever students failed to repay their loans because of financial hardship, death, or any other reason. For low-income students, the federal government would also pay interest on the loans to the lenders while students were still enrolled in school.

NCHELP first proposed a new federally guaranteed loan program for all students regardless of income.[47] The new loan program would become known as unsubsidized Stafford loans because the federal government would guarantee against nonrepayment but would not subsidize the interest payments for the loans while students were in school. Second,

NCHELP pushed to increase the cap for total borrowing. Congress ultimately decided to double the caps for both subsidized and unsubsidized Stafford loans from close to $30,000 to over $70,000 in 2016 constant dollars.[48] Third, NCHELP proposed eliminating the cap for the federal Parent Loan for Undergraduate Students (PLUS) to allow parents to borrow however much a college charged for tuition, room, and board.[49]

NCHELP also pushed aggressively for the federal government to maintain the guarantee subsidies so that Sallie Mae and the banks would receive support to provide most of the expanded federal student loan programs. The Federal Credit Reform Act of 1990 had changed federal accounting rules in ways that made it possible for the federal government to directly lend to students at a much lower cost without having to record it as deficit spending.[50] Sallie Mae and consumer banks, however, won policy changes to maintain the costlier guarantee subsidies from the federal government to private lenders. This victory would give the private lenders an incentive to advocate for policies in the coming two decades that would further expand borrowing and increase the cost of borrowing for students. These policies would include regular increases in borrowing caps, higher interest rates, and restrictions on borrowers' ability to discharge debts they could not afford to pay.[51]

Intimate Ties in Action: The Bankers Enlist Colleges and Lawmakers

The more assertive leadership by Hough, Dean, and other lenders around the 1992 reauthorization was a clear and decisive change from 1976 and 1979 legislative battles over federal college aid. To push through their policy agenda, however, the bankers also enlisted the support of universities and, of course, lawmakers. After coping with a distributional squeeze for more than a decade, colleges and Democrats were more open to supporting student loan expansion as an alternative to expanding Pell Grants and state appropriations. Most colleges and lawmakers, however, initially favored the expansion of student loans through direct lending by the US Department of Education rather than through guarantee subsidies. To win support for guarantee subsidies, Hough and Dean would explicitly present their proposals as solutions to distributional pressures. Hough and Dean would also employ both personal and intimate ties from the collegiate backgrounds of their coalition and from the business relationships between lenders and college financial aid administrators.

Private colleges were the most aggressive in supporting loan expansion and in acquiescing to the costly proposition that private lenders receive federal guarantees to do most of the lending. Private colleges were represented by the National Association of Independent Colleges and Universities (NAICU). NAICU explicitly supported loan expansion because Pell Grant expansion had failed. Jane Wellman, NAICU's executive director at the time, told me in an interview,

> The membership in NAICU, one of the first things it was explained to me very clearly, we're here to get money out of the bill and the only way there's going to be money in this bill is in the loan program. We don't particularly care whether it's bank based or fed based, as long as the dough is there.[52]

During the 1980 reauthorization fight, NAICU simply signed on to the testimony of the broader ACE, which opposed student loan expansion. In the 1992 reauthorization debate, however, NAICU instead offered its own testimony to underscore its support of loan expansion.[53]

The elimination of federal grant support for middle-income students in the 1980s was cited as a key reason for NAICU's support of expanded loan programs. The president of NAICU, Dr. Richard Rosser, directly linked his call for expanded student loans to the spending constraints on Pell Grants in his testimony:

> Students from middle-income families need subsidized loan programs to finance the costs of higher education over the long term. These students have been virtually disenfranchised from federal grant programs.[54]

On this basis, NAICU endorsed the lenders' proposal to lift the cap on PLUS loans for parents. NAICU did not explicitly endorse the lenders' proposal to create a new unsubsidized federal loan program for students of all income levels. However, NAICU made a similar proposal to expand access to subsidized Stafford loans to higher-income students.[55]

While NAICU led the charge among colleges for loan expansion, ACE followed suit with its first strong position in support of loan expansion. ACE presented a "consensus position" as the "national umbrella association representing all sectors of American higher education," including the respective associations for nonprofit private schools, public universities, community colleges, and for-profit schools.[56] The consensus position backed all the loan proposals put forward by NAICU. Similarly to this new openness to student loans, Berman has shown that universities also warmed to the marketization of scientific research when government funding tightened.[57]

Many public universities, however, supported the direct provision of expanded federal loans by the US Department of Education rather than private lenders. Direct loan provision by the Department of Education would save several billion dollars by eliminating subsidies to private lenders. The savings and simplified administration of loans could be used to make loans cheaper for students or to subsidize expanded Pell Grants.[58]

Against arguments that a direct loan program would be cheaper and more efficient, the bankers drew on the same free-market mythologies that had animated the mobilizations for tax cuts and financial deregulation. For example, Sallie Mae's Hough invoked free-market efficiencies to justify his proposal, even though the proposal involved government subsidies and Sallie Mae had been created by the federal government itself. On October 29, 1991, Hough testified to the Senate Committee on Labor and Human Resources that "no matter how one designs a centralized, federally administered program, it cannot possibly compete with the incentives that drive private sector entities."[59]

Hough and Dean also employed a set of personal and impersonal ties to win support from colleges and lawmakers for their policy proposals. These activities became particularly visible when newly elected US President Bill Clinton proposed to eliminate the guarantee subsidies in 1993 as part of national service legislation on which he had campaigned for president. Removing the guarantee subsidies would make federal student loans unprofitable for private banks. As a result, these private financiers would have left the federal government to make all federal student loans directly at a lower cost to both students and taxpayers. *Newsweek* reporter Steven Waldman was embedded in the Clinton administration's effort to pass the national service legislation, and he documented the political warfare over the bill.

Dean drew on a mix of ties, for example, by organizing lobbying activities that included both private lenders affiliated with the Consumer Bankers Association and financial aid administrators employed by colleges. In doing so, Dean drew on the ties forged between lenders and aid administrators through the economic activity of calculating, financing, and awarding financial aid packages. At one level, these ties are relatively impersonal and transactional. At another level, the relationship between lenders and aid administrators provided Dean and the Consumer Bankers Association with intimate private information about the fears that financial aid administrators had about the ability of the Department of Education to effectively administer loan aid. Playing on these fears, Dean and his allies hammered points about the Department of Education's administrative capacity in testimony and comments in the media.[60] In addition to what Waldman documented in 1993, a 2007 internal Sallie Mae memo detailed plans to use the exact same strategy to defend the guaranteed loan subsidies.[61] The memo listed Sallie Mae's number one strength for its political campaign as its "vast school customer base" even though Sallie Mae's customers technically are their student borrowers.

Dean and Hough also drew on intimate college alumni ties in building their political coalition. Hough himself had an elite educational pedigree with an undergraduate degree from Stanford and an MBA from MIT. Hough was also an Olympic medalist in rowing, one of the elite prep school sports that Rivera has shown investment bankers tend to relate to when hiring new recruits.[62] But to reach deeper into the Clinton administration, Hough hired financial industry lawyer Jerry Hultin because Hultin had attended Yale Law School with Clinton. Hultin wrote speeches for Hough in 1993 about the proposal to eliminate loan guarantee subsidies and used his friendship with Clinton to hand-deliver the speeches to the president.[63] To help defend the loan guarantee subsidies, Dean similarly hired William Blakely, the lobbyist for the United Negro College Fund. With leadership from Blakely, most historically Black colleges and universities supported continued guarantee subsidies to the private lenders who had come to finance the loans for their student aid packages.

Recent scholarship has suggested that legislators with elite educational backgrounds tend to get their legislation passed at higher rates in the US Congress.[64] Is it possible that the high rate of elite educational backgrounds among financiers has helped them to win policy-making fights, such as the battle over student loan guarantee subsidies? If so, have social status and alumni connections to other elites given financiers this advantage? More cases would help us to evaluate this conclusively, but we can say that student lenders sought to exploit university ties in their political mobilization.

The Consequences of Banker Power for Student Debt

As we saw, the distributional pressures on US colleges created the essential conditions for lawmakers to shift in 1992 to a loan-based system for financing US higher education. Sociologist Gretta Krippner has suggested that preceding waves of financial deregulation were ad hoc solutions adopted by policy makers to address such distributional problems.[65] In the case of student loans, we also do not see any grand design by bankers to construct the US student loan system long before the 1992 expansion. Nevertheless, bankers and banking organizations were clearly the lead movers in seeing the opportunity to construct a new system with themselves at its center. NCHELP, led by Hough of Sallie Mae and Dean of the Consumer Bankers, crafted the major proposals that were endorsed by colleges and universities and incorporated into the 1992 reauthorization of the HEA.

This leading role for bankers in student loan expansion resembles what

Sarah Quinn has shown with policies to privatize Fannie Mae, using similar guarantee subsidies for mortgage-backed securities in 1969. In that case, "bankers . . . asserted that they would only invest in the MBSs [mortgage-backed securities] with some kind of government guarantee." Bankers eventually won mortgage guarantee subsidies in the political negotiations over Fannie Mae. Noting the importance of banker political power, Quinn writes, "Lenders benefited greatly from extensive access to and influence over government officials."[66] In other words, bankers acted as agentic rent seekers in both the 1969 Fannie Mae privatization and 1992 student loan reforms.[67]

Under the policy changes adopted in 1992, student loan borrowing financed expanding college enrollment across public, private, for-profit, and community colleges alike. The creation of Stafford loans without interest rate subsidies for higher-income students dramatically expanded the availability of student loans for middle-class students. The doubling of the caps on all Stafford loans also allowed students from all income backgrounds to borrow more. Finally, the elimination of borrowing caps on PLUS loans allowed parents and eventually graduate students to borrow more still. As was shown in figure 3.1, annual federal loan borrowing per full-time equivalent student grew from around $2,000 during the 1980s to more than $7,000 in 2011. Because loans were also used to pay for increased overall enrollments, total annual borrowing ballooned even more from $20 billion in the 1980s to $120 billion at its peak in 2011.

In the chapters ahead, we will see how the expansion of federal student loans also fueled widening inequalities between the different strata of US higher education. At the top, parental wealth and the hoarding of university endowments shielded students from many of the negative repercussions of student debt. For example, 81 percent of first-year Ivy League undergraduates did not borrow at all during the 2016 academic year.[68] At the bottom, the expansion of student loans encouraged Wall Street investors to capitalize on a massive expansion of for-profit colleges that would leave millions of disadvantaged students in debt without improving their employment prospects on average.[69]

In the middle, the expansion of federal student loans enabled public universities, which enroll over 62 percent of four-year degree seekers, to pay for rising enrollment demands with loan-financed tuition revenue.[70] Under these arrangements, the percentage of US residents age twenty-five to twenty-nine with a bachelor's degree increased from 23 percent in 1990 to 36 percent in 2017.[71] The price was a new loan burden for most of those other than the wealthiest students. In 1975, just one in eight students at any type of college borrowed using federal student loans.[72] By 1992, the share of students with debt from public universities had increased to 25 percent. By 2016, 64 percent of graduating seniors at public universities had student debts. The average debts for students also grew in size. And students from underrepresented racial and ethnic groups and from less-wealthy households tended to borrow at the highest rates.[73] As a result, most students now left school with debts that disadvantaged them relative to wealthy students and elite private college students, who overwhelmingly left college debt-free. This student debt disadvantage is a new economic inequality that was virtually nonexistent before the 1990s.

Although loans helped public universities to meet rising enrollment demands, the expansion of student loans failed to completely alleviate the distributional pressures on public universities. Chapter 6 will detail how these persistent resource pressures compounded the consequences of increased student loan borrowing. First, state and federal lawmakers continued to reduce per-student spending on Pell Grants and direct appropriations.[74] At the same time, many states placed limits on the extent to which public universities could offset funding shortfalls with student loan–financed tuition increases.[75] Hindered by these resource constraints, graduation rates at public universities ranged from just 42 percent to 49 percent during the years of student loan–financed expansion.[76] States also continued to push substantial shares of qualified students into underfunded community colleges from which they were less likely to progress to a bachelor's degree.[77] As a result, a majority of borrowers never actually attain a bachelor's degree.

Some economists have argued that students rarely borrow too much because, on average, the earnings gains from college are higher than the costs of repaying student debt.[78] While the latter claim may be true on average, a majority of borrowers do not receive commensurate wage gains from their borrowing because they never actually attain a bachelor's degree. In fact, scholars have found negative effects on graduation rates from debt as some students who borrow heavily early in college will hesitate to take on further debt to complete college.[79] With many borrowers failing to graduate, 46 percent of all borrowers have missed payments on federal student loans even since the 2008 recession subsided.[80] And more than one million federal student loan borrowers have defaulted annually since the 2008 financial crisis, including 27 percent of students at nonselective four-year public and private colleges in the most recent years for which data are available.[81] Among students from low-income backgrounds who left public universities in 2013, only 47 percent had repaid any principal without defaulting after three years compared to 67 percent of higher-income students.[82] Just 31 percent of low-income community college students repaid any of their debt within three years.

Student Loan Politics without Bankers

Would policy makers have turned to student loans were it not for the political intervention by Hough, Dean, Sallie Mae, and the Consumer Bankers? The demise of the banks' loan guarantee subsidies in 2010 provides what social scientists call a counterfactual—a sort of alternate history to consider what might have been. Ten years of student loan politics since the end of the guarantee subsidies suggest that the expansion of student debt and its consequences would have been less severe were it not for financiers' involvement in the 1992 loan reforms.

You might expect that the banks were eventually driven out of the federal student loan programs by public outrage over mounting student debt. In actuality, the banks were done in when the 2008 financial crisis obliterated their mythology that private financial markets and institutions operate best with minimal government intervention and regulation.[83] Following financial deregulation, America's largest investment and commercial banks merged into the consolidated financial service corporations that we met in chapter 2.[84] In the early and mid-2000s, the consolidated banks engaged in widespread fraud and herd behavior involving mortgage-backed securities that inflated a massive real estate and financial bubble.[85] The bubble burst in 2007, triggering the worst global financial crisis and economic downturn since the 1930s.[86] Amid this collapse, the banks became unable to raise capital for mortgages by selling bonds and other securities because no one could trust that the banks would actually pay out on them. And the same problem rendered the banks and Sallie Mae completely unable to finance any federal student loans.[87] As a result, the US Department of Education took over direct funding of nearly all new federal student loan origination by 2009. With the federal government already directly funding almost all student loans, the banks mounted little resistance to an amendment to the 2010 Affordable Care Act that finally eliminated the federal student loan guarantee subsidy to private lenders.[88]

A series of developments since 2010 reveals how the elimination of subsidies to private banks reduced political and budgetary pressures to finance higher education through student loans with adverse terms for borrowers. These shifts provide us with some counterfactual insights for how problems from rising student debt since the 1990s might have been mitigated were it not for the successful political mobilization of the bankers. First, the elimination of the guarantee subsidy saved $62 billion over ten years. The amendment to the 2010 Affordable Care Act used much of this savings for a $36 billion increase in Pell Grant funding.[89] Pell Grants still fund a much smaller share of the price of college than they did in the 1970s, and financial need requirements still exclude many middle-class students who would have been Pell eligible before cuts in the 1980s. Still, the elimination of the private bank role made possible the largest federal nonloan investment in undergraduate education since the 1970s.

Meanwhile, the elimination of the bank role made it easier for the Department of Education to offer lower interest rates and loan forgiveness for millions of borrowers.[90] First, the elimination of the bank role freed up funds for the department to offer forgiveness and lower interest rates. Second, the banks had politically opposed programs to reduce loan burdens such as income contingent repayment (ICR) because the program was associated with direct lending. With the banks out of the federal student loan system, they no longer had an incentive to oppose programs like ICR. In this reconfigured political ecology, amendments to the Affordable Care Act also included provisions to expand ICR through a broader set of income-driven repayment plans, in which new borrowers pay no more than 10 percent of their income toward loans and have all outstanding debts forgiven after twenty years. Enrollments in income-driven repayment plans subsequently increased from 13 percent of new borrowers in 2014 to 32 percent in 2020, with growing enrollments among high-balance, low-income borrowers.[91] As a result, the federal government is now lending more than will be eventually repaid by these borrowers.[92]

In chapter 7, I will return to how the elimination of private banks from the federal student loan program may provide greater political space for imagining alternative ways to finance higher education. It is revealing that the expansion of both Pell Grants and income-driven repayment loan relief survived Republican President Donald Trump, even with Republicans controlling both houses of Congress for the first two years of his administration. Sallie Mae executives and other student loan financiers have also been remarkably silent on increasingly popular proposals to cancel student debt and make college debt-free. Had politicians credibly advanced debt-free proposals in the pre-2010 student debt system, subsidized lenders likely would have spent hundreds of millions of dollars to politically stop them in their tracks. With banks mostly out of the student loan system, proponents for alternative financial aid arrangements have a fighting chance.

4.

The Top

How Universities Became Hedge Funds

On June 5, 2015, Harvard University President Drew Gilpin Faust gleefully announced that the university had received its largest-ever donation—$400 million from hedge fund investor John Paulson. The gift, Faust said, "will change Harvard and enhance our impact on the world beyond."[1]

While Paulson's gift grabbed bigger headlines, another hedge fund billionaire was doing just as much to build Harvard's financial stockpile behind the scenes. Seth Klarman of the Baupost Group hedge fund had signed on as an honorary chair when the Harvard Business School (HBS) announced its $1 billion fundraising campaign in 2014.[2] HBS also named its new conference center after Klarman in recognition of his donation to a fund for the project.[3] Another managing director from Klarman's Baupost Group, Scott Nathan, served on the Harvard Corporation Committee on Finance to advise the university on matters including its endowment.[4] By 2017, as Klarman gained status and prestige from these Harvard ties, the university had also given his Baupost Group $1.96 billion in endowment funds to manage.[5] Under a typical hedge fund contract, Baupost would earn tens or hundreds of millions of dollars for managing this investment.

Harvard, Baupost, and Klarman's mutually beneficial relationship reaches back to the birth of the hedge fund sector. Just after Klarman graduated from Harvard Business School, HBS adjunct professor Bill Poorvu recruited him to run the newly formed Baupost.[6] Over the subsequent twenty-six years, Baupost would earn an average 20 percentage point compounded annual rate of return for itself and investors like Harvard (and Yale, which had invested $700 million in Baupost as of 2017).

Between the 1980s and the financial crisis of 2008, these spectacular earnings elevated hedge fund managers and their cousins in private equity

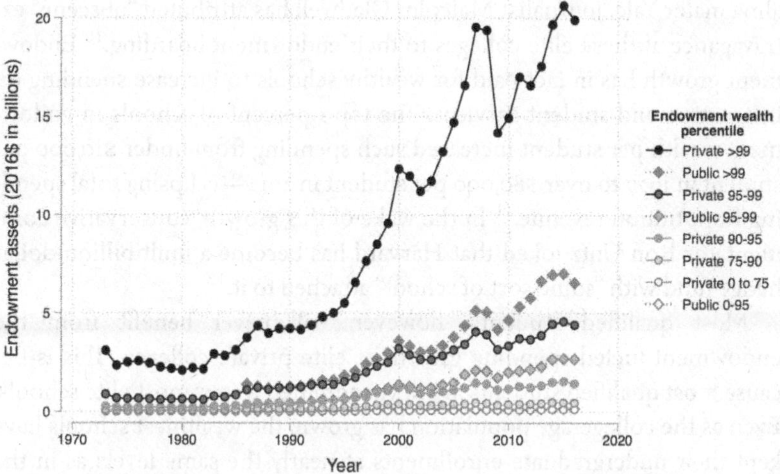

FIGURE 4.1 Total endowment wealth by endowment wealth percentile

NOTE: Data on endowment wealth are from the Council for the Advancement of Education Survey, the National Association of College and University Business Officers Survey, and the Integrated Postsecondary Education Data System. See note 7 for further details.

to the pinnacle of America's new financial oligarchy. But the rise of hedge funds and private equity also transformed US higher education by providing massive new financial surpluses for the most elite colleges. The endowments of America's most elite private universities have almost uniformly grown by 500 percent or more in the last forty years (in 2016 dollars, which are used for dollar amounts throughout the book). Figure 4.1 illustrates this exponential growth for the wealthiest 1 percent of schools alongside more plodding growth for almost all schools below the ninety-fifth percentile for endowment wealth.[7]

Economist Charles Clotfelter has shown that rising endowment wealth is sharply stratified according to the admissions selectivity and average SAT scores of enrolled students.[8] Echoing Clotfelter's findings, there is substantial overlap between the most endowed schools and the Times Higher Education (THE) thirty top-ranked private universities whose boards are profiled in chapter 2. Harvard, Yale, Stanford, Princeton, and MIT made up five of the six schools above the ninety-ninth percentile in all years since 1973. Members of the top thirty in 2017 made up twenty-two of the twenty-three schools in the top 5 percent for endowment wealth in 1973.[9]

The increase in endowment wealth at the top has led to a growing divergence in resources between highly selective private universities and the rest of the higher education system. In a scathing commentary about his alma mater Yale, journalist Malcolm Gladwell has attributed "obscene" extravagance at these elite colleges to their endowment hoarding.[10] Endowment growth has in fact paid for wealthy schools to increase spending on instruction and student services. The top 1 percent of schools in endowment wealth per student increased such spending from under $10,000 per student in 1977 to over $80,000 per student in 2012—eclipsing total spending from tuition revenue.[11] In the wake of this growth, conservative commentator Ron Untz joked that Harvard has become a multibillion-dollar hedge fund with "some sort of school" attached to it.[12]

Most qualified students, however, will never benefit from the endowment-fueled spending growth at elite private colleges. This is because most qualified students are never admitted to our most elite schools. Even as the college-age population has grown, the wealthiest schools have kept their undergraduate enrollments at nearly the same levels as in the 1970s, including for students from underrepresented communities.[13] As was noted in chapter 2, thirty-eight top private colleges today enroll more students from the top 1 percent of the nation's income spectrum than from the bottom 60 percent.[14] The transformation of elite college endowments into fast-growing hedge funds has reinforced this inequality.

But how is it that elite college endowments became hedge funds, and why has this phenomenon been confined to exclusive private universities? The Baupost-Harvard relationship encapsulates a pair of inequality-generating dynamics that must be unpacked to explain the elite endowment boom. The first dynamic we must understand is *the high-finance advantage*—how private information and trust from the social circuitry of finance boosts investment returns for the managers of private equity, hedge funds, and elite university endowments.[15] This advantage enabled both fund managers and elite universities to attain substantially higher investment returns between the 1980s and the 2008 financial crisis. The second inequality-generating process is *philanthropic homophily*, by which increasingly wealthy financiers disproportionately boosted donations to the endowments of their own elite alma maters.

Intimate university social ties are central to the high-finance advantage and to philanthropic homophily. Like most people in the economy, private equity, hedge fund, and endowment managers use cultural connections and social relationships in their economic exchanges. These social ties are constantly renegotiated through economic life itself. But they are also imported from parallel social organizations like country clubs and especially universities. Social ties and culture from college and elsewhere build trust and reciprocity, defining who is in the elite by also necessarily defining who is out. Sociologist Frederick Wherry has shown that people also make and maintain intimate in-group ties by exchanging private information.

New financial elites like Klarman and endowment managers like Yale's

David Swensen needed trust and private information from this social circuitry for their new investment strategies. Private information was essential because they planned to buy companies and financial assets that they thought were undervalued according to public information and prevailing wisdom. They needed high levels of trust from investors and partners because they borrowed large amounts of capital in order to increase both the potential returns and potential losses of their investments. They also needed investors to trust that the strategy would produce larger average returns over time despite large, inevitable losses on some investments and in some years. As a result, private equity and hedge fund managers raised critical early capital from wealthy individuals and endowment managers with whom they had close social ties, including from college. In subsequent years, private equity and hedge fund financiers returned the favor with increased donations to the universities that minted them.

Endowments and the High-Finance Advantage

Top endowment managers started down the path to private equity and hedge fund investment in response to private university financial woes in the 1960s. In 1969, former Harvard dean of faculty and Ford Foundation President McGeorge Bundy commissioned a report on how university endowments could best be managed. Entitled "Endowment Funds: The Law and the Lore," the report responded to widespread depreciation of real endowment asset values in the 1950s and 1960s.[16] Prior to the report, endowment managers believed they should manage endowments to simply maintain their total value over time. This preservation of endowment values would provide "intergenerational equity" by providing comparable levels of resources for the university's mission from one generation to the next.[17]

Bundy transformed endowment management, arguing that endowments should instead seek to maximize endowment investment returns. The strategy diversified endowment investments to include stocks and bonds. Bundy also called for reinvesting capital gains to further grow endowments. This radical change in thinking would eventually lead endowment managers to make some of the earliest investments with private equity and hedge funds.[18]

Financial Deregulation, Automation, and Institutional Investors

Three political and economic shifts combined in the 1980s to make it possible for private equity and hedge funds managers to deliver higher returns for endowments and other investors.

First, academics and financiers developed new types of transactions and computational methods for betting on which investments would deliver the largest returns. Second, deregulation and finance-related tax cuts let the new financiers use debt to make these investments at an unprecedented scale—and to keep more of the profits. Third, institutional investors—the people who managed investments for institutions—embraced the idea in the Bundy report that they should seek to maximize returns on their funds. University endowment managers were the first major institutional investors to turn to private equity and hedge funds with this motivation. They were later followed by even larger pension funds.

Echoing the 1969 Bundy endowment report, financiers and academics developed new ideas and technologies in the 1970s for a small staff of financial professionals to manage larger, riskier, and more complex financial portfolios. DePaul University alum and hedge fund pioneer Edmund O'Connor commissioned research by Princeton economists Burton Malkiel and Richard Quandt in 1969 to build support for the creation of a derivatives exchange. O'Connor used the report to enlist Harvard alum and Securities Exchange Commission attorney Milton Cohen. Cohen then convinced the Securities Exchange Commission to let the Chicago Board of Trade establish its derivatives exchange in 1973.[19] Separately, MIT economists Fischer Black, Robert C. Merton, and Myron Scholes developed new practices for pricing and trading derivatives. They developed their approach to derivative pricing in consultation with hedge fund pioneers like Columbia MBA Michael Goodkin and University of Chicago economist Harry Markowitz. Goodkin and Markowitz's hedge fund also developed one of the first computer programs for arbitrage trading.[20]

Separately, financial economists like Michael Jensen created new ideas about how to value and financially manage companies to increase their profitability for shareholders.[21] These new ideas about shareholder value would pave the way for leveraged buyouts as the primary investment technique of private equity in the 1980s.[22] Private equity investors also used new computing technology to obtain and analyze greater amounts of public and private data on risks and opportunities associated with potential investments.[23]

The new conservative-business coalition successfully promoted financial deregulation from the 1970s onward. Financiers were well represented in the coalition by leaders like Wharton alumnus Charls Walker of the American Council on Capital Formation. Their agenda reorganized the rules for US finance around the new ideas and technologies for maximizing investment returns. The creation of the derivative exchange by the Chicago Board of Trade itself required regulatory changes by the Securities

Exchange Commission. Congress and regulators also loosened constraints on junk bonds and other debt vehicles.[24] These changes allowed investment managers to leverage capital from their investors with debt to make bigger investments. Steep cuts to capital gains taxes in the late 1970s simultaneously allowed investors, investment managers, and recipients of investment to retain more of their investment returns than ever before.[25] As part of the broader shift in US tax policy, Congress eliminated a 2 percent excise tax on university endowment investment returns in 1984.[26]

Finally, institutional investors—including pension funds and endowments—provided a new source of capital for high-risk, high-return investment strategies. Most capital for private equity and hedge funds today is provided by pension funds. Wealthy individuals and the wealthiest college endowments, however, provided essential early capital to establish the new funds when their ability to produce high returns was still uncertain.[27]

For example, most Ivy League schools began investing in venture capital in the early 1970s. Venture capital firms are both a forerunner and variant of contemporary private equity funds. They tend to invest in younger, privately held companies such as technology start-ups. Prior to the Employment Retirement Income Security Acts of 1974 and 1978, however, pension funds could not even hold stock or high-risk bonds in their portfolios.[28] Most corporate pensions and public employee pension funds therefore did not begin investing in private equity (including venture capital) or hedge funds until the 1980s and 1990s, respectively.[29]

The pipeline from the Ivy League to Wall Street led Yale to become one of the first endowments to dramatically expand its alternative investments and realize greater returns. After earning both a BA and PhD in economics from Yale, David Swensen worked for Lehman Brothers and Salomon Brothers surrounding their earliest financing of leveraged buyouts and currency derivatives.[30] Six years later, Yale hired Swensen to run its endowment. Under his stewardship, Yale became a leader in endowment investing with private equity and hedge funds.

But Yale was not alone. Data from the National Association of College and University Business Officers Endowment Survey shows that elite ties facilitated critical early investment in alternative investment activities by an array of wealthy college endowments, beginning with venture capital investments in the 1980s.[31] In 1988, 315 colleges and universities responded when the survey asked for the first time whether they had invested in venture capital firms. Fifty-eight schools (18 percent) reported investments in venture capital firms, and fourteen schools (4 percent) reported investments in other private equity firms in 1988. Data on board members for twenty-three of the highest-ranked private universities and twenty-nine highest-ranked liberal arts colleges in 1989 show that schools were more likely to have investments if they had board ties to the new high-finance funds.[32] Of schools with high-finance board ties, 54 percent reported investments in venture capital—21 percentage points higher than for the schools without board ties.

Intimate Ties and University Investing

Private equity and hedge fund managers probably would have eventually found other investors if they hadn't received early capital from university endowments, but university investment helped tip the scales and give fund managers their first big successes. And the new high-finance funds likely took off earlier than they would have otherwise. Why then did endowment managers provide the new financiers with their largest source of early capital? By answering this question, we can see *how* the new financiers used intimate ties and private information to make their fortunes.

Initially, fund managers like Klarman of Baupost Group and Harvard turned to wealthy individuals for capital. But there was no public directory of people who were willing and able to provide large amounts of capital for investment strategies that were unproven and carried risks for substantial losses.[33] Elite private universities provided social connections so that private equity and hedge fund managers could raise capital from wealthy individuals willing to take such risks. Baupost got its first $27 million in capital from wealthy Bostonians who orbited the Harvard Business School. Baupost cofounder and HBS adjunct professor Bill Poorvu contributed capital from his success as a real estate investor.[34] Another local millionaire and HBS adjunct professor, Jordan Baruch, also invested.[35] A fourth Baupost cofounder, Harvard professor Howard Stevenson, has a book on fundraising that echoes how hedge fund managers use social ties and private information to raise capital. In it, Stevenson writes, "If you've done your homework, people say yes more often." Doing your homework requires "finding the right prospects" and understanding their motivations.[36]

University social ties also helped private equity and hedge fund managers to raise capital from university endowments on top of wealthy alumni networks. First-person accounts show these social ties involve exchanges of valuable private information and the validation of social status. Further details about Yale's early investment in the hedge fund of alumnus Tom Steyer are revealing. Steyer told the *New York Times* in 2007 that he began his courtship of investment by the Yale endowment in his hedge fund after learning of fellow Yalie David Swensen's appointment to lead the school's endowment at a 1988 homecoming football game.[37] Two years later, Swensen provided Steyer's Farallon Capital with $300 million, a third of its total investment capital. Steyer ultimately related the story of Yale's early investment to the *Times* as private information that could convey the status honor of his most important first investor. "David told us: 'I don't see why we would give you any money. You might shut down after a bad year,'" Steyer told the *Times*, validating Swensen's shrewdness as a trail-blazing investor. Swensen finally invested after Steyer "swore that he wouldn't shut down." Consecrating the intricate exchange of capital, private information, and reputation, the *Times* entitled the story with Steyer's interview "For Yale's Money Man, a Higher Calling."

Swensen's initial reservations about Steyer closing his hedge fund show how university social and cultural ties helped the new financiers secure investors despite the risk and high uncertainty about their new strategy. While top private equity and hedge funds have consistently delivered higher returns than have conventional investments over the long run, they do so by tolerating more volatility and large losses in the short run. This has remained true in the twenty-first century. For example, the Sun Capital and Cerberus Partners private equity firms lost hundreds of millions of dollars when Mervyns went bankrupt in 2008 following their $1.25 billion leveraged buyout of the company.[38] The Long Term Capital Management hedge fund founded by the MIT economist and hedge fund pioneer Robert C. Merton itself collapsed in 2000 after losing $4.6 billion in four months around investments affected by the Asian financial crises of the late 1990s.[39] The potential for investors to suffer such huge losses is intrinsic to the use of debt leveraging to increase the size of investments and potential returns.[40]

Based on in-depth interviews and ethnographic observation of a major hedge fund, Megan Neely has shown that university social ties help high-finance fund managers to tolerate risks through patrimonial arrangements.[41] As Neely writes, "Patronage is an ingrained feature of the industry. Overwhelmingly white and male investors become patrons, passing on their wealth to carefully groomed protégés who look like themselves." Neely even documents that hedge fund professionals routinely refer to top hedge funders as "chief" and "king."[42]

Journalists have also found that financiers on elite university boards steer their schools' endowment managers toward mutually beneficial investment opportunities. In addition to Harvard's investment in Baupost while managing director Scott Nathan served on Harvard's board, Brown, Columbia, Cornell, Penn, Princeton, and Yale all disclosed in 2013 that they had investments involving at least one trustee on their board.[43] In defense of the practice, Dartmouth general counsel Robert B. Donin said to the *New York Times*, "Dartmouth is proud that some of the world's leading money managers are Dartmouth alumni." Donin added that investments with private equity and hedge funds were "based on a manager's strategy, expertise and performance history," not board ties.[44] Yet Dartmouth held investments in six different funds with ties to its board members in 2013, including Leon Black's Apollo Global Management.

Even if endowment managers' choices are ultimately based on expected returns, board ties can help endowment managers learn of lucrative investment options. Having proven themselves, top private equity and hedge fund financiers today only invite a select few investors like endowments to participate in their funds. This is in part because financiers closely guard their strategies and performance data as valuable information that a competitor might exploit. Consistent with this, Todd J. Zywicki, a Dartmouth trustee, said that several of the investments with trustees' firms were presented as "special opportunities."[45] Zywicki later criticized the practice as a conflict of interest.

Echoing Donin and Zywicki, a top financial administrator with one of the oldest and most elite British universities attributed his school's lack of private equity and hedge fund investments to a lack of connections. Asked why his university did not follow the lead of the Ivies, he told me in a correspondence, "We did not have the contacts with Wall St hedgies." He added, "We did not have the scale to be welcome as Wall St hedgy customers."

Inversely, disclosure requirements have limited the extent to which public universities invest with top private equity and hedge funds. In 2004, University of Michigan (U-M) leaders actually lobbied the state to exempt its endowment from public disclosure requirements. U-M's chief lobbyist told the *Detroit Free Press* that they did so because private equity and hedge fund managers with investments from the university worried that "companies were trying to access deeper information about their competitors through us."[46] Nearly every Michigan legislator voted for the bill, and Democratic governor Jennifer Granholm signed the bill into law. University of Michigan chief investment officer Erik Lundberg in 2018 explained the importance of secrecy around the information that flows between endowment managers and outside fund managers, including via university board members: "The reality is nobody gives away their secrets," said Lundberg. If U-M revealed the performance and fees of the funds it invested in, he argued that private equity and hedge fund managers would deny the university access to their highest-yield investments "at a tremendous cost."

Consistent with the reporting above, private universities with more private equity and hedge fund trustees moved larger shares of their endowments into these types of funds in the early 2000s. Nearly all the other top thirty private universities followed suit over the next decade by increasing their investments in private equity and hedge funds. Figure 4.2 illustrates the transformation. The top half and the bottom half of the figure each have eleven panels, one for every year from 2003 to 2013, the only years for which full data is available. In the top half, each panel plots a circle for each of Times Higher Education's thirty top-ranked private universities. Each university is plotted on the *y*-axis according to the share of their endowment invested in private equity and hedge funds for the given year. Each university is plotted on the *x*-axis according to the share of university trustees who owned or managed private equity and hedge funds. The dashed line in each panel represents an ordinary least squares regression estimate for the relationship between the two dimensions. This shows that from 2003 to 2007, the investment share and the board share were strongly correlated. For every 10 percentage points more that a school's board seats went to financiers, a school averaged between 6.6 and 8.8 percentage points more of its endowment invested in private equity and hedge fund investments. As the decade wore on, nearly all the top thirty private universities added more financiers to their boards. But even the schools that added the fewest financiers to their boards imitated the financier-led boards by increasing the share of their endowments invested in private equity and hedge funds to an average of 60 percent.

The bottom half of figure 4.2 shows that the top thirty THE public universities had no equivalent relationship between board membership and early investment in private equity and hedge funds. The public top thirty did increase the average share of their endowments in such funds from 20 percent to just over 50 percent. At Michigan, this involved a nine-member investment advisory board. Lundberg invested Michigan endowment funds with the firms of four of the nine members of the advisory board, including alumnus Sandy Robertson's Francisco Partners private equity fund. But Michigan's governing Board of Regents is directly elected by citizens of the state. So as with most public universities, the governing board with ultimate authority over the University of Michigan did not have any such financiers as regents.

Outside of the top thirty, other universities eventually followed suit after watching elite schools cash in on private equity and hedge fund investments in the 1990s and early 2000s. Figure 4.3 charts the average share of a school's portfolio in alternative investments by endowment wealth percentile from 2000 to 2013. Schools above the ninety-ninth percentile increased the share of their portfolios in alternative investments from 30 percent in 2000 to nearly 70 percent from 2009 onward. The wealthiest schools maintain the highest shares of alternative investments. But even the least wealthy

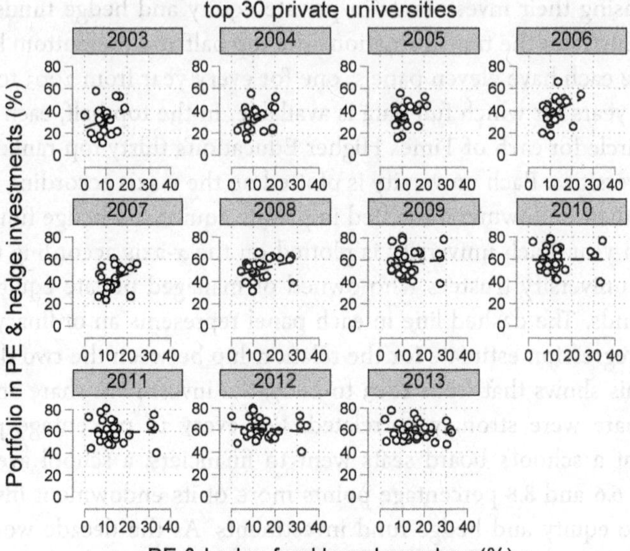

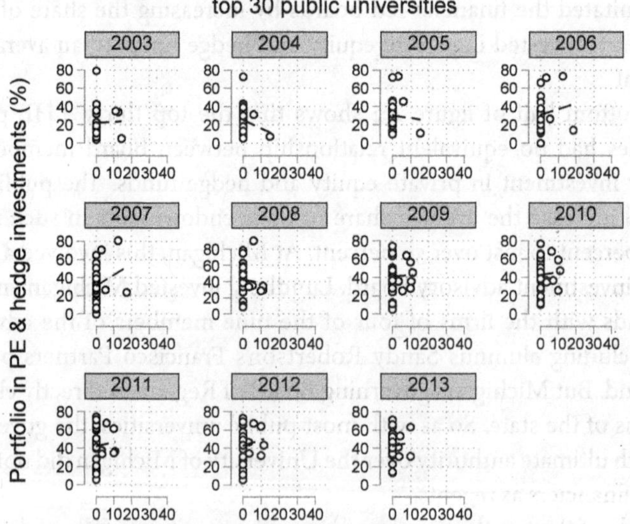

FIGURE 4.2 University private equity and hedge fund investments and board shares

NOTE: Data on endowment investments from NACUBO endowment survey. Data on board membership from Eaton and Gibadullina (2020).

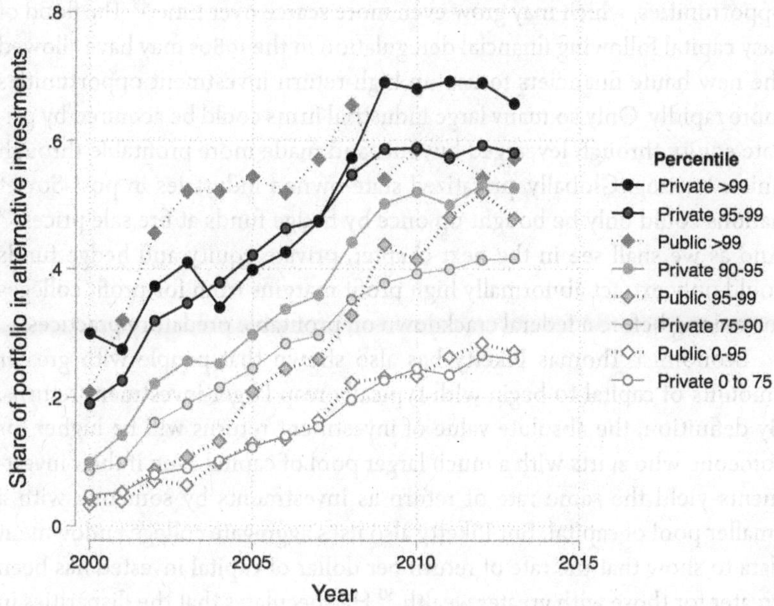

FIGURE 4.3 Private equity and hedge fund investment over time by endowment wealth

NOTE: Data on endowment investments and endowment asset size from NACUBO endowment survey.

schools increased their investments in alternative assets from 5 percent of their portfolio to over 25 percent of their portfolio during the period.

University Ties and the High-Finance Advantage

Poorer and less elite schools, however, may have arrived too late to the high-finance party. Consistent with assertions by Donin at Dartmouth and Lundberg at Michigan, lower-status schools with few links to high finance may have few paths to gain access to top-performing private equity and hedge funds. There have also been some indications that even the top fund managers have lost some of their advantage since the 2008 financial crisis. The booming returns of the 1990s and 2000s came at the cost of systemic financial risks that precipitated the 2008 financial crisis. And financial re-regulation under President Barack Obama may have clipped the wings of private equity and hedge funds by curtailing debt leveraging for their largest speculative bets.[47]

Economists have also shown that private equity and hedge fund managers look for high returns in sectors that have only a limited number of such opportunities, which may grow even more scarce over time.[48] The flood of easy capital following financial deregulation in the 1980s may have allowed the new haute financiers to use up high-return investment opportunities more rapidly. Only so many large industrial firms could be acquired by private equity through leveraged buyouts and made more profitable through union busting. Globally, privatized state-owned industries in post-Soviet nations could only be bought up once by hedge funds at fire sale prices.[49] And as we shall see in the next chapter, private equity and hedge funds could only extract abnormally high profit margins from for-profit colleges for so long before a federal crackdown on profitable predatory practices.

Economist Thomas Piketty has also shown that people with greater amounts of capital to begin with typically reap larger investment returns. By definition, the absolute value of investment returns will be higher for someone who starts with a much larger pool of capital even if their investments yield the same rate of return as investments by someone with a smaller pool of capital. But Piketty also uses aggregate college endowment data to show that the rate of return per dollar of capital invested has been greater for those with greater wealth.[50] He speculates that the disparities in returns arise because the wealthy can tolerate more short-term risk, have greater bargaining power over their investments, and enjoy economies of scale in the management of larger pools of capital.[51] Others have suggested that elite schools are able to recruit financial managers with greater skill from their talented alumni, independent of having more resources to hire the best investment managers.[52]

Finer endowment detail than Piketty's show that investment returns have a positive association with high-finance board ties for private universities on top of their association with endowment size.[53] But the data further show that this association also may have weakened after the 2008 financial crisis. This is illustrated in figure 4.4, which plots this relationship for the THE top thirty private universities and top thirty public universities. Figure 4.4 uses the same structure as figure 4.2 but plots universities each year according to their investment returns on the *y*-axis and board shares on the *x*-axis. The figure shows that from 2003 through 2008, the private universities had annual investment returns that averaged 2 percentage points higher for every 10 percentage points more of their board seats they awarded to private equity and hedge fund managers.[54]

The lower half of figure 4.4 shows that there is no comparable relationship between returns and financier board ties at public universities from 2003 to 2013. This supports the argument by Lundberg that private equity and hedge fund managers do not give their secrets away to public universities because of public disclosure requirements.[55]

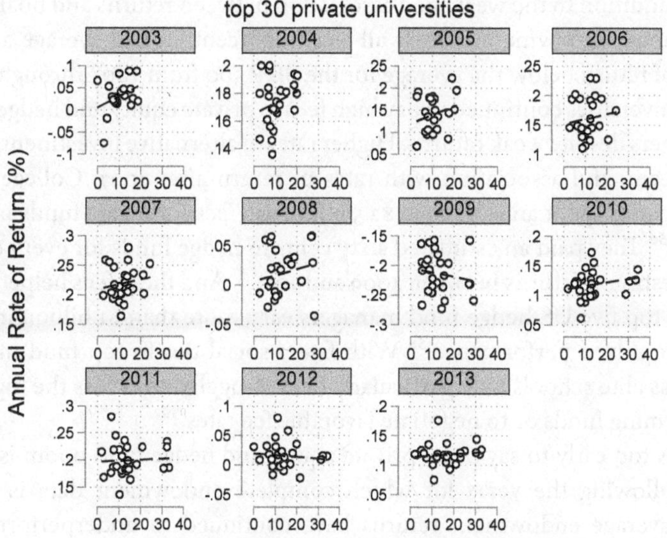

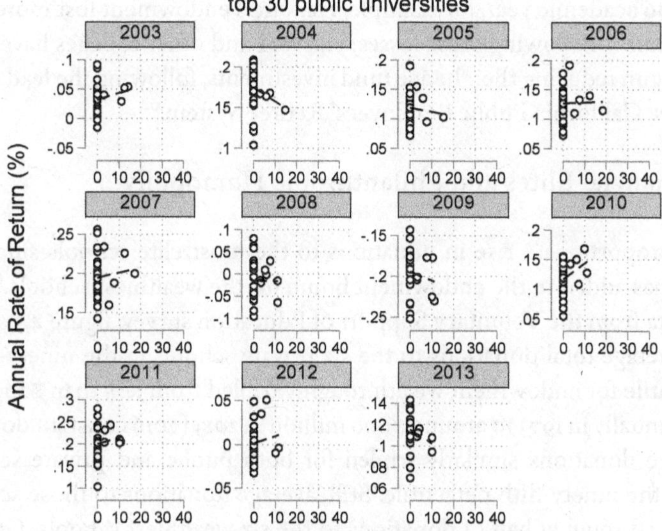

FIGURE 4.4 Annual rate of return and private equity and hedge fund board members, 2003–2013

NOTE: Data on endowment investments from NACUBO endowment survey. Data on board membership from Eaton and Gibadullina (2020).

In addition to the weakened association between returns and board ties after 2008, endowments across all wealth percentiles had average annual rates of return below the average for the S&P 500 from 2008 through 2013. But universities continued to pay high fees to private equity and hedge fund managers despite weak returns. Higher rates of alternative investment show no meaningful association with rates of return after 2007. Colleges and universities spent an estimated $2.5 billion on fees for hedge funds in 2015 alone.[56] They paid an estimated sixty cents to hedge funds for every dollar in investment returns between 2009 and 2015.[57] And these fees helped each of the top five US hedge fund managers earn more than $1 billion in 2015 despite mixed performance.[58] With fewer social ties to top fund managers, less elite schools may particularly have struggled to access the highest-performing funds or to negotiate favorable fee rates.[59]

It is too early to say if the private equity and hedge fund boom is over. But following the years for which complete endowment data is available, average endowment returns have continued to underperform the S&P 500.[60] The downturn in endowment performance has even reached into the ranks of elite schools. When the S&P 500 grew by 1.4 percent in the 2016 academic year, for example, Harvard's endowment lost more than $2 billion.[61] Following these losses, Harvard and other colleges have actually begun reducing their hedge fund investments, following the lead of the massive California Public Employees' Retiree System.[62]

Financial Elites and Philanthropic Homophily

A disproportionate rise in donations to the most elite schools since the 1970s has added to the endowment boom for the wealthiest schools.[63] Using data from the Voluntary Support of Education survey, figure 4.5 shows that average total donations to the six private schools in the ninety-ninth percentile for endowment wealth roughly tripled from less than $200 million annually in 1973 to around $600 million in 2013 (2016 constant dollars). Average donations similarly tripled for both public and private schools above the ninety-fifth percentile. Still, average donations to those schools remained roughly half of donations to the six wealthiest schools. Growth of average donations drops precipitously among both public and private schools below the ninety-fifth percentile and particularly among schools below the ninetieth percentile for endowment wealth.

The rise in donations accelerated endowment growth at the top because wealthier private schools consistently direct a larger share of donations to their endowments than do other universities. The growth of donations therefore helped expand the endowments of wealthy schools. Data from

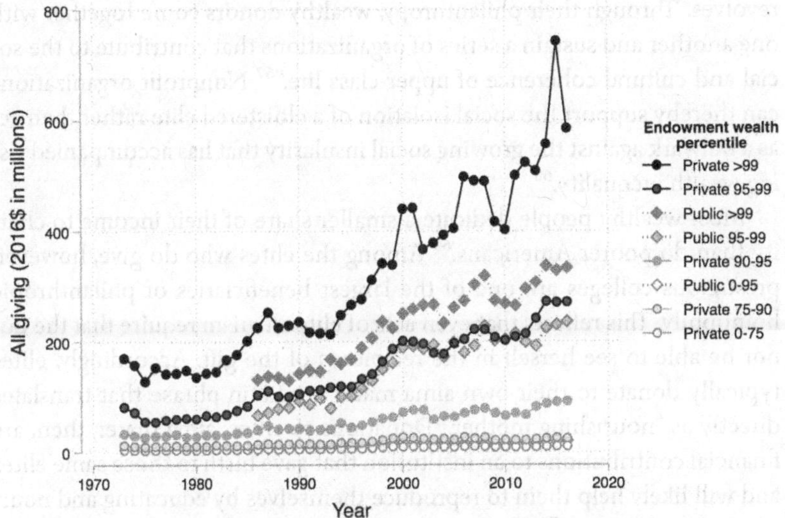

FIGURE 4.5 Average annual donations by endowment wealth percentile

NOTE: Data from Voluntary Support of Education survey.

the Voluntary Support of Education survey since 1973 shows that private schools above the seventy-fifth percentile for endowment wealth have consistently been able to steer about 35 percent of their donations to their endowment.[64] Only about 20 to 25 percent of donations have gone to endowments at public schools and less-wealthy privates during the period.

Amid the rising fortunes of the superrich, the particular growth of donations to elite colleges and their endowments reflects what I call a philanthropic homophily. Social scientists have shown that the giving of gifts is motivated by altruism, expected reciprocity, and social status accrued by those who engage in visible acts of generosity.[65] The idea of philanthropic homophily flows from the insight that altruism, reciprocity, and status benefits in philanthropy all occur within the social world of the donor.[66] Potential status benefits require appreciation of the gift by others who occupy the same social space, be it a country club, an alumni gathering, or a college board meeting. In the case of higher education, this status can be bestowed through the naming of endowed faculty positions or buildings, as we saw with Harvard Business School's new conference center Klarman Hall.

Educational and cultural organizations often provide social worlds in which philanthropic homophily can occur. As sociologist Francie Ostrower concluded from a study of ninety-nine wealthy donors in New York, "Nonprofit organizations are focal points around which upper-class life revolves. Through their philanthropy, wealthy donors come together with one another and sustain a series of organizations that contribute to the social and cultural coherence of upper-class life."[67] Nonprofit organizations can thereby support the social isolation of a cloistered elite rather than act as a bulwark against the growing social insularity that has accompanied rising wealth inequality.[68]

Most wealthy people dedicate a smaller share of their income to charity than do poorer Americans.[69] Among the elites who do give, however, prestigious colleges are one of the largest beneficiaries of philanthropic homophily. This reflects that even acts of elite altruism require that the donor be able to see herself in the recipients of the gift. Accordingly, elites typically donate to their own alma mater—a Latin phrase that translates directly as "nourishing mother." Donations to elites' alma mater, then, are financial contributions to an institution that gave birth to those same elites and will likely help them to reproduce themselves by educating and nourishing their children.[70] In other words, donations to one's alma mater epitomize philanthropic homophily in that donors are giving to institutions in which they can see themselves. Even if donors will not send their own children to their alma maters, they can see themselves in their colleges' students, who hail from mostly elite backgrounds, and in the life transformations those students experience while at college.

Philanthropic homophily also takes a reciprocal form in higher education via admissions preferences. Financiers figure prominently in reporting by journalist Daniel Golden on the children of university donors and trustees who receive favorable treatment in admissions. For example, private equity billionaire Robert Bass joined Stanford's board in 1989, having previously attended its business school.[71] By 1991, Bass had given $25 million to the university.[72] Then, in 1998, Stanford admitted one of Bass's children despite grades and an SAT score (1,220) that were lower than those of seven of her classmates who were denied admission.[73] Her SAT scores were also below the average for admitted students. Bass's daughter ultimately enrolled at Harvard, where Bass then became cochairman of the parent fundraising committee.[74]

Consistent with financiers' high rates of elite university ties, the limited data available on philanthropic giving by the wealthy also show that financiers donate to universities at higher rates than do other members of the superrich. The Chronicle of Philanthropy's Philanthropy 50 has tracked the fifty largest annual donations from such Americans every year since 2000. Among the Philanthropy 50, giving by financiers made up 31 percent of donations and 33 percent of dollars given during this period. And among donations by financiers, 31 percent of donations and 43 percent of total dollars went to colleges and universities. In contrast, among donations from outside of finance, just 24 percent of donations and just 25 percent of dollars went to higher education.[75] In other words, financiers make up a disproportionate share of the biggest philanthropists. And they direct much greater shares of their giving to universities than do wealthy philanthropists from other sectors.

Tracking the broader growth of financier wealth and philanthropy, schools with more private equity and hedge fund managers on their boards consistently received more financial gifts to pad their endowments from 2003 through 2016. Figure 4.6 uses the same structure as figure 4.2 but plots the THE top thirty universities each year according to their total donations on the *y*-axis and board shares on the *x*-axis. The figure shows that private equity and hedge fund board shares are positively associated with donations in all years except 2003 for private universities. There is also a positive association for public universities after 2008. Overall, every 10 percentage points more in board seats awarded to private equity and hedge fund managers are associated with 6 percent more in donations to a school.[76]

A final sign of philanthropic homophily in the rise of wealthy endowments is stasis in the privileged composition of undergraduate student bodies at elite private colleges. Princeton University is a particularly telling example. Between 1973 and 2016, Princeton's endowment grew by 847 percent, from $2.3 billion to $22.2 billion in 2016 constant dollars. With no business school, law school, or medical school, undergraduate education is even more central to Princeton's mission than at the nation's five other wealthiest schools. At the same time, far more qualified students graduate from high schools across America today than did in 1973. But with overflowing coffers from its endowment boom, Princeton enrolls only about 29 percent or three hundred more new first-year undergrads today than it did in 1973. As a result, Princeton was able to spend from its endowment approximately $110,176 *per student* (including graduate students) on university operations in 2013. Yale, Harvard, and Stanford similarly spent $95,065, $89,824, and $66,736 per student, respectively, from their endowments in 2013. In fact, most elite private schools have dramatically increased subsidies per student from their endowments by keeping undergraduate enrollments flat amid soaring endowment wealth.[77]

Public universities with large endowments, however, have expanded their undergraduate enrollments substantially over the last four decades.[78] This pattern has extended even to highly prestigious institutions such as the University of California, Berkeley. UC Berkeley enrolls low-income students at nearly twice the rate of Ivy League schools and has enrolled almost as many low-income students as the entire Ivy League combined in recent

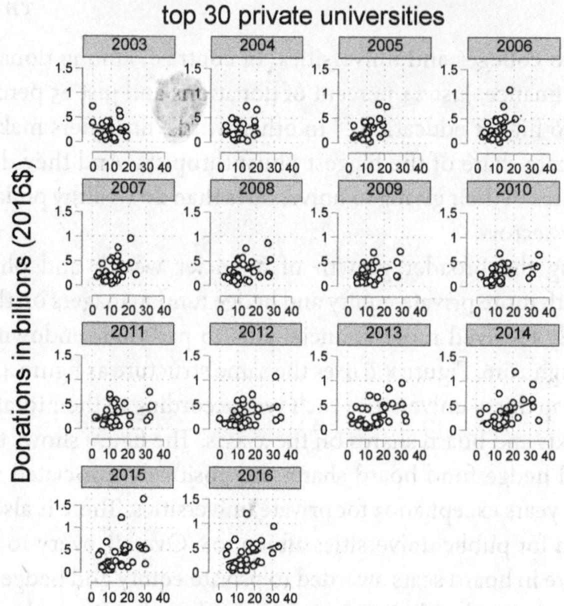

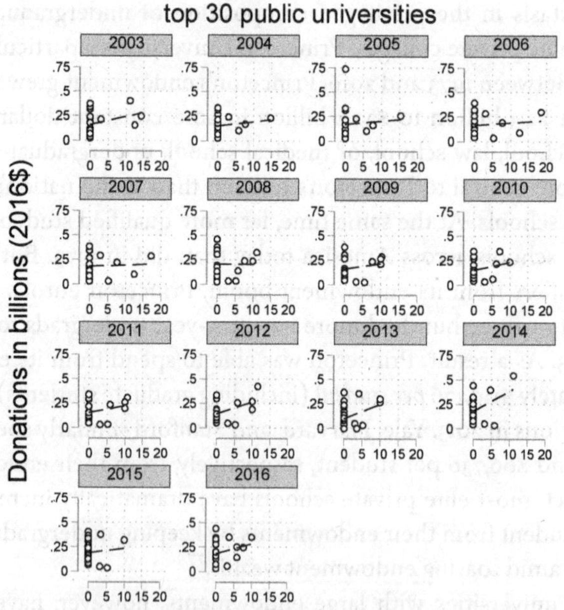

FIGURE 4.6 Annual donations and private equity and hedge fund board members, 2003–2017

NOTE: Donation data from the Voluntary Support of Education Survey. Data on board membership from Eaton and Gibadullina (2020). For further details, see text.

years.[79] Lower-status institutions linked to large endowments such as nonflagships in the University of California and University of Texas systems have increased enrollments even more, especially among underrepresented racial and ethnic groups. Economist Raj Chetty has documented that these public institutions are the greatest engines of educational mobility in the US postsecondary system.[80] As we shall see in chapter 6, the persistence of this greater function of educational mobility reflects public political pressures and university social ties to nonelites among even the financiers who have helped lead public institutions.

At elite private schools, the preservation of small and well-off undergraduate student bodies has effectively hoarded endowment growth mostly for the children of donors, board members, and others from similar backgrounds. Increased endowment spending by elite schools supports high faculty salaries and small class sizes for these students.[81] But it is the very exclusion of nonelites that elevates the status of these institutions. That status is the precious commodity that these schools offer to wealthy donors. High rates of educationally beneficial expenditure are therefore coupled with low undergraduate enrollment levels, legacy admissions, and application advantages for athletes in club sports such as lacrosse and field hockey. Under these policies, African American, Latinx, and low-income students remain woefully underrepresented at Princeton and other elite schools. For example, Black students made up 15 percent of the US college-age population but only 9 percent or less of first-year students at Stanford and every Ivy League college as of 2015.[82] So it is that alma maters remain a familiar sight to the financial elites they helped produce, ensuring that donations will continue to feed their growing endowments.

After Hedge Funds

While donations from finance have continued to flow to the wealthiest schools, the disparity in endowment investment returns declined in recent years.[83] Could it be that the era of private equity and hedge funds is waning?

The prospects for high investment returns may depend on the balance of power in the United States and other polities where financiers and their allies have prevailed since the late 1970s. As Piketty writes in his opus, "The history of inequality is shaped by the way economic, social, and political actors view what is just and what is not, as well as by the relative power of those actors."[84] Endowments and private equity and hedge fund managers are permitted to retain much greater profits from their investments because of substantial cuts to the capital gains tax in the late 1970s and early 1980s. The future of US tax policy remains uncertain. But proposals to close capital gains tax loopholes and regulate private equity funds, such as Senator Elizabeth Warren's "Stop Wall Street Looting Act," have proven popular with voters. Proposals to tax wealthy endowments have also gained steam. While the 2018 tax reform signed by President Donald Trump expanded tax advantages for private wealthy investors, it also placed a 1.4 percent tax on the wealthiest college endowments for the first time since 1984.[85] At the same time, some state governments in the United States are moving to close state tax loopholes for capital gains that Trump had also opposed but never acted on.[86]

Consistent with Piketty's argument, private equity and hedge fund managers reaped some of their greatest pretax windfalls around other shifts in political power. These political shifts changed market rules in ways that allowed a company or some other asset to be purchased and made much more profitable by those with access to capital. For example, automation and a political offensive by business weakened unions in the 1970s and 1980s. This opened the door for private equity to acquire unionized industrial firms through leveraged buyouts and increase the companies' market values through union busting, factory closures, and cuts to workers' wages and social benefits.

The role of private equity and hedge fund managers in US deunionization illustrates how the rising wealth accumulation at the top of society can be linked to rising deprivation at the bottom. Anthropologist David Harvey refers to the extraction of such windfall profits as "accumulation by dispossession." Some primarily think of accumulation by dispossession as only happening early in the development of capitalism: peasants are forced from communal lands as agrarian capitalists amass sufficiently large landholdings to accumulate enough surplus capital to reinvest in technological advances. Another way to think of accumulation by dispossession is as something that happens recurrently in capitalism, particularly when state power or technological change provides an opportunity for those with capital. Since the 1980s, financial deregulation and the lowering of barriers to global investment allowed private equity and hedge fund managers to move vast new stores of capital into investments afforded by such opportunities.

If the political balance of power shifts, fewer new opportunities may arise for large-scale accumulation by dispossession. As was noted earlier, the flood of deregulated capital since the 1980s may have used up many of the opportunities for big returns. In recent years, hedge funds and elite endowments have faced campus protests for their collaboration around state-aided investments that may deliver returns for investors while punishing the less fortunate. Even David Swensen, the exalted pioneer of Yale's alternative investment strategy, has been swept up in controversy over the university's investments in fossil fuels, for-profit prisons, distressed Puerto Rican bond debt, and home foreclosure activity.[87]

Ironically, neither student activists nor scholars have taken much note of comparable investments in predatory for-profit colleges at the bottom of the US higher education system. The private equity and hedge fund partners of elite endowments became the largest owners of for-profit colleges in the 2000s. Under their ownership, for-profit colleges extracted billions of dollars in windfall profits from the expanded federal loan programs chronicled in chapter 3. In the process, they saddled millions of students who were disproportionately low-income, Black, and Latinx with large student debts while providing almost no discernible educational or economic benefit.

Elite university endowments did not cause private equity and hedge funds to ransack disadvantaged communities via for-profit colleges. But with an average of 60 percent of their endowments invested in private equity and hedge funds during the for-profit college boom, elite endowments likely accumulated returns from this wealth extraction from the bottom of the US higher education system. By helping private equity and hedge funds get off the ground earlier, endowments also helped to hasten the broader shift to financial arrangements for maximizing profits via the dispossession of workers and consumers. This involved intimate social ties—often rooted in university networks—between financiers like Klarman and his Baupost partners. But the social circuitry of finance also connects these collaborative ties between elites at the top to the dirty work of extraction at the bottom of the economy—and of the higher education system. These extractive connections differ from the elite ties of financiers, but they are also social. By looking next at Wall Street's invasion of the for-profit college sector, we will see how they operate.

5. The Bottom

A Wall Street Takeover of For-Profit Colleges

Kim Tran grew up just fifteen miles from New England financier Jonathan Nelson. The daughter of two refugees from Vietnam who never went to college, Tran attended a public high school in Wakefield, Rhode Island. By her own account, Tran struggled through high school. When she graduated in 2009, she only knew that she wanted a career involving visual arts. Tran's sister convinced her that the best way to build a career around her passion was to study applied arts in college.

While separated by a social chasm of race, class, and gender, Nelson has professed a desire to use his wealth to support educational opportunity for disadvantaged students such as Tran. Like most private equity billionaires, Nelson has reaped large rewards from his elite education. Nelson received a BA in economics from Brown University and an MBA from Harvard before founding the investment firm Providence Equity Partners in 1989.[1] The firm's success turned Nelson into Rhode Island's only billionaire and an avowed education philanthropist. He has signed on to Bill Gates and Warren Buffet's Giving Pledge to give away half of his personal wealth in his lifetime.[2] Since 2000, Nelson has also served on the Brown Board of Trustees. The campus recreation center is named after him in honor of his $25 million donation for its construction.

But Nelson's educational philanthropy never reached Tran. Instead their paths crossed as financiers expanded their reach into the bottom strata of US higher education: for-profit colleges. In 2006, Nelson's investment firm partnered with Goldman Sachs and private equity behemoth KKR to buy the Education Management Corporation (EDMC). In 2009, Tran enrolled at one of EDMC's schools, the New England Institute of Art (NEIA). Ultimately, in many ways, the encounter left Tran worse off than if she had never gone to college at all.

Accelerating from the 1990s onward, the Wall Street takeover of for-profit colleges illustrates how intimate and impersonal ties can together organize predatory financial extraction from a widening range of domestic and global domains. Scholars have previously shown how rising investor power contributed to declining wages and job security for industrial workers.[3] But few studies have considered another mechanism by which finance may widen inequality—the expropriation of wealth from consumers and from government-subsidized social programs such as health care and higher education.

Reporting requirements for colleges that use federal student aid programs offer a unique source of big data to see how financiers might extract wealth from consumers and social programs. Because academics and the media tend to focus on their own prestigious alma maters, few have used this data to grasp the scale of this upward redistribution of wealth in higher education and its particular consequences for working-class students, women, and communities of color. Enrollments surged at for-profits from less than five hundred thousand annually in the 1990s to more than two million in 2010. Figure 5.1 plots the percentage of all US undergrads enrolled at community colleges, state universities, private nonprofit colleges, and for-profit colleges. The for-profit share of enrollments grew from around 5 percent to 12 percent at their peak in 2011. That year, for-profits enrolled more Black and Latinx students than did nonprofits and nearly as many women. For-profits also enrolled more low-income students, including 42 percent of Pell recipients, than did all other types of schools. Most of these students, including Tran, were saddled with debts they have scarce hope of repaying, as their credentials came with little detectible career benefit.

To understand how this educational disaster occurred, we also need to examine personal accounts from former for-profit college managers and students. This will reveal how financial cultures and social structures helped financiers like Nelsen (and even university endowments) to accumulate wealth with impersonal detachment from sometimes intimate exploitations of students like Tran.[4] But before we can see these intimate and impersonal ties in action, we need to revisit two broader political and economic shifts that encouraged the Wall Street takeover of for-profit colleges: the expansion of federal student loans and the rise of the shareholder value movement among investors and corporate managers. Understanding the roles of loan expansion and shareholder value will help us to grasp how intimate and equitable financial ties among elites are connected to intimate but exploitive relationships with nonelites. Building on separate lines of research by sociologists Tressie McMillan Cottom, Frederick Wherry, and Viviana Zelizer, I develop a new idea of unidirectional intimacy to explain the latter ties between financiers and nonelites.

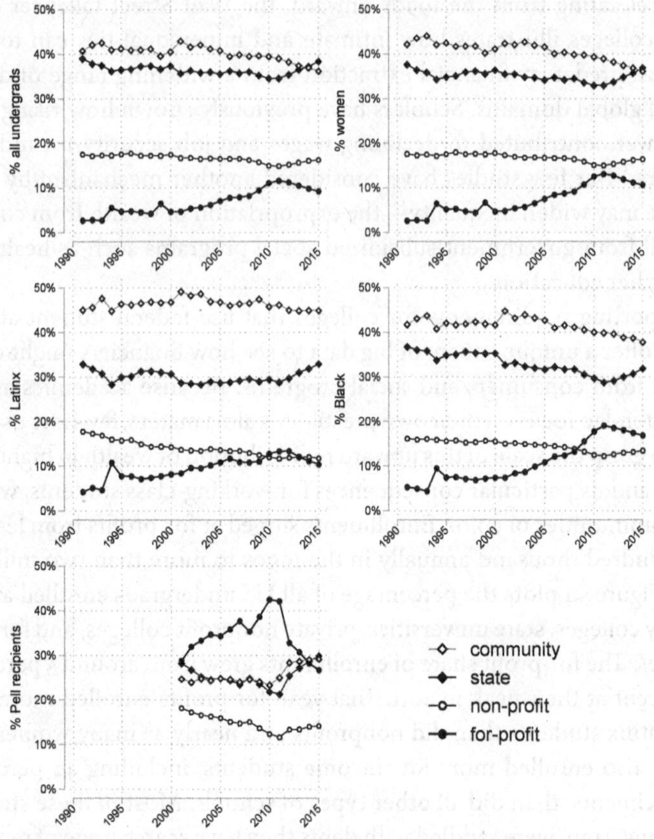

FIGURE 5.1 Percentage of US undergrad enrollments by sector

NOTE: Lines represent the percentage of all US undergraduate students in a given group who were enrolled in a given sector. Pell estimates are for full-time first-year undergraduate students only, for which more years of data are available. Estimates use IPEDS data. Data and code: https://github.com/HigherEdData/bankersintheivorytower.

Student Loan Expansion as Deregulation

Economic sociologists argue that deregulation opens the door to predatory corporate behaviors by eliminating not all regulations but regulations that powerful people and their companies do not like.[5] The link between student loan expansion and for-profit college predation is a case in point. As I detailed in chapter 3, the US Congress implemented new subsidies and regulations at the beginning of the 1990s to provide greater capital for federal student loans, in part from private lenders like Sallie Mae and Wells Fargo. But Congress simultaneously eliminated regulations that restricted who could get the loans and in what amounts.[6]

The political decision to increase federal student lending was not driven primarily by for-profit colleges, but it had the most pernicious effects in the for-profit sector. Congress primarily adopted the student loan expansion at the behest of private lenders, public universities, and nonprofit colleges. For-profit colleges only enrolled around 5 percent of US students at the time, but they were eligible to enroll students using the expanded loan programs. The availability of these loans made an intrinsic problem with education even worse—it is very difficult to evaluate the quality and value of a college degree program.[7]

The legal scholar Henry Hansmann singled out education in 1980 as an example of how markets for opaque goods are rife with opportunities for preying on consumers.[8] Hansmann's thinking suggests a definition for predation as the sale of goods whose substandard quality and uncompetitive price cannot be accurately assessed without "undue cost or effort." When it comes to such goods, from subprime mortgages to health care to education, consumers cannot evaluate the quality of a good by simply going for a test drive or kicking its tires. Nor can you return a college degree for a refund if it turns out to be worthless.

Students from educationally underserved communities, like Tran, can particularly struggle to evaluate the value of a given college program. In separate studies, sociologist Laura Hamilton and anthropologist Caitlin Zaloom have shown that even middle-class parents with college degrees rarely make economistic decisions when deciding how much to borrow or where to send their children to college. Rather, choices about college are often guided by social status aspirations and what scholars have called the "education gospel"—a sacred belief in the emancipatory power and value of education. Sociologist W. E. B. Du Bois partly attributes this faith in the power of education to centuries of resistance against prohibitions on Black literacy as a form of social control under slavery and Jim Crow.[9] The education gospel can sometimes light a path to educational and career mobility. Many for-profit college students are drawn to the schools because of their vocational emphasis in fields such as business administration, graphic design, health care, and cosmetology.[10] When she finished high school, for example, Tran knew only that she wanted a career involving visual arts.

But sociologist Cottom points out that for-profit colleges can exploit a belief in education when students lack resources to evaluate a college. In a variety of economic sectors, consumers have often relied on nonprofit alternatives to for-profit enterprises when the quality of goods is difficult to judge. Examples include credit unions for financial products, nonprofit hospitals, and private nonprofit colleges. In such markets, consumers trust that the absence of a profit incentive will ensure that a nonprofit will not exploit the opacity of what they sell through overpricing or shirking on quality.[11] None of the for-profit college students that I interviewed in this study, however, even knew their school was a for-profit when they enrolled. Tran even told me, "My parents were not aware there was such a thing as for-profit schools."

The federal student loan expansion made it even easier for for-profits to enroll students without students understanding the schools' prices and quality, or lack thereof. With the expanded federal student loans, for-profits could enroll students at zero upfront price to the student, despite charging higher tuition rates than other institutions.[12] Tran and the other students I interviewed reported that they had little understanding of the terms of their loans or what it would take to pay them off. For example, another NEIA art student, Alyssa Brock, said, "Everyone's mindset was just like, well yeah, it's college. It's going to cost money, but it's good debt and you'll pay it off once you get a really good job in graphic design."

In sum, loan expansion reduced the market incentive for for-profit colleges to compete on price or quality for students. By itself, however, loan expansion would not have pulled as many students into for-profit schools. Nor would Tran have gone to NEIA. Despite their for-profit status, many for-profit colleges have long operated under the management of dedicated owner-educators who previously worked in the vocational fields for which they trained students. NEIA, for example, was operated from 1962 to 1988 by local television producer Victor Best as the Northeast Broadcasting School.[13] Even at the peak of the for-profit college boom, schools were less likely to exploit federal student loan programs if they remained under the "privately held" ownership of educators like Best.

Before the 1990s, nearly all for-profit colleges had privately held ownership without any ownership stake for outside investors. But following the loan expansion, outside investors like Nelson used new ownership structures and ideas from the shareholder value movement to invade the for-profit college sector, suck up student loan subsidies, and wreak havoc on the lives of students like Tran.

Private Equity, Hedge Funds, and the Spread of Shareholder Value

Before the shareholder value movement of the 1980s, privately held ownership and publicly traded corporate ownership were the principal ownership forms of the US economy. The executives of publicly traded corporations also enjoyed substantial independence from the investors who owned shares in their company.[14] Under these ownership arrangements, corporate executives had latitude to accommodate the interests of employees and their communities. Through rising unionization, workers even negotiated for greater shares of corporate profits.[15] But as I discussed in chapter 2, in the 1980s, a movement grew among investors to demand that executives maximize their "shareholder value," a term for how much profit can be claimed by someone who owns a stock or other type of share in a company.

The shareholder value movement transformed industrial corporations in ways that help to explain the rise of predatory for-profit colleges. Initially, private equity firms like Nelson's played a central role in transforming industrial corporations. They did so through a new form of private equity ownership in which investors used newly deregulated types of debt to seize controlling shares in companies and take them private—something that ends the trading of company shares on the stock market.[16] These buyouts were commonly known as hostile takeovers. For example, the private equity firm KKR bought the food manufacturing giant RJR Nabisco in 1988. KKR thought they could increase RJR Nabisco's value by making it more efficient and profitable. KKR then employed common shareholder value tactics to increase the company's value by selling off less profitable divisions, closing plants, breaking unions, and eliminating forty-five thousand jobs. Private equity owners also employed these types of implicit contract violations to expropriate creditors and suppliers before reselling the firm at a profit on the stock market.[17]

While hostile takeovers directly reoriented firms toward shareholder value maximization, the threat of hostile takeovers led to an obsession with shareholder value throughout publicly traded corporations.[18] Corporations linked executive compensation to shareholder value through stock options and locked in a commitment to shareholder value through debt-financed stock buybacks that deterred hostile takeovers by making them costlier.[19] Hedge funds also created additional pressures by using debt and derivatives to reward and punish companies with large-scale stock transactions based on their shareholder value maximization.[20] Hedge funds further used their stock and bond holdings with other institutional investors, like pension funds, to push for profit maximization.[21]

But after successfully extracting large shares of wealth from industrial corporations, private equity investors, followed by hedge funds, turned to other domains.[22] Eventually, there were fewer unions left to break and few industrial corporations that could be made more profitable. Private equity instead moved its investments to other sectors where government subsidies or a lack of market competition made windfall profits possible. For example, Nelson initially specialized in investments that sought to corner telecom markets, such as acquisitions of the predecessors to T-Mobile and a German cable broadcaster.[23]

Few publicly traded corporations operated in subsidized sectors like health care and higher education before the rise of private equity ownership. Accordingly, private equity shifted from hostile takeovers of publicly traded corporations to acquisitions of privately held firms like the Northeast Broadcasting School.[24] Private equity managers then tried to make the privately held firms more profitable and take them public through an initial public offering on the stock market. In this way, private equity began to spread the culture and short-term profit demands of the shareholder value movement to sectors beyond the historical reach of publicly traded corporations. Following the expansion of federal student loans in the early 1990s, private equity investors had a golden opportunity to bring shareholder value to for-profit colleges.

While the culture and incentives of shareholder value help explain why financiers would seek to exploit the opacity of education and the expansion of federal student loans for profit, it does not fully explain *how* investors like Nelson would do this. To unpack this process, we need to look more closely to see how financiers weave together a variety of intimate and impersonal ties.

Financiers' Intimate Ties in Action

Both critics and proponents of what some still refer to as "free markets" have characterized market actors as cold, calculating, and self-interested.[25] But as we saw in chapters 2 and 4, intimate ties are crucial to the social wiring of high finance. Just as Tom Steyer needed his Yale connections to raise early funds for launching his hedge fund in 1988, private equity firms draw heavily on intimate social ties to raise capital and make investment decisions. Shared identities and social networks with other elites provide trust and reciprocity between fund managers, potential investors, and sources of the private information that funds use to find undervalued investments.[26] The elevated value of these intimate elite ties in high finance helps to explain why financiers hail from the Ivy League at such higher rates than others among the superrich—and how finance maintains inequality at the top.

It is easy to lose track of financiers' intimate ties when contemplating the scale at which private equity transformed US for-profit colleges. Figure 5.2 illustrates how the growth of for-profit enrollments from the 1990s onward occurred almost exclusively under private equity and publicly traded ownership. During this period, private equity investors acquired eighty-eight different for-profit college companies and 994 colleges that they consolidated into chains. They took twenty of these firms public, accounting for 57 percent of all thirty-five publicly traded firms that operated in the sector

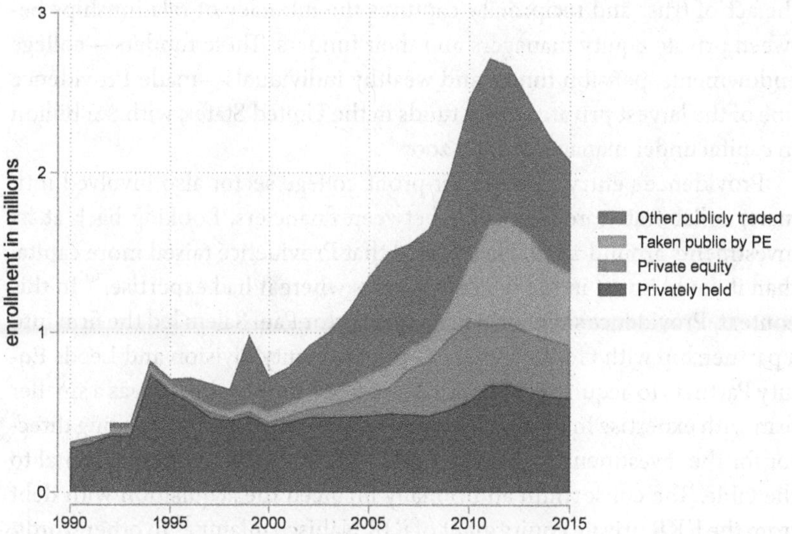

FIGURE 5.2 Total enrollment in millions by ownership type

NOTE: Data from IPEDS and my database on for-profit college ownership. Data and code: https://github.com/HigherEdData/bankersintheivorytower.

after 1990. Private equity and hedge funds also took large stakes in publicly traded firms that were not initially taken public by private equity. For example, the Tiger Management hedge fund held $414 million in shares in the University of Phoenix in 2010 when Phoenix's enrollments topped two hundred thousand.[27] Figure 5.2 includes the enrollments of University of Phoenix in the "other publicly traded" category for companies that were publicly traded but not initially taken public by private equity.

We can see the importance of financiers' intimate ties by looking more closely at how Nelson built up Providence Equity Partners before buying EDMC in the largest-ever acquisition of a for-profit college chain. Nelson cofounded Providence Equity with his Brown classmate Glenn Creamer in 1989. In 1992, they also recruited Brown alum Paul Salem, who would become one of Providence's top executives. Nelson, Creamer, and Salem all boast MBAs from Harvard as well. The firm focused on media and communications investments by developing insider knowledge of the sectors. In 2007, the *New York Times* described the firm as "closely knit."[28] Every year, Nelson took the firm's staff on a ski trip to the Alta resort in Utah. And one of Nelson's largest investors, Haim Saban, separately told the *Times* that he gave Nelson part of his share in a German cable acquisition in 2003 because "I was so impressed by his ideas."[29] While Saban speaks of Nelson's ideas, the act of trust and reciprocity captures the intimacy of relationships between private equity managers and their funders. These funders—college endowments, pension funds, and wealthy individuals—made Providence one of the largest private equity funds in the United States, with $21 billion in capital under management by 2007.

Providence's entry into the for-profit college sector also involved intimate, collaborative relationships between financiers. Looking back at its investments around 2006, Nelson said that Providence raised more capital than it could invest in the telecom sectors where it had expertise.[30] In this context, Providence's senior managing director Paul Salem led the firm into a partnership with Goldman Sachs's private equity division and Leeds Equity Partners to acquire EDMC for $3.4 billion in 2006. Leeds was a smaller firm with expertise in for-profit colleges. Goldman Sachs's managing director for the investment, also a Harvard MBA, brought additional capital to the table. The consortium additionally financed the acquisition with debt from the KKR private equity giant of RJR Nabisco infamy.[31] In other words, financiers across multiple firms did not coldly compete against each other. They collaborated, drawing on trust from shared networks and identities to exchange insider knowledge and access to capital.

Aided by an earlier round of private equity investment, EDMC had already grown into one of the largest for-profit college companies in the country with eight differently branded chains, seventy-seven colleges, and 64,592 students. EDMC had purchased the Northeast Broadcasting School in 1999 and rechristened it the New England Institute of Art.[32] But with capital from the 2006 buyout, EDMC ramped up its recruitment further, more than doubling its enrollment to a peak of 142,846 students in 2012. EDMC had already used federal student loans to increase tuition at NEIA from $14,826 in 2000 to $21,241 (2016 constant dollars). After the buyout, EDMC increased tuition to a peak of $24,583 by 2010, Tran's second year at the school.

But even as tuition increased, graduation rates fell at NEIA from over 60 percent in the 1990s to 48 percent for students who started school in 2005 and ultimately to just 34 percent for students who started school in 2011, the last year that NEIA reported graduation rates.[33] Median earnings for students six years after they left NEIA fell from $43,494 for students leaving school in 1998 to $30,044 for students leaving school in 2007. The share of borrowers who could repay at least one dollar of their loans without defaulting within three years of leaving school also collapsed from 67 percent in 2007 to 44 percent in 2013.

These latter shifts stem in part from the slow recovery from the 2008 recession. But the downward trends at NEIA and investor-owned for-profits more broadly were not paralleled by comparable declines at privately held for-profits, which were free of investor ownership. Average earnings after school and loan repayment for NEIA students were also lower for students who came from low-income households and left school after 2010 than for students from low-income households who left school before the 2008 recession. On top of these declining and substandard outcomes for students, the US Department of Justice sued EDMC in 2011, alleging that EDMC had illegally paid its recruiters entirely based on the number of students they enrolled.[34] The Massachusetts attorney general filed a separate suit against EDMC and NEIA in 2018, alleging that recruiters had defrauded students with misrepresentations of job placement rates and financial aid.[35] By 2017, 166 former NEIA students joined more than one hundred thousand for-profit college students nationally in filing claims with the US Department of Education to have their loans forgiven because of alleged fraud.[36]

Intimate Ties in For-Profit College Predation

It is also tempting to write off the injuries suffered by Tran and hundreds of thousands of other for-profit students as an impersonal act by investors who are only intimate with other elites. This again misses the critical role of intimate ties that Wherry and Zelizer have shown in a variety of economic exchange relationships.[37] In their recruitment, investor-owned colleges commonly deprived students of private information about the school and its owners that would be essential for bilateral intimacy. But accounts from Tran and other students reveal that recruiters still had to cultivate intimacy and trust in order to lure students into signing up for debts that they rarely could repay. This exploitive deployment of intimacy reflects the idea that it is those who know us best who can hurt us the most.[38]

According to Tran and other students, recruiters shared private information about their personal backgrounds before becoming recruiters. The recruiters also learned about students' lives and families when trying to sign them up. Tran and Brock, another NEIA student, both said that recruiters called them "every single day" after they initially spoke to the admissions office. Tran said, "It made me feel special." Brock said that her recruiter also cultivated a relationship with her family. "It helped that the admissions guy we had been talking to the whole time had gone to Colby College and my mom had spent a semester at Colby College, so they were like, 'Oh my god!'"

The recruiters used the closeness they cultivated to make a more persuasive case that students should enroll. They assured Tran that she would have "small classes, having teachers paying attention to you, specialized majors."

The recruiters also promised that with an NEIA degree, the school would help her get a job in animation. Another NEIA student, Don Quijada, told his recruiter that he had briefly been at University of New Haven to study music production, "but it's not really what I expected, I haven't got to see the studio at all my first semester." After the recruiter learned this, "the main thing the guy promised me was as soon as you start classes, it's hands on you're in the studio." Brock, the other NEIA student I spoke to, said the recruiter told her, "Don't worry. Take out the loans and then you're going to get a really good job in graphic design and you're going to be able to pay everything off."

Tran, Brock, and Quijada all said that they found out quickly after enrolling that the school was not what they were promised. Brock and Tran said they had to borrow much more than they expected. Brock borrowed $80,000 using both federal and private loans. About her parents borrowing to pay for NEIA, Brock said, "To this day, they will not tell me how much they took out." Tran said she borrowed $30,000, and Quijada said he borrowed $60,000.

Tran and Brock liked some of their instructors, but Tran told me, "None of the instructors actually had any professional experience, and I couldn't even get an internship. . . . They weren't teaching us the specialized skills that employers said they wanted." Tran also said that class sizes in her animation major increased to more than sixty students as NEIA recruited more students without adding faculty. In his two years at the school, Quijada said he never got any time in a sound studio as his recruiter had promised.

Tran, Brock, and Quijada all left NEIA before completing a degree. Brock made it to the final semester when her work-study job at NEIA was eliminated. With her loans "maxed out," Brock began commuting an hour for a retail job at Forever 21 and struggled to come up with the funds that NEIA required students to pay out of pocket for her graphic design final art project. By her third year at NEIA, Tran realized that none of her classmates were actually getting jobs in applied arts, so she withdrew. Because most of his borrowing went to tuition, Quijada became homeless and received poor grades during his second year at NEIA. As a result, NEIA did not allow Quijada to reenroll in his third year.

Tran, Brock, and Quijada still do not have jobs in the fields they enrolled to study. Unable to repay their loans, all three are still holding out hope that their debts will ultimately be cancelled. Reflecting the intimacy of their interactions with recruiters, faculty, and aid officers, they feel a mix of betrayal and understanding. About the recruiter who her mom bonded with, Brock said, "I still think he's a cool guy. Like, I don't really hold it against him. I feel like he was just doing his job."

Unidirectional Intimacy and Organizational Obfuscation in Investor Ownership

Nelson's and Tran's stories reveal very different forms of intimate ties at the top and bottom of Wall Street's takeover of for-profit colleges. Nelson's intimate relationships in the closed world of Ivy League financiers were mutually beneficial with equitable power balances. Nelson built a management team from his Brown and Harvard networks. Saban took a chance on Nelson as his firm grew beyond its boutique origins and stuck with him even after major losses. Leeds and Goldman Sachs pooled private information and capital with Nelson and Providence in the acquisition of EDMC. The intimate relationships between NEIA recruiters and students like Tran, however, were highly unequal and exploitative. The recruiters gained substantial private information and trust from students as cutouts for investors and their management team. Recruiters provided misleading information about NEIA's programs and student outcomes, taking advantage of students' limited college options, sparse knowledge about for-profit colleges, and embrace of the education gospel.

Why do the intimate ties among financiers work so differently than intimate ties between their subordinates and for-profit college students? And how are these two sets of intimate relations connected? I view the connection between these elite and nonelite social links as connected by what I call a unidirectional intimacy that is promulgated by the financial governance of corporations. Under financial governance, the organizational hierarchy of for-profit college chains transmits valuable private information about students to investors and their management team. Executives and investors, in turn, filter this private information through the logic of shareholder value maximization. This one-way transmission and shareholder value filtering of private information, unidirectional intimacy, enables financiers and their management team to simultaneously exploit students' private information while maintaining impersonal social detachment from the consequences for students.

Consider first how investor-owned colleges constructed a one-way flow of private information about their students. Investor-owned for-profit colleges hired executive personnel exactly for this purpose. For example, Corinthian Colleges recruited Bill Buchanan as its chief marketing officer in 2004. Buchanan had previously built the credit card division of Providian and led marketing for the subprime lender Greenpoint Mortgage. According to a former Corinthian vice president who I interviewed, Buchanan "knew how to market, especially to a kind of low-income mass market."[39]

In 2006, Corinthian hired CEO Peter Waller from PepsiCo, where he had previously directed marketing for Kentucky Fried Chicken and was then president of Taco Bell. Likewise, EDMC appointed former First Interstate Bank marketing director Craig Swenson to lead its Argosy University chain following Nelson's buyout. For its new CEO, EDMC hired Todd Nelson, who had risen to be CEO of University of Phoenix's parent company, itself a pioneer in marketing to low-income students.[40]

The executives installed by the investor-owners of Corinthian and EDMC incorporated digital technologies to create disciplined assembly lines for extracting private information from students—and turning that information into new recruits. These structures provided a model for other private equity–owned colleges, which, on average, employed nearly twice as large a share of their employees in sales than did other for-profit schools.[41] A former vice president at Corinthian Colleges described how recruitment for its chain of campuses became nationally centralized during the years when it was publicly traded. Centralization of marketing used national advertising campaign development, targeted cable ad buys, internet search advertising, and call center support to follow up on and pass along to campuses "warm leads" who responded to the ad campaigns. Corinthian became "the highest-volume advertiser on a lot of channels from 10 p.m. to 3 a.m.," the former vice president said. He described one component of the recruitment strategy as the "popcorn challenge":

> If you let a lead sit for twenty-four hours, the conversion rate was X. If you got back to them within eight hours, the conversion rate was 2X. If you got back to them within the amount of time it took to cook a thing of popcorn in the microwave, three minutes, you had like 4X.

EDMC built its marketing operations on the same ideas. When EDMC's chief marketing officer Joe Charlson left in 2010 to form his own lead acquisition subcontractor, he advertised "speed is life" as the new company's second guiding principle.

As we heard earlier from Tran, Brock, and Quijada, recruiters gathered further private information from the leads and used it to enroll students as quickly as possible. Even Corinthian's television and digital advertising incorporated generalized knowledge of student social insecurities and career focus gleaned from private interactions. The Corinthian vice president said to me about their advertising, "The bottom-line message was, you know, you can do it. [short laugh] Like we know who you are, we know that you are good enough to do this. . . . The picture of the scrubs and the, you know, clean buildings and the, everything was very, you know, purposeful, all the imagery."[42] Tran's recruiter learned more details of her parents' concerns around student debt and career outcomes. Brock's recruiter developed a relationship with her mother around having both lived in Maine. Quijada's recruiter promised he would have immediate access to the in-studio education he wanted but would never receive.

Inversely, investor-owned companies and their executives used a combination of obfuscation and secrecy to deny students private information about their schools. To begin with, major investor-owned schools rarely made it clear to students that they were for-profit. One investor-owned firm went so far as to name its schools American Public University and American Military University. Corinthian and EDMC also used a popular obfuscation strategy among investor-owned schools whereby a parent company would maintain multiple brands offering exactly the same degree, sometimes even within the same geographic market. The Corinthian vice president told me the operation of multiple brands was intended as a hedge against the reputational risks of maintaining poor educational practices:

> So, if you had one school that got into regulatory trouble, as long as you had a brand that was just local, that contagion wouldn't spread to the other brands. You know, ultimately, that was why, this is, you know, if you were trying to just, you know, continue to operate substandard schools. [short laugh][43]

When I asked if Corinthian still suffered brand damage despite the multibrand strategy, the vice president responded:

> I don't, I mean, only because literally we became a national news, but we were having local problems all throughout this time. You know, like one campus here would get into trouble or something like that. And it never, I mean, this whole like brand contagion thing that, you know, didn't ever. . . . It took a long time before it ever impacted anything.[44]

Eleven of the twenty-five largest and five of the ten largest for-profit college companies employed a multibrand strategy in 2012.[45] In 2007, Kaplan alone awarded health care degrees under twenty-six separate brands. These investor-owned for-profit colleges strove to learn all they could about the private lives of their students and potential recruits, but they acted in ways that made it harder for students to learn even public information about themselves.

While investor-owned college executives carefully used private information to recruit students, investors like Nelson can use a shareholder value logic to filter out unpleasant information about the social consequences of their schools for students. Interviews and public statements by two high-level managers at EDMC and the investor-owned Florida and Midwest Career Colleges show how this works. In an anonymous email correspondence, the manager at Florida and Midwest Career Colleges told me,

> [When] presenting annual results to investors, I told Managing Partner of PE firm [*sic*] that I wanted to address all the compliance and regulatory achievements. He laughed and said, "They don't care about that. All they want to know is how much money you made them."[46]

Later, investor pressures pushed the company to boost enrollments by eliminating entrance exams to confirm students had the high school–level scholastic skills needed to begin Florida Career's programs. In other words, financiers participated in governance decisions for Florida Career by excluding students' educational outcomes from their consideration entirely.

Corinthian and EDCM managers reported similar investor filters and pressures. The Corinthian vice president told me of the late 2000s when the company sought to enroll more students than it could possibly serve, "We had a lot of financial pressure, you know, from our investors primarily, to expand and try and capture all of this growth and demand that was happening in the market."[47] EDMC's CFO for eighteen years, Robert McDowell, says he resigned after Nelson's 2006 buyout because of "calls from Wall Street analysts to pursue growth opportunities that could undermine academic quality."[48]

The Price of Unequal Intimacies

More than a decade after NEIA recruited them, Tran, Brock, and Quijada are still paying a price and have little to show for their years spent at the school. Each student has had accomplishments, but their successes are in spite of their experience at NEIA, not because of it. Tran has started her own freelance illustration business but is still searching for full-time employment in Rhode Island. Brock has abandoned applied work and works at an SPCA animal rescue in Massachusetts. Quijada started his own business in New Haven, The Laboratory Studio, to help hip-hop and R&B artists record and promote their music.

While they strive to build careers, Tran, Brock, and Quijada are all burdened by unpayable student debts. In fact, all three say they owe more today than they originally borrowed because of compound interest. Tran has only avoided default because all $30,000 of her debt was in federal student loans eligible for the federal income-driven repayment program, which reduces payments for low-income borrowers. After originally borrowing $80,000 in total, Brock still owes $44,000 on her federal student loans, and her private student loans have ballooned to more than $100,000 after four years in default, with interest continuing to accrue. Quijada's debt has similarly increased from $50,000 to $60,000 because of defaults on private loans. Even though he paid off one of his private loans, Quijada has been unable to secure a credit card or even a forty-dollar monthly line of credit from a music equipment vendor. Deprived of credit, Quijada has built his business with one arm tied behind his back.

In a series of articles, my research collaborators and I have shown that what Nelson and EDMC did to Tran, Brock, and Quijada is the norm, not the exception, for what investor-owned colleges did to their students over the last two decades. The studies linked data from an array of sources on the ownership and organizational behaviors of all 14,303 for-profit, private non-profit, state, and community colleges that were eligible to enroll students with federal student aid between 1987 through 2016. In the endnotes for this chapter, you can find links to the papers, data, and statistical software code for the analyses.[49] The papers show that schools under private equity and publicly traded ownership were more likely to behave in predatory ways across a variety of measures. These groupings of investor-owned schools were more likely to spend a lot on recruitment, obscure their identities with multiple brands for the same product, charge higher tuition rates, load students with more debt, employ fewer faculty per student, and be subject to student claims and law enforcement actions for fraudulent recruiting.

With high rates of predatory behavior, investor-owned for-profits also had the worst student outcomes even when we control for their students tending to come from lower-income households and disadvantaged racial and ethnic groups. Figure 5.3 presents averages for a variety of student outcomes after regression adjustments for these student body characteristics.

Average student outcomes were worse at investor-owned colleges across almost all measures than at either nonprofit and public institutions or at other privately held for-profits. Compared to other for-profits, students at investor-owned schools took on 40 percent more debt and had graduation rates that were 12 to 18 percentage points lower. Students at investor-owned for-profits had average earnings after school that were comparable to those at privately held for-profits but 9 percent lower than the average for community college, state university, and nonprofit college students. This comports with audit studies that have found job applicants with a for-profit degree are no more likely to get a call back than applicants without a degree.[50]

Potential economic gains for students from investor-owned schools are also dubious given that their share of student borrowers who repaid any

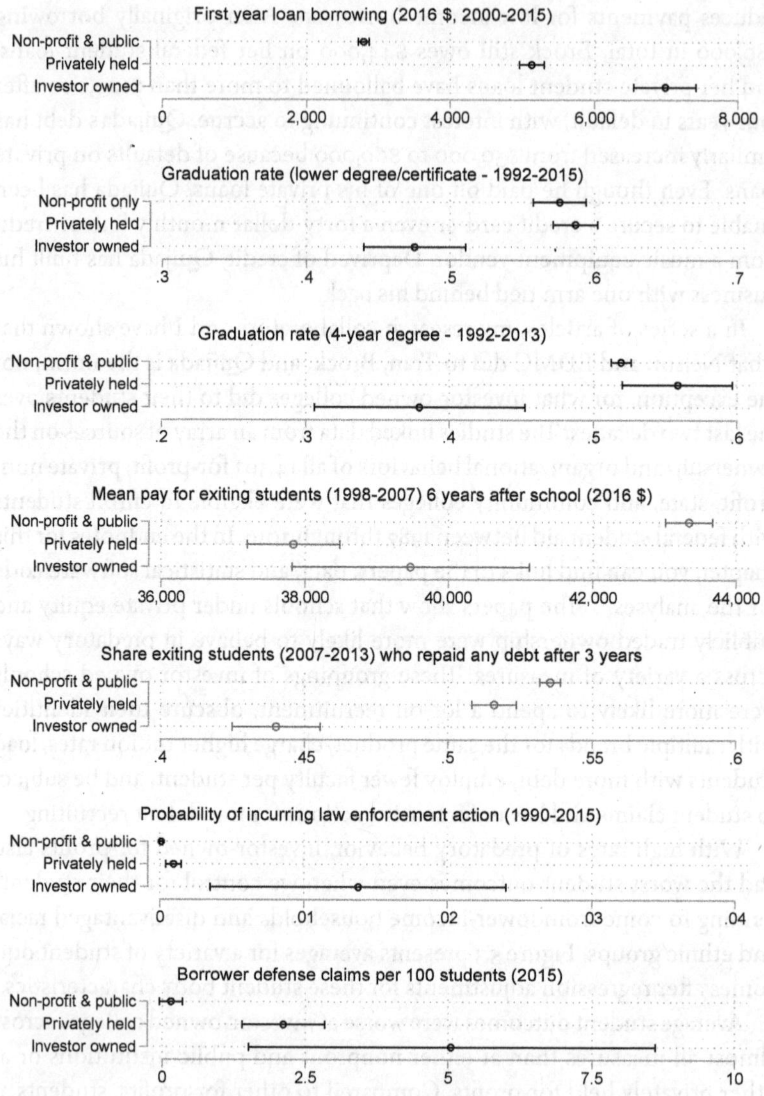

FIGURE 5.3 Average student outcomes adjusted for student body characteristics

NOTE: All average student outcomes are OLS regression adjusted with white student body share, Latinx student body share, Black student body share, average student financial need, selective admissions, highest degree offered, state effects, and year effects held constant at their means. Ninety-five percent confidence intervals are estimated using robust standard errors clustered by parent company or system. Nonprofit and public institutions include community colleges except for estimates of lower degree/certificate graduation rates for which accurate community college data are not available. Data and code: https://github .com/HigherEdData/bankersintheivorytower.

debt after three years was 8 percentage points lower than at other for-profits and 10 percentage points lower than at public and nonprofit institutions. Finally, investor-owned schools were ten times more likely than other for-profits to become subjects of fraud-related law enforcement actions and averaged twice as many borrower defense loan cancellation claims. In short, enrollment at investor-owned schools was on average a disaster for the millions of students who passed through their doors over the two decades bracketing the turn of the millennium.

The millions of negative student outcomes at investor-owned schools play a large and underacknowledged role in the US education system's production of widening race, class, and gender inequalities. Recall that figure 5.1 showed how Black and Latinx students at for-profits outnumbered their counterparts at nonprofit institutions at the apex of for-profit expansion. Low-income students at for-profits outnumbered low-income students in all other sectors for most of the first decade of the twenty-first century. More than 75 percent of these for-profit enrollments occurred at investor-owned colleges during the sector's peak years.

It is difficult to disentangle the for-profit college fleecing of Black, Brown, poor, and female students from the failure of society to provide these students with other viable options. Yet there are signs that the investor-owned targeting of these students may draw them away from better schools. Students primarily choose for-profits over community colleges, which also have open admission but provide much better labor outcomes.[51] States ravaged community colleges with budget cuts from 2000 until only recently, restricting access to the classes needed to complete a credential quickly.[52] But I show in a paper with economists Sabrina Howell and Constantine Yannelis that investor-owned schools also lured students away from community colleges.

Some for-profit college executives have denied that such recruitment involves racial or other identity-based targeting. The former vice president of Corinthian, however, told me,

> This is what my group did; it was we had to use mapping software that had census block data in it. And you could, you know, locate a school; you could draw a twenty-mile ring around the school for in terms of commuting time. And if you located it in the right demographic, you could predict how many students would; and you had these six programs, you know, you could predict how big the school would be.[53]

In a follow-up correspondence, the former vice president clarified that his team did not use race and ethnicity metrics in its targeting models. Instead, the team used "market saturation (e.g. existing enrollments/capita in similar programs in the market), household income, educational attainment, and age cohorts."

Targeting students for recruitment on the basis of their social identity could advance equity objectives if investor-owned schools provided recruits with better educational and economic outcomes. But such targeting by investor-owned colleges is predatory when coupled with low spending on instructional support, high student debt requirements, and abysmal outcomes. The Corinthian models are predatory in that they explicitly target students on the basis of class via household income and educational attainment metrics. But such criteria also lead to the locating of schools disproportionately in communities of color as the communities that are most underserved by nonprofit public and private colleges. As a result, Cottom has noted that there is "no intent required" when it comes to predatory targeting on the basis of race.[54]

We need more research to learn how intersectional structures of race, class, and gender may further intensify inequalities from for-profit college predation.[55] We already know, however, that investor-owned schools affected Black students in especially pernicious ways because of the racial wealth gap. The policy scholar Fenaba Addo and sociologists Jason Houle and Daniel Simon have shown that Black borrowers particularly struggle to repay student loans because of their disproportionate enrollment at for-profit colleges. Black students' college debts are compounded by a lack of parental household wealth to draw on for assistance with repaying loans.[56] Like Tran, Brock, and Quijada, these pressures left the average Black student loan borrower who began school in 2004 with 113 of their original debt in 2016, compared to 65 percent for white students.[57] By 2016, 49 percent of the 2004 nationwide cohort of Black students had defaulted on their loans, and default rates only worsened among Black students who enrolled in 2012 after the end of the 2008 recession.[58] In sum, student debt from investor-owned for-profits played a central role in reproducing the racial wealth gap that originated in part from housing and loan discrimination in the twentieth century.[59]

Impersonal Beneficiaries of Finance's Unequal Intimacies

The interviews and public statements by former EDMC, Corinthian, and Florida and Midwest Career managers show that private equity and hedge fund managers used a unidirectional and organizationally filtered intimacy to extract profits from Tran and millions of other for-profit students. The social circuitry of finance, however, also impersonally distributed these profits to elites and even nonelites who lacked any knowledge whatsoever of the private lives of for-profit students. These impersonal ties radiate out from private equity firms, hedge funds, and other asset managers to millions of people who invest capital with them via pensions and 401(k)s. Shareholder value logics are the transistors of this circuitry, connecting impersonal ties to unidirectionally intimate ones.

Take, for example, the case of widespread investment in for-profit colleges by nonprofit and public universities via private equity and hedge funds. As we learned in chapter 4, the most elite private universities invested earliest in these funds and have reaped the largest returns because of favorable terms and the size of their endowments. The most elite private universities increasingly use shell companies to obscure such investments.[60] But the *Wall Street Journal* revealed in 2017 that Columbia University had investments with Renaissance Technologies, the largest hedge fund investor in EDMC in 2013.[61] Brown and Princeton reported in a 1990 endowment survey that they were among the first universities to invest in the Tiger Management hedge fund, which went on to become the largest shareholder in University of Phoenix.[62] And in 1988, Cornell invested with the private equity firm TA Associates, which acquired Florida and Midwest Career Colleges in 2004. By the 2000s, however, even public universities and smaller private schools invested substantial shares of their endowments with such firms. At least seventeen college endowments, ranging from Oberlin and Swarthmore to Purdue and the University of New Hampshire, had invested just in the funds involved in Nelson's 2006 buyout of EDMC.[63]

University endowment investments did not cause the Wall Street takeover of for-profit colleges. Nor did predation by investor-owned schools like EDMC by itself cause the rising concentration of wealth at elite private endowments that we saw in chapter 4. To be sure, investments in for-profit colleges were highly profitable. From 2003 to 2012, gross profit margins at publicly traded firms in the sector averaged 55 percent, significantly higher than the 33 percent average gross margin across ninety-nine major industries in the United States (standard deviation: 14 percent; median: 31 percent). But I have never encountered any signs that university endowment managers particularly sought out opportunities to invest in for-profit colleges. In fact, I have found no evidence that endowment managers or other university leaders had any awareness at all that their portfolios included private equity and hedge fund investments in for-profit colleges.

The apparent ignorance of endowment managers to their for-profit college holdings shows how the logic of shareholder value maximization can impersonally link disparate people and organizations to invidious strategies for profit extraction. Shareholder value proponents argue that those with capital should always invest it where it will yield the highest rate of return. This logic enables owners of capital to indirectly transact on woefully unequal terms with those who lack capital, such as most workers and for-profit college students. But knowledge of the intimate dirty work involved in profit accumulation, such as defrauding underserved students, need not be transmitted across the transistor of shareholder value logic.

Members of the Princeton Resource Committee recently invoked the impersonal detachment of shareholder value in response to protests over university investments in for-profit prisons. The committee wrote, "Investment policy includes a strong presumption against any action that is intended to take a position or play an active role with respect to 'external issues of a political, economic, social, moral, or legal character.'"[64] They added that "issues" should only be considered if they have "attracted 'considerable, thoughtful, and sustained' campus interest." Even then, "the University must refrain from using divestment . . . to pressure either companies or governments to adopt particular policies."

The shareholder logics of the Princeton Resources Committee and most institutional investment funds provide a transistor to impersonal detachment through a potent mythology.[65] They posit that the guiding principle of shareholder value maximization itself plays no "active role with respect to 'external issues.'" It follows that their selection of investment funds that maximize returns will have no influence on the policies of the companies or governments that receive their capital. No doubt, the incentive structure of financial deregulation encourages endowment managers to embrace this illusion. But just as lawmakers advanced financial deregulation with little engagement by those outside of finance, university endowment managers adopted shareholder value logics with nothing that resembled "'considerable, thoughtful, and sustained' campus interest."

Via shareholder value logics, elite university endowments and the largest holders of capital have expropriated far greater amounts of wealth from workers and social groups outside of the for-profit college sector. Beyond their role in breaking labor unions in the 1980s and 1990s, private equity investors have recently invaded other socially important sectors, including health care and housing.[66] But the investments of endowments in predatory colleges provide an especially vivid illustration of the varied intimate and impersonal ties involved in these upward transfers of wealth.

While elite private universities experienced few downsides from shareholder value, the detachment of less elite institutions left them blind to a pitfall of the for-profit colleges in which they invested. For-profit colleges achieved their unusually high profit margins not only by expropriating students but also by sucking up public subsidies that could have otherwise gone to public institutions. At their peak, more than 25 percent of Pell Grant awards, nearly $10 billion annually, went to for-profit colleges.[67] The federal government also provided nearly $20 billion annually in loans to for-profit college students—only a fraction of which has been repaid. Meanwhile, state governments steadily reduced their appropriations to public universities and community colleges. In other words, student loan expansion was followed by exactly what public university leaders had worried about until the end of the 1980s—the replacement of federal and state funding for public institutions with loans and other subsidies that for-profit colleges could capture.

The leaders of public and nonprofit universities have done curiously little to stop investor-owned colleges from diverting public subsidies and preying on underserved students. Rather, we will see in the concluding chapter that a diverse coalition of students, education labor unions, and civic organizations has turned the national policy discussion toward principles of equity and empowerment in higher education financing. Tran, Brock, and Quijada have all themselves participated in this movement through the ten thousand–member strong We Are AI Facebook group of former EDMC Art Institutes students. Together, they won major reforms to reduce student loan burdens and protect for-profit college students under the Obama administration. These reforms precipitated the cancellation of billions of dollars in associated student debts and the closure of EDMC, Corinthian Colleges, ITT Tech, and other predatory chains.[68] The coalition also won surprising victories to slow the restoration of predatory for-profit colleges under the for-profit-friendly Trump administration.

But before we turn to the broader coalition that is reimagining higher education from below, we need to look more closely at the public universities that make up the massive middle of US higher education. These institutions enroll 62 percent of all US bachelor's degree seekers. The diversion of public subsidies to for-profit colleges contributed to a squeeze on these schools since the 1990s. Facing this squeeze, public universities themselves looked to financiers and financial markets for solutions to their resource shortfalls. While their turn to finance in no way matched the shareholder value revolution in for-profit colleges, the exploitive combination of the intimate and impersonal in finance culture conflicted with the public ideals and governance structures of state universities. This conflict was nowhere more explosive than in California, home to the nation's largest public higher education system. We turn next to this case of the public university as an alternative ideal and organizational form to the social circuitry of finance.

6. The Middle

A Hidden Squeeze on Public Universities

On July 29, 2003, California's state legislature passed a budget cutting $250 million or 8 percent of the state's $4 billion annual funding to the University of California.[1] Private equity billionaire Richard Blum had been appointed to the University of California (UC) Board of Regents a year earlier by Democratic governor Gray Davis. Looking back, Blum described a crisis for UC with "the budget going to hell in a hand basket."[2] Little did he know the legislature would cut nearly $2 billion more, almost half of state funding for UC, over the next eight years. Nevertheless, Blum sensed the proportions of the escalating financial squeeze on the UC system.

Consistent with their rising wealth and power nationally, financiers like Blum played a leading role in how UC responded to state budget cuts from 2003 to 2011. They did so from the Board of Regents and from the university system's c-suites. As creatures of the financial world, they drew on the shareholder value template they applied in their professional lives. As Blum told one interviewer, "I decided that this place needed to be shaken up and restructured, and I set out to do that." To do so, Blum soon became chair of the Board of Regents and brought in a team of market-oriented reformers, led by new UC President Mark Yudof.

The UC restructuring effort ignored the ways that financier tax avoidance and subsidy capture were depriving public universities of state and federal funding. This squeeze included the diversion of resources via endowment tax breaks for wealthy private institutions, tuition subsidies to for-profit colleges, and subsidies for student lenders. The private and technical nature of high finance obscured the relationship between these diversions and declining state funding for public higher education. But I will show that a large factor in cuts to California's public universities was financiers' increasing exploitation of the state's property tax loopholes.

While Blum did not challenge these diversions of fiscal resources from UC to the financial sector, he differs notably from his Ivy League counterparts. Critically, the financiers in UC leadership are often themselves products of the California public education system. As a result, they are anchored by the system's public ideals of universality and affordability. And they are connected both publicly and intimately to a much broader swath of society by the far-reaching shared identities and alumni networks that public universities create through mass enrollment of nonelites. Consistent with their stronger ties to nonelites, Blum and his team sought to preserve and even expand a public university mission that differs fundamentally from the core tradition of elite private schools.

With their split orientations between private finance and public purpose, UC's leaders tested the limit to which contemporary financial market structures and ideas can support equity in higher education. This task was complicated by deep budget cuts that coincided with rapid growth in the number of California high school graduates who wanted to attend college. UC leaders responded to this challenge through increasing reliance on two areas of finance: (1) student loans as a source of tuition revenue and (2) direct bond market borrowing to finance facilities expansion and repair. Under this strategy, UC kept pace with other US public universities between 2000 and 2007—with twice the undergraduate enrollment growth rate of the top thirty US private universities. Between 30 percent and 50 percent of undergraduates at each UC campus continued to come from Pell Grant–eligible low-income households compared to just 15 percent at the top thirty private universities. UC used grants to these students to limit increases to already high levels of student debt for low-income students as it increased loan borrowing among upper-middle-class students. While maintaining mass enrollments, UC also kept education-related spending per student well above the US average for public universities. This spending included targeted programs to support low-income students. As a result, UC maintained high graduate rates for low-income students across most of the system, with low-income graduation rates approaching 90 percent at UC Berkeley.[3]

Ultimately, however, increases in student debt and bond borrowing failed to mitigate access and affordability impacts from state and federal funding shortfalls. UC's new model maintained large inequalities in student debt between white and wealthy students who rarely borrow compared to low-income, Black, and Latinx students. These inequalities arose earlier after the 1992 loan expansion in place of adequate per-student federal funding growth, but UC enshrined these inequalities in its new financial model. At the same time, UC in-state enrollment growth failed to keep up with college-age population growth and was effectively frozen after 2007 amid the onset of the global financial crisis and catastrophic state budget cuts. This pushed a malapportioned share of students into the California State University (CSU) and community college systems. Underfunding and overenrollment adversely affected graduate rates and student loan repayment rates in both the CSU and community college systems.

The UC system is an ideal case for studying the extent to which student debt and university bond borrowing can advance educational equity amid the fiscal squeeze on public universities. As the most prestigious public university system in the world, UC has more "market power" to attract students who will pay higher tuition rates including with student loan debt. This means UC has the maximum ability of a public university to use student debt and tuition from higher-income students to subsidize access and lower college prices to lower-income students. Californians also have an unusually strong ideal that UC should be an affordable institution for educational mobility for all Californians. This provides the strongest possible cultural framework for politicians and university leaders to tailor the use of student debt and bond borrowing for social equity. California's strong ideal around UC as a public university also makes the tensions between this ideal and financiers' ideas more legible in university deliberations about student debt and bond borrowing. Particularly abrupt cuts to state funding in the 2000s made financial choices even more immediate and visible and their results easier to compare.

Reflecting the state's strong public ideals and governance structures, there is a detailed public record of the financiers, financial ideas, and financial organizations involved. In addition, I am able to go beyond the public record with interviews with university officials and other stakeholders.

This chapter will explain UC's response to the financial squeeze as follows. First, I expand on how UC is an ideal typical case for how public universities can foster social mobility and create extensive social ties that connect elites to people from diverse backgrounds. This section also documents how public universities faced challenges from rising demand in the 2000s. Second, I explain how financier tax avoidance and public subsidy capture contributed to declining state revenue and budget cuts to public universities in California. Third, I detail how Blum, Yudof, and other UC leaders tried to preserve equity and affordability by using student debt and bond borrowing to solve the problem of state funding cuts. Fourth, I use data for all US public universities to show that increasing bond borrowing and student debt tends to do little if anything to help universities meet rising enrollment demand. The new burdens of student debt, however, are highly unequal across class and race even within UC. I conclude the chapter by discussing how the relationship between financializing changes and commercializing changes could gradually build counterpressures to the public mission of the university.

Public Universities, Extensive Intimate Ties, and Rising Demand in the 2000s

Public universities are the massive middle of the US higher education system, conferring 62 percent of bachelor's degrees in recent years.[4] These institutions create lifelong identities and social ties that connect both elites and nonelites. They do so by enrolling students from a much broader array of class backgrounds than do top private universities. And they are typically more affordable than nonelite private institutions. Consistent with these features, public universities are by far the largest postsecondary engine of social mobility.[5]

Public university expansion in California also carried forward longstanding ideals that foster intimate ties among alumni that are both more diverse and more extensive than elite private university social ties. California lawmakers and UC President Clark Kerr, a labor economist, codified a commitment to universal higher education access and affordability in the 1960s with a state Master Plan for higher education. Later in the 1960s and 1970s, Black Panther George Mason Murray, Mexican American Student Confederation leader Manuel Delgado, future Oakland mayor Jean Quan, and others led a wave of Third World Liberation strikes across CSU and UC.[6] With considerable success, they pushed university officials to expand the Master Plan promise to underrepresented racial groups.

In the 1990s, conservative activists convinced California's majority white electorate to roll back the state's expansion of access at the state's more selective campuses by banning affirmative action in admissions to UC and CSU. Nevertheless, California at the end of the 1990s still enrolled larger shares of college students at its public universities than almost any other state—and used high levels of state spending per student to charge some of the lowest tuition rates in the country.

In the 2000s, public universities in California and the rest of the nation faced a new challenge of surging enrollment demand. College-age population growth fueled this growing need. But demand also grew as stagnant wages for blue-collar and service professions amplified the appeal of the education gospel that college is a path to economic empowerment.[7] In California, total high school graduations began a new growth spurt in the 2000s. Figure 6.1 shows that the share of California students who were college ready when they left high school also increased. This is measured as the share of students who met California's A-G requirements for admission to

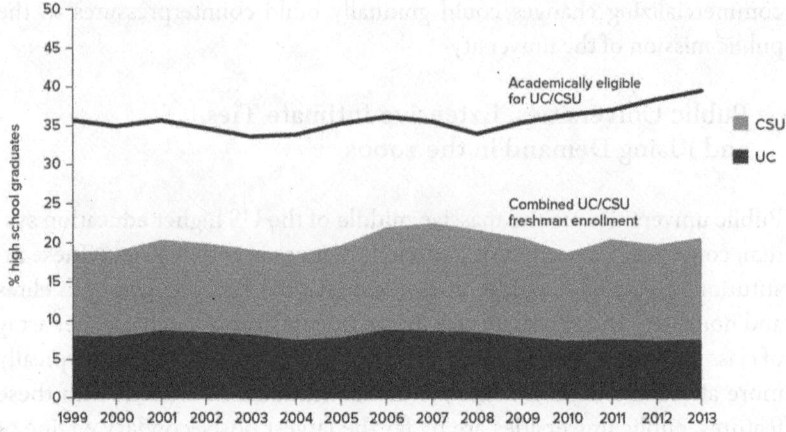

FIGURE 6.1 Public university enrollments and college readiness among California high school graduates

NOTE: Used with permission from the Public Policy Institute of California; Jackson, Bohn, and Johnson (2016).

CSU and UC. But the share of new high school graduates who enrolled at CSU remained flat, and it actually declined for the UC system from 2006 to 2013. State funding cuts and stagnation are the primary reason that both CSU and UC failed to keep up with demand. Financiers contributed to these shortfalls via tax avoidance and subsidy capture that steadily eroded the tax base for funding public services and public universities in the state.

State Funding Cuts, Financier Tax Avoidance, and Financier Subsidy Capture

The private and technical nature of high finance has obscured financiers' role in declining state funding for public higher education. Behind this curtain of financial opacity, government funding for universities was undermined by both tax avoidance and public subsidy capture by financiers—including those who managed elite university endowment portfolios and who acquired for-profit colleges. In this way, cuts to public universities and other public programs are directly linked to the growing share of profits retained by the financial sector since 1970.

California state funding cuts partly resulted from the same financier tax evasion that has reduced federal coffers. Private equity and hedge funds took off in the 1980s in large part because of cuts to capital gains taxes. Fund managers use the carried interest loophole to reduce their federal income tax liability by around half or $180 billion annually.[8] Beyond avoiding taxes on their own income, private equity and hedge fund managers pressure the companies they own to increase tax avoidance.[9] A recent study shows that lax Internal Revenue Service enforcement for wealthier taxpayers reduces federal tax revenue by another $100 billion annually.[10]

In California, financiers particularly exploit state property tax caps. Under these caps, businesses pay taxes as though their properties still had the same assessed market value as they did in 1979 or whenever the property was last transferred between owners.[11] Private equity funds routinely structure their acquisitions and mergers in ways that prevent property value reassessments even when businesses change hands.[12] Property reassessment sometimes depends on the capacity of county tax assessors to identify ownership changes involving private equity. This county-level variation is informative in the case of the Bain Capital and KKR private equity acquisition of Toys R Us in 2005. Following the acquisition, Los Angeles County reassessed that the Toys R Us store in Bell Gardens should be taxed at $0.44 per square foot. In neighboring Ventura County, the assessor left the property tax rate for two Toys R Us stores in the cities of Oxnard and Ventura at their respective 1997 and 1996 rates of $0.11 and $0.19 cents per square foot. Property values tend to be much higher in wealthy Ventura than in Bell Gardens, where the poverty rate exceeded 27 percent in the 2000 census. But by slipping under the radar in Ventura, Toys R Us's private equity owners paid a property tax rate that was lower by two- to fourfold. Overall, California property tax caps cost the state between $7 billion and $11 billion annually.[13] Private equity likely used similar property tax avoidance techniques when they acquired dozens of for-profit colleges in the state, such as the Heald College chain, DeVry campuses, and the state's EDMC Art Institutes.

As major investors in private equity and hedge funds, elite university endowments receive greater returns from financier tax avoidance. In 2017, the Paradise Papers leak revealed that most major university endowments go a step further by setting up offshore shell companies to avoid taxes on their investment activities. Endowments are already tax exempt, but they partner with private equity and hedge funds to borrow additional money to invest. Endowments pay taxes on the money they earn that way because it is not related to their educational mission—unless they hide that money with the help of offshore investment corporations.[14] On top of offshoring, private universities began to bolster their endowment investments and returns through indirect tax arbitrage involving their access to tax-exempt bonds. The overall tax revenue lost to endowment tax exemptions is $20 billion annually without accounting for offshoring tax avoidance.[15]

As a result of tax avoidance, California state revenue steadily declined as

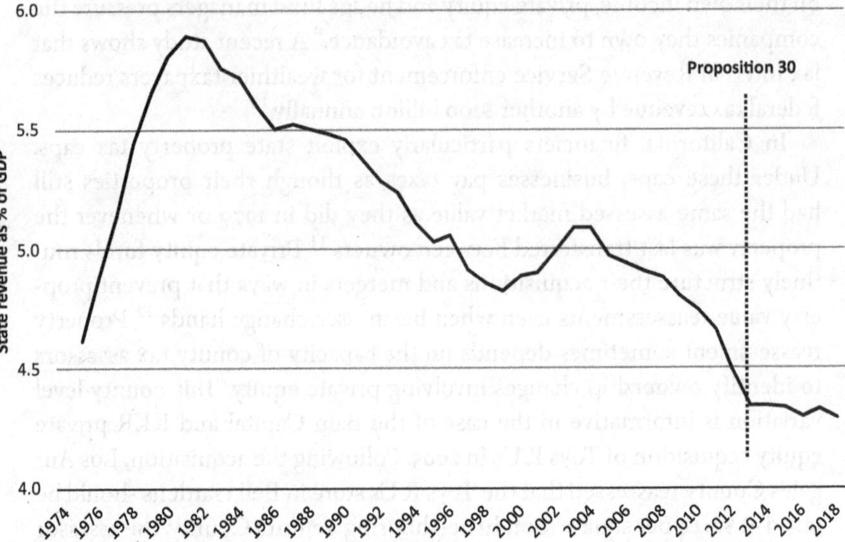

FIGURE 6.2 California state revenue as a percentage of GDP (five-year rolling average)

NOTE: Data from federal Bureau of Economic Analysis and California Legislative Analyst Office.

a share of state gross domestic product (GDP) in the forty years since 1980, even as tax rates held steady or increased. This is plotted in figure 6.2. The ten-year rolling average of state revenue as a share of GDP peaked in 1979 at just short of 6 percent and then declined from 5.5 percent in the 1980s, to 5 percent in the 1990s, to 4.9 percent in the 2000s, and finally to 4.3 percent in the 2010s.[16] California only halted this decline in state revenue with the 2012 passage of Proposition 30, a new income tax on millionaires—including financiers. Chapter 7 will chronicle how public university stakeholders helped pass the tax through a social process I call bargaining with bankers.

As declining tax revenue shrank the pot to pay for state programs, lawmakers prioritized social welfare and prison spending and reduced the share of the state budget going to higher education. Starting in 2001, lawmakers cut state appropriations to UC from over $4 billion or about $20,000 per student to just over $2 billion or about $10,000 per student in 2011.[17]

Unlike in the domain of health care, Congress did not establish entitlements in the 1960s or 1970s to guarantee federal funds for expanding higher education demand. As a result, federal funding growth for higher education did not offset state funding cuts in California. Federal expenditures on subsidies to for-profit colleges and universities with large endowments also came at the expense of public universities like UC and CSU. For-profit colleges captured 25 percent of all Pell Grant expenditures at their peak in 2011—$10 billion annually. For-profit colleges in California alone captured $2 billion in federal Pell Grant tuition subsidies. For perspective, the $10 billion in Pell Grant spending on for-profit colleges and the $20 billion in federal tax exemptions for endowments alone could pay for doubling Pell Grant awards to low-income public and nonprofit university students nationally. Doubling the current average annual grant of $4,160 per Pell recipient would cover nearly all the college expenses that low-income public university students currently use loans for.

For-profit colleges also increasingly captured state subsidies at the expense of public institutions in the early 2000s. In the period that California cut over a billion dollars from UC and CSU, the state also increased spending on Cal Grants for for-profit college students to a peak of $116 million in 2011. Cal Grant rules allowed for-profit colleges to absorb all Cal Grant dollars as tuition revenue. In 2012, lawmakers cut Cal Grant funds going to for-profits by 50 percent by banning the most predatory schools from using the program. Lawmakers did so in part to avert cuts to Cal Grants for UC and CSU students despite state revenue shortfalls. The explicit tradeoff in this decision illustrates how at least some of the state and federal support for endowments and for-profit colleges came directly at the expense of public institutions.

Private Ties and Shareholder Value Logics in UC's Turn to Finance

Why were California's university leaders unwilling or unable to get lawmakers to end financier tax evasion and subsidy capture instead of cutting state funding for higher education?

Part of the answer is that financiers and their cultural logics had also gained an increasingly prominent position among state political elites and University of California executives. They offered what seemed like easier solutions to state budget cuts: student loan–financed tuition hikes and bond borrowing increases.

Even the financiers involved, however, differed in fundamental ways from those who predominate on Ivy League boards and among for-profit college investors. Critically, they often held intimate ties to nonelites because they, themselves, had attended UC. Reflecting this social position, they promoted financial market transactions and organizational management as strategies to advance a public mission that differs radically from the role of private universities in the reproduction of elites. In this way, the efforts of these financiers and their backers tested the extent to which financial market ideas and structures can advance equity in higher education.

Blum played one of the most central roles in the UC system effort to meet rising enrollment demand despite a decade of state budget cuts. Blum recounted his own role in dozens of hours of interviews he gave between 2009 and 2014 for a UC oral history initiative. Democratic governor Gray Davis appointed Blum to the UC Board of Regents in 2002. In 2006, Blum became chairman of the Board of Regents. Davis appointed Blum amid a round of budget cuts on the heels of a recession—a recession exacerbated by a tech-sector bubble in California inflated by investment banks and private equity funds. Blum had gone to public schools in San Francisco before attending UC Berkeley for college and business school starting in 1953.[18] Married to US Senator Dianne Feinstein since 1980, Blum has long had extensive intimate ties at the intersection of finance and politics. He has said these ties were central to his appointment to the UC board:

> I could have obviously, with my wife as a U.S. senator, served on a lot of things. I just told Gray Davis, before he got elected—I helped him with a couple of things. He said, "If I can ever do anything for you, let me know." I said, "Yes, put me on the Board of Regents."[19]

Blum has been remarkably forthright about the social and economic benefits of becoming a regent. He also claims a sense of reciprocal duty in exchange for the status one gains from an appointment. "It's as close as you can come to knighthood in California," Blum said. But he adds, "I knew what the University of California had done for me. I knew what it had done for a lot of my friends. I just felt that it was the best education for the money you could get anywhere in the world, and to the extent I could provide some help, I wanted to do it."

To "provide some help," Blum invoked the ideas and relationships he had accumulated as a private equity fund manager. Blum's financial orientation trained his attention on a variety of solutions other than ending tax avoidance by investors and the companies they own. Nor did UC executives, other UC regents, or state lawmakers show any understanding or appetite for confronting declines in state tax revenue. Blum observed that collecting more taxes—from financiers or other prosperous California residents—was politically complicated by a state constitutional requirement for a two-thirds vote of the legislature or a popular referendum for any tax increase. With more than one-third of state assembly members and senators, a conservative Republican minority could block all attempts at tax increases. Instead, Blum called for steady increases in tuition, expanded bond borrowing, and UC spending cuts.[20]

By Blum's own account, he drew on his private financial ties to replace top UC executives and directly tap financial markets. Blum particularly thought that UC could thrive by borrowing much more from bond markets with more independence from state oversight:

> I brought the guys in from Lehman Brothers who knew the university. They said, "No, your debt capacity is not a billion dollars. If you're willing to go down to A credit, it's probably eleven billion dollars."[21]

On July 13, 2003, the Lehman consultants recommended that the university increase borrowing by issuing new "general revenue bonds" backed by a broader swath of UC's assets and future income—but not by state tax revenue. Previously, the university only borrowed directly with revenue from bond-funded assets like dormitory fees as collateral. UC also borrowed against state tax revenue using state public works bonds, but this borrowing required more public oversight via the legislature. On top of the move to general revenue bonds, Lehman recommended that UC use variable rate bonds in conjunction with derivatives known as interest rate swaps to borrow at lower effective interest rates. The Board of Regents adopted the policy and nearly tripled the UC bond borrowing from $5 billion at the time of the Lehman report in 2003 to $14 billion in 2011.

UC's move toward general revenue bonds over state public works bonds shifted the orientation of UC executives away from popular democratic engagement via the state legislature and toward an autonomous governance relationship with financial markets. This idea resembles the shareholder value revolution that shifted the focus of corporate executives toward an obsession with their stockholders rather than with consumers, workers, or community stakeholders. This more direct relationship with financial markets aligned with Blum's vision for university autonomy. In Blum's view, university autonomy is not just about faculty having the freedom to determine what they research, publish, and teach. Rather, university autonomy also should give UC regents and executives the freedom to set tuition rates and make financial allocations without political meddling. Consistent with this view, Blum criticized Governor Davis—who appointed Blum—because he was "much more in the face of the university for this, that and the other thing. Didn't want fees to increase." On the other hand, he praised California's next governor, Arnold Schwarzenegger: "Arnold has never, ever said anything to us about fees one way or the other. You got to do what you think is right," said Blum.[22]

Blum and the UC Board of Regents brought in a new executive team to manage UC and its relationship with financial markets more in accordance with the logic of finance. In 2008, the regents hired University of Texas system chancellor Mark Yudof as UC system president. Yudof had risen to prominence for deregulating tuition rates in Texas.[23] In 2009, UC hired former Lehman Brothers managing director of public finance Peter Taylor as chief financial officer and former JPMorgan managing director of public finance Nathan Brostrom as executive vice president of business operations. Taylor was also a UCLA alumnus who had served as a UC regent from 1999 to 2001. Blum described the criteria for borrowing established by the new leadership team as follows:

> Forget all the debt caps. They don't matter anymore. Each campus should come to us. If you want to build a building, I only care about two things. One, is it going to fall down? And two, is it financially sound?[24]

Under Taylor's management, the June 2011 newsletter of the UC Capital Markets Finance Department elaborated, "The Regents have agreed with bondholders to set rates, charges, and fees in each Fiscal Year so as to cause General Revenues to be in an amount sufficient to pay the principal of and interest on GRBs [general revenue bonds] for that Fiscal Year." The number one source of such revenues listed in the newsletter was "gross student tuition and fees."

Consistent with its pledge to pay bond debts with tuition increases, UC increased net tuition revenue per full-time equivalent student from $4,643 in 2003 to $11,468 for the fiscal year that began in 2011 (2016 constant dollars). Net tuition revenue is the revenue retained by a university after using some tuition revenue to subsidize grants to low-income students. Bond buyers took note of UC's new commitment to increasing tuition revenue. For example, the credit rating agency Moody's wrote in September 2012 that UC deserved an AA rating for its bond issues because it could leverage its "powerful student market position" to "compensate for state funding cuts by raising tuition dramatically" and by "growing non-resident tuition, differentiating tuition by campus or degree, and increasing online course offerings."[25]

Expanding UC's borrowing capacity offered a new source of capital for facility expansions to enroll more students. Unlike UC's patrons in state government, however, bond borrowers made no demands that UC increase in-state enrollments. As a result, UC was able to effectively freeze in-state enrollments from 2008 forward even as borrowing grew exponentially for other purposes. For example, Blum "rallied a few regents with me" to require construction of a new Memorial football stadium to begin in 2010.[26] Over resistance from UC Berkeley chancellor Robert Birgeneau, Blum argued that a new stadium was needed because the existing stadium could not safely withstand an earthquake. UC ultimately borrowed $445 million under a plan that Blum attributes to Brostrom, who was UC Berkeley chief financial officer at the time. UC covered the repayment costs in part by negotiating with other PAC-12 schools to increase revenue from television rights for their athletic teams. But borrowing for projects like Memorial Stadium used up borrowing capacity for other investments needed to increase enrollments. When the new stadium opened in 2012, UC in-state enrollments had been frozen for five years.

The combined annual principal and interest payments for UC borrowing then doubled from $435 million in 2003 to more than $1 billion in 2011—almost as much as the cut to state appropriations in this period. Some of these investments paid for themselves, such as the construction of thousands of new student housing units at UCSD. But who ultimately paid for borrowing that did not generate adequate revenue to repay itself? And what occurred with revenue from capital projects that exceeded the original borrowing costs—such as profits from the expansion of UC's academic medical centers, where annual operating margins tripled from just over $200 million in 2003 to over $600 million in 2010?

The implicit logic of finance suggested that UC should invest borrowing and excess returns wherever those allocations would generate the largest further investment returns. Blum himself expressed concern about this dynamic in 2010, agreeing with his interviewer that UC borrowing would "skew the kind of buildings you had." Blum added,

> It absolutely hurts the humanities. I think it's a major concern. This is increasingly a research-professional university, but you need all that other stuff. So how do you fund it?[27]

UC leaders also took policy and political actions in support of grant aid for low- and middle-income students that demonstrated concerns about student debt under the new model. As Board of Regents chair, Blum asked UC Berkeley Chancellor Birgeneau to lead the UC Affordability Working Group in October 2007, on the eve of the global financial crisis. While not a UC graduate, Birgeneau was the first in his family to graduate from high school and had earned his undergraduate degree at the public University of Toronto.

In March 2008, the working group issued a report proposing to reduce student loan borrowing and the actual price of attending UC for low- and middle-income students. Few policy analysts or researchers understood at the time that even moderate amounts of student loan debt were risky for low-income borrowers and other underrepresented students. A research consensus has only recently emerged that these borrowers face higher risks because of lower graduation rates, lower household wealth, and labor market disadvantages. Nevertheless, the working group report called for prioritizing reductions in prices and loan burdens for low-income students and undocumented immigrants.

The working group proposed to reduce prices for low- and middle-income students through increases in state- and university-funded grant aid programs. We may never know if the proposals could have effectively reduced college costs were it not for massive budget cuts brought on by the 2008 financial crisis. But UC and the California state government did implement grant aid policies that may have prevented even larger increases in student debt. UC used increased tuition rates and increased out-of-state enrollments to expand grant aid, first at UC Berkeley under Birgeneau and later UC-wide. Perhaps more importantly, Birgeneau, Blum, and Yudof all followed the lead of the UC Student Association in publicly opposing any cuts to California's large Cal Grant aid program for low-income students. They maintained their opposition to Cal Grant cuts even as they accepted a reduction in direct state appropriations to UC from $3.5 billion to a nadir of $2.2 billion in 2011.[28]

At the same time, the working group proposal illustrates the difficulty in reconciling financial logics with public ideals of access. The regents and the working group explicitly opted not to support tax reforms that might provide revenue to fund the proposal. As we shall see in chapter 7, the UC regents and executive leadership would reverse course and endorse a millionaire tax increase after large-scale protests against student debt and tuition hikes in 2011. Even with greater nonelite ties and public ideals among financiers in UC leadership, it took collective action by nonelite stakeholders to create a political context in which the financiers could support such a tax.

Unequal Consequences in UC Access

The squeeze on public universities had unequal consequences in California and nationally across students of different race and class backgrounds. In California, tens of thousands of qualified but socially disadvantaged students were diverted into CSU colleges and community colleges with fewer resources. Across the country, including at UC, low-income students at public universities took on debts that they struggled to repay. Wealthier students at both public universities and private schools tended to leave college debt-free.

In California, the UC system increased in-state enrollments more slowly than did community colleges and the less-selective CSU system. UC kept pace with other US public universities from between 2000 and 2007. But UC effectively froze new in-state enrollments from 2007 to 2016 even as Blum's team tripled UC's outstanding bond debt. In contrast, California community colleges increased enrollments during the financial crisis, and CSU resumed enrollment growth in 2011. These divergences involved a process called crowd out. Crowd out perversely rations state higher education funding by pushing more students into lower-status and less-funded strata of the higher education system, which also have the least capacity to raise private funding.[29] Chapter 5 detailed how crowd out pushed hundreds of thousands of students into predatory for-profit colleges. Tens of thousands of qualified students were similarly redirected into underresourced CSUs and community colleges.

Figure 6.3 details enrollments at UC, CSUs, and California community colleges between the 2001 and 2019 academic years. From 2001 to 2016, annual new enrollments of in-state students actually grew fastest at CSU if we include new transfer students to CSU from California community colleges. During this period, new enrollments at CSU grew 77 percent from 74,142 to 131,212. Enrollment of in-state first-year students grew by 60 percent at California community colleges from 122,084 to 195,409, with community college enrollment particularly surging during the 2008 recession. New enrollments at UC tracked average enrollment growth for public universities in other states from 2001 to 2007, increasing 24 percent from 38,646 to 48,069. Following its freeze on new in-state enrollments, UC boosted new in-state enrollments by another 20 percent or 7,925 students in 2017. In the rest of the United States, average public university frosh enrollment growth was between that of CSU and UC at 38 percent. Even before 2017, however, the UC in-state enrollment growth rate was roughly double the enrollment growth rate at the thirty most selective private universities (not included in figure 6.3).

During this period, UC campuses continued to enroll far more low-income students than did elite private institutions. The share of students from low-income households ranged from over 30 percent at UC Berkeley to more than 50 percent at UC Riverside and UC Merced. As a result, even UC Berkeley alone enrolled nearly as many low-income undergraduates as the entire Ivy League combined.[30]

Still, qualified low-income students were disproportionately pushed into California's community college system by limited UC enrollment

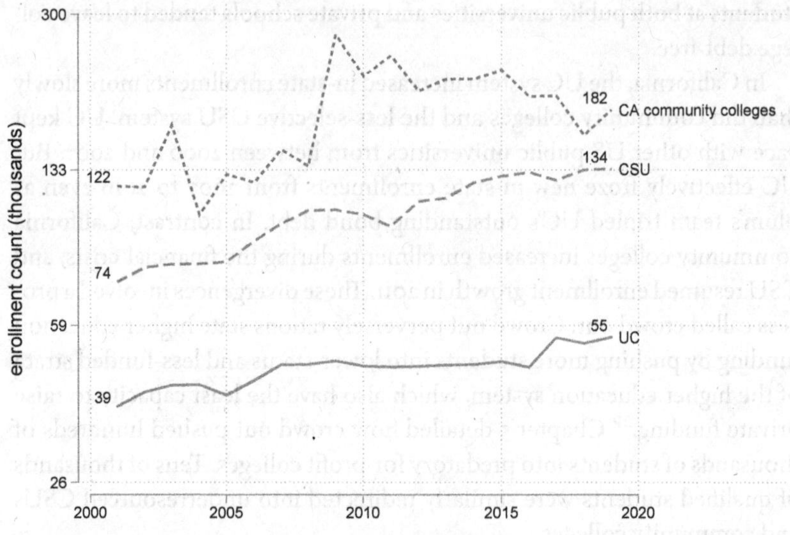

FIGURE 6.3 Total new undergraduates from in state

NOTE: Community college count is first-time full-time students from in state in IPEDS. UC and CSU published data sum new in-state frosh and new California community college transfers. Enrollments are plotted on log scale on the y-axis to illustrate relative growth year to year. Data and code: https://github.com/HigherEdData/bankersintheivorytower.

growth. Nearly 90 percent of California community college students have household incomes below $48,000 annually. Almost 70 percent of them have household incomes below $30,000.

Low-income students redirected into community colleges are especially less likely to complete degrees than are equivalently qualified students that UC admits directly. Community colleges commonly do not offer enough courses for students to transfer within two years and have low faculty-to-student ratios that adversely affect student persistence.

Graduation rates are also constrained because community college students have full-time paid employment at much higher rates than do UC students. Under the California Cal Grant program, tuition is essentially free for a majority of low-income students at both UC and the state's community colleges. But low-income UC students receive additional aid to cover cost-of-living expenses.[31]

Unequal Consequences in Student Debt

Like public and private universities nationally, UC used student debt in financial aid packages to pay for tuition increases in the years after Blum's appointment in 2002. This again had unequal consequences. Borrowing among low- and middle-income students had already risen substantially by the beginning of the 2000s. It continued to rise in the 2000s with most of the borrowing growth at UC occurring among upper-middle-class students. The overall share of students who borrowed at UC tracked a national increase in the share of students who borrow at public universities from 42 percent in 2001 to 52 percent in 2015.

Figure 6.4 uses more detailed data available from 2000 onward for UC borrowing by income group. This reveals that a UC education remained debt-free for just one group: wealthy students whose parents could cover the cost of college. Figure 6.4 also shows that student loan borrowing at UC had already increased substantially for lower-income groups by 2000 under the 1990s expansion of federal student loans.

The 1990s growth in borrowing occurred even though in-state tuition and fees remained below $6,500 in 2016 constant dollars. This reflects that a substantial share of loan borrowing at public universities goes to cover the cost of nontuition basic needs like food and housing. Accordingly, figure 6.4 shows that 76 percent of UC graduates from households

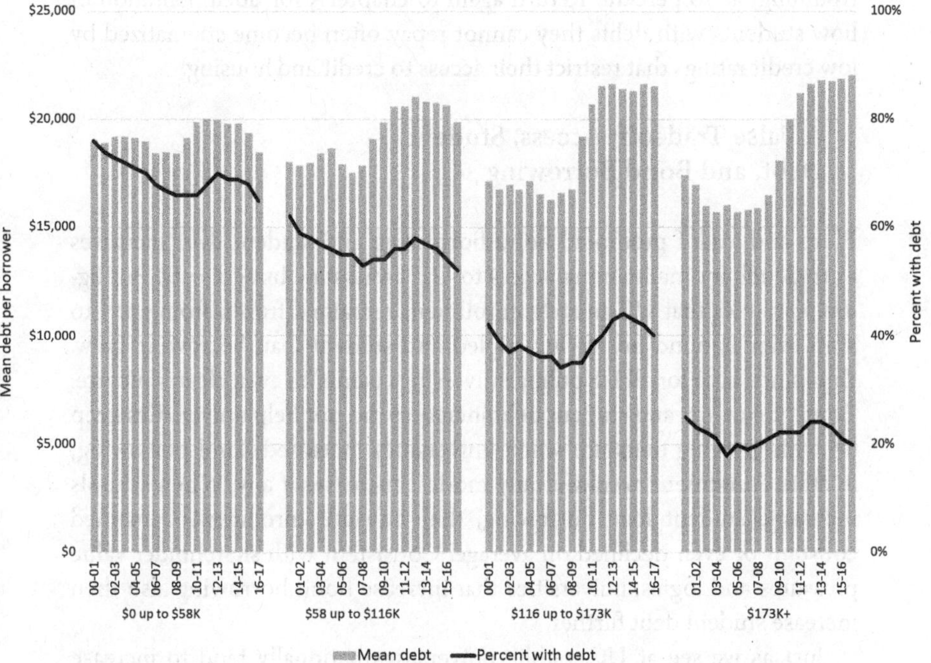

FIGURE 6.4 Student loan borrowing rates and average debt amounts by income category

NOTE: Figure used with permission from UC Office of the President. Data from student loan borrowing rates and average debt amounts by income category UC Corporate Student data system.

with income below $58,000 left school with student debt in 2000. Their average debt was $19,041. The share of these students with any borrowing actually fell by 11 percentage points in the following years as the state and UC expanded grant aid programs for the lowest-income students. Nevertheless, borrowing by low- and middle-income UC students remained 32 to 45 percentage points higher than for wealthy students during this period.

Data on borrowing by race shows parallel inequalities at UC but are only available for the 2017 academic year. Among UC graduates, 66 percent of Latinx graduates and 67 percent of Black graduates had student debt, compared to just 40 percent of white graduates.[32] As I detail in chapter 5, the racial wealth gap and labor market inequalities have left most Black borrowers unable to repay any of their debt even after ten years.

Students from low-income backgrounds have also struggled to repay debts at increasingly disastrous rates. Among low-income borrowers at US public universities who left college in 2013, less than 50 percent had repaid at least one dollar of principal without defaulting after three years. The repayment rate for low-income borrowers in 2013 was better at UC, but still troubling, at 70 percent. Return again to chapter 5 for documentation of how students with debts they cannot repay often become stigmatized by low credit ratings that restrict their access to credit and housing.

A False Tradeoff: Access, Student Debt, and Bond Borrowing

Blum and Yudof promoted bond borrowing and student debt increases as tradeoffs for maintaining access to UC amid state budget cuts. But figure 6.3 shows that UC in-state enrollment remained frozen from 2007 to 2016 even as bond borrowing tripled and student loan borrowing grew. Data since 2001 for all US public universities paints an even clearer picture. Bond borrowing and student debt increases did not help universities keep up with growing demand: when universities increased bond borrowing, in-state enrollment averaged only modest increases if any. When schools increased student loan borrowing, their in-state enrollments remained constant or even declined on average. Consistent with shareholder value pressures and logics, universities that increase bond borrowing also then increase student debt further.

Just as we see at UC, public universities nationally tend to increase student debt and bond borrowing when they are squeezed by state funding reductions. This is shown in panel A of figure 6.5. The left-hand plot in panel A uses a regression adjusted marginal estimate model to show

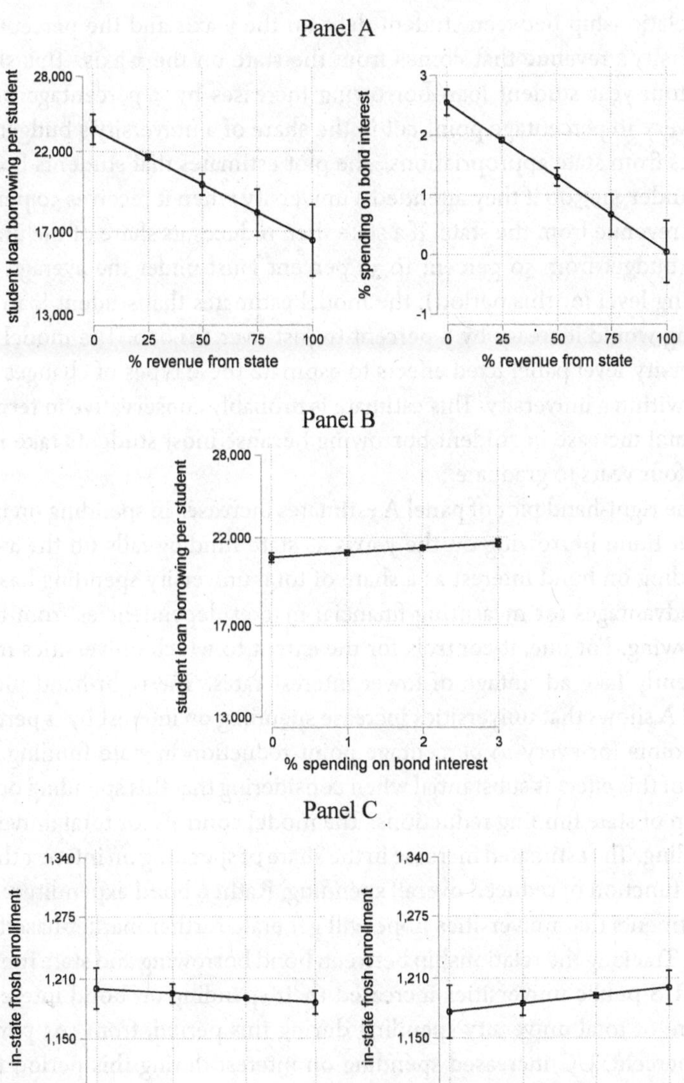

FIGURE 6.5 Regression estimates for enrollments, student debt, bond interest, and state funding

NOTE: Longitudinal OLS regression–adjusted estimates using robust standard errors. Estimates include school fixed effects and controls for year effects, total revenue per student (log), undergraduate admission rate, and state college age population by race and ethnicity (log). Models use data from 2001 through 2016 for 424 public universities (reporting in some cases at the system level, $N = 5{,}144$). Data and code: https://github.com/HigherEdData/bankersintheivorytower.

the relationship between student debt on the *y*-axis and the percent of a university's revenue that comes from the state on the *x*-axis. This shows that four-year student loan borrowing increases by 4 percentage points for every 10 percentage point cut in the share of a university's budget that comes from state appropriations. The plot estimates that students borrow just under $19,500 if they attended a university when it receives 50 percent of its revenue from the state. If a state then reduces its share of the university's budget from 50 percent to 30 percent (just under the average state funding level for this period), the model estimates that student loan borrowing would increase by 8 percent to just over $21,000. The model uses university-level panel fixed effects to estimate these types of changes over time within a university. This estimate is probably conservative in terms of the total increase in student borrowing because most students take more than four years to graduate.

The right-hand plot of panel A estimates increases in spending on interest for bond borrowing on the *y*-axis as state funding falls on the *x*-axis. Spending on bond interest as a share of total university spending has several advantages for measuring financial market dependencies from bond borrowing. For one, it controls for the extent to which universities might prudently take advantage of lower interest rates. The right-hand plot of panel A shows that universities increase spending on interest by .2 percentage points for every 10 percentage point reduction in state funding. The scale of this effect is substantial when considering that this spending occurs on top of state funding reductions. The model controls for total university spending. The estimated increase in the share of spending on interest thus is not a function of reduced overall spending. Rather, bond expenditures are investments that universities hope will generate further market-based revenue. Tracking the relationship between bond borrowing and state funding cuts, US public universities increased their spending on bond interest as a share of total university spending during this period, from 1.25 percent to 2 percent. UC increased spending on interest during this period from 1.5 percent to a peak of 2.7 percent in 2013.

Bond borrowing receives much less public scrutiny than tuition and student loan increases that students feel directly. But when public universities increase spending on bond interest, they also tend to increase student debt further still. This is consistent with the shareholder value incentives for universities to repay bond borrowing through tuition, room, and board charges paid for by student loans. Panel B of figure 6.5 shows that student loan borrowing increases by about 1 percent point for every 1 percentage point increase in the share of university spending that goes to bond interest.

The scale of the bond and student debt relationship suggests only radical increases in bond borrowing are likely to independently cause large increases in student debt. But bond-driven growth in student debt comes on top of student debt increases caused directly by state funding cuts. As shown in panel A, universities that raise student debt in response to state budget cuts are also more likely to increase bond borrowing. As a result, increased bond borrowing tends to compound increases in student debt by universities in response to state budget cuts.

UC leaders contended that maintained access was worth the price paid by students for increased student debt and bond borrowing. Panel C of figure 6.5, however, shows that neither increased student debt nor increased bond borrowing lead to meaningful increases in in-state enrollment. The left-hand plot of panel C shows that in-state frosh enrollment actually tends to decline slightly as universities increase student loan borrowing. The right-hand plot of panel C shows that schools increase enrollments on average by less than one percent for every percentage point increase in the share of their budget devoted to bond interest. The large and overlapping confidence intervals for both plots in panel C, however, signal that neither relationship is statistically significant. The model for estimating both plots in panel C controls for state funding levels and for the college-age population size in the state of each university. The absence of increased enrollment thus is neither a function of associated state funding cuts nor declining college demand.

In sum, universities increase student debt and bond borrowing in response to state funding cuts. Universities also intensify student debt increases further when they expand bond borrowing. But neither student debt nor bond borrowing have any systematic benefit for meeting growing demand for university access.

The Public University, Financialization, and Commercialization

The connective power of public universities emanates from the ideal of their universality. The ideal holds that all members of society benefit from the public university. Even before state funding cuts and rising dependence on student debt, this entitlement was stratified. Admission competition channeled less-advantaged students into CSUs and community colleges that had fewer financial resources than the UC. Still, even prestigious University of California campuses continue to enroll far more low-income students than do elite private schools both in total and as a share of their overall enrollments. UC thus figures powerfully in the California dream as a broadly attainable path to social mobility. Californians from all walks of life routinely experience this as a universal benefit via social interactions with family members, coworkers, neighbors, and civic activists who are among the millions of UC alumni living in the state. In contrast, Californians rarely encounter alumni from elite private institutions that enroll few students overall and fewer students still from less-advantaged social backgrounds.

But the universal ideal of the public university also holds that all members of society are expected to help pay for it. Financial deregulation and tax avoidance have undercut this universal ideal that all should pay for the public university. Financiers have effectively been allowed to secede from the public that pays for the public university. This secession lets financiers hoard ever greater resources at their private alma maters, mostly for the education of their own children and a fraction of the upper middle class.

The reduction of financial-sector tax obligations to public universities then pushed UC and other public universities to embrace proposals from financiers like Blum to financialize and commercialize even the public university. These dual transformations have created counterpressures on the ideal of UC universality. But California has not privatized UC as some have suggested. Privatization is the transfer of ownership to private individuals.[33] Ownership can be thought of both as formal organizational control and a claim on the profits of an organization. For-profit colleges, then, are the clearest example of a privatized college. Private nonprofit colleges might also be conceived of as privatized in that they are formally controlled by a private body of college trustees. We refer to such organizations as nonprofits, however, because their controlling board members do not have personal claims to the profits of the school like an investor would.

With a few exceptions (more on that in a moment), UC remains a public university today because private individuals have no claim on its profits and because UC's governing board is selected through a representative democracy. State-owned organizations can be highly commercialized without being privatized. Much like public universities that charge tuition, publicly owned transit systems, public utilities, and public hospitals charge fees in exchange for transportation, electricity, water, and medical services to a mix of customers. What these organizations can charge is regulated to varying extents. They also may sometimes be subsidized to charge below-market rates to consumers. These public organizations are also typically governed by bodies selected through representative democracy such as gubernatorial appointments to the UC Board of Regents. Few observers would refer to these publicly owned organizations as privatized. In fact, antiprivatization movements commonly arise when governments attempt to sell off publicly owned commercial organizations.

Public governance and the public ideal pressured UC leaders, lawmakers, and even financiers like Blum to maintain affordability and access even while commercializing tuition rates and financializing student debt and bond borrowing practices. After 2011 student protests chronicled in the next chapter, UC leaders modestly reduced student loan borrowing by lower-income students even as they radically increased tuition revenue. They did so by using tuition from wealthier students and state funding of Cal Grants to increase grant aid to lower-income students. Birgeneau has argued further that UC Berkeley enrollment of low-income students has declined because of a freeze on tuition since 2011. "If you freeze tuition then you remove revenues that support both our low-income workers and support our low-income students," he told me in an interview.[34] Tuition freezes, in his view, require Berkeley to choose between either spending cuts or the enrollment of out-of-state students in place of in-state students who tend to have lower family incomes. Birgeneau says that inadequate growth in tuition revenue also deprived UC Berkeley of revenue needed to further reduce actual prices for low-income students in accordance with the Working Group report.

But there is a problem with the hope that public universities could use higher tuition to fully realize their public purpose despite the financier-led secession from taxes. It is particularly dubious that most public universities could use tuition-financed grant aid to adequately reduce student loan borrowing by low-income students. This is because the majority of public universities lack enough prestige to attract enough wealthy students to pay higher tuition rates. We can see this even within the UC system. UC Berkeley, UCLA, and UC San Diego have all maintained out-of-state enrollments at more than 20 percent of undergraduates since 2014. These students pay a higher out-of-state tuition rate that helps to subsidize enrollment of low-income students, primarily from California. But UC Riverside and UC Merced, UC's lowest-status campuses, enroll less than 5 percent and less than 1 percent of students from out of state, respectively.

Nationally, more prestigious public universities have not typically increased affordability or enrollments when they were given more freedom to increase tuition. For example, University of Virginia (UVA) has long been allowed to charge tuition rates that were 20 percent higher or more than tuition at UC Berkeley. Yet the actual annual price to attend UVA after financial aid (including the price of housing, food, and basic needs) has averaged around $9,500 for low-income students since consistent federal survey data became available in 2015. UC Berkeley's actual annual price for low-income students has remained around $1,000 lower than UVA's despite a much higher cost of living. UC Berkeley has also increased its total in-state enrollments at around twice the rate as UVA after accounting for community college transfers. And low-income students have never exceeded 15 percent of UVA undergrads even though Virginia's standard poverty rate (based only on income) was just 2.7 percentage points lower than California's in 2018. Despite recent declines, 30 percent of UC Berkeley undergraduates are from low-income households.

Direct borrowing from bond markets also has similar limitations as a financializing solution to state funding cuts. It is harder for less prestigious universities to borrow at favorable rates from bond markets if they cannot promise credibly to repay those debts by enrolling more wealthy students at high tuition rates. Consistent with this dilemma, UC's Merced campus had to resort to using public-private partnerships to capitalize an expansion that has provided much of UC's enrollment growth in recent years.[35] Birgeneau has opposed such arrangements that give long-term leases and rights for on-campus buildings and services, including dormitories and dining halls. "I have always opposed handing over university facilities to for-profit third parties. In the end you do not exercise total control and there is no way of knowing what the pitfalls might be," Birgeneau told me in an interview.

As Birgeneau fears, there is at least one exception in which the commercialization or financialization of public universities may lead to a perverse form of privatization: public-private partnerships to deliver online degree programs. Public records act requests have shown that most such programs at public universities almost always rely on subcontracts with for-profit online program managers (OPMs). Some private equity–backed OPMs like Kaplan and Zovio (formerly Bridgepoint) pivoted to OPM subcontracting after facing regulatory sanctions for operating predatory for-profit colleges. Other major OPMs like Pearson face shareholder value pressures as publicly traded corporations. One study found that 50 percent of public institutions' OPM contracts split tuition revenue with the OPM provider, and 41 percent of their contracts give the for-profit OPM control over recruitment.[36] OPMs also sometimes provide financing for new online degree programs. These arrangements exploit a loophole in the federal ban on paying commissions to college recruiters.[37] OPM contractors appear to already be cashing in on these arrangements. From 2012 to 2018, enrollments in entirely online programs at public and private nonprofit colleges and universities went from being nonexistent to enrolling nearly 2 million undergrads, equivalent to total enrollments for the entire for-profit college sector at its 2011 peak. We also have early signs that outcomes for OPM students may be just as bad as for-profit college outcomes. For example, graduation rates were just 4 percent at Arizona State University (ASU) Online for the only year it has reported data for a full cohort.[38] But 45 percent of

ASU Online students borrow an average of $5,000 for every year enrolled. This borrowing partially flows to Pearson via a tuition sharing OPM agreement with ASU.

In sum, Blum and Yudof's approach to tuition, student loans, and bond borrowing—despite their commitment to UC's public ideals—has failed to extract contributions to public higher education from financiers commensurate to their growing tax avoidance. In the end, few of the wealthiest financiers will ever pay higher tuition rates for their children to attend public universities, because they rarely send their children to public universities at all.

We will have to look elsewhere for political and policy strategies regarding how to equitably finance higher education and the public ideal of universality. The sociology of innovation suggests that people most often invent effective solutions to social problems when they engage with diverse others who have sufficient shared identities and cultures to collaborate. As we have seen, California's public universities, including the UC system, provide just these sorts of shared identities and cultures to a remarkably diverse array of students, education workers, policy makers, and even financiers. So, it should come as no surprise that Californians advanced one of the first major tax policy shifts toward restoring equity in higher education and finance. Reflecting their own public university ties and ideals, Blum and Yudof eventually endorsed Proposition 30, the 2012 income tax increase on millionaires that finally stopped a decline in state tax revenue as a share of GDP. Birgeneau also endorsed Proposition 30 and penned a 2015 op-ed calling for California to close the property tax loophole commonly exploited by private equity investors.[39] The 2012 tax increase—extended in 2016—helped pay to freeze tuition, reduce student loan borrowing, and restore UC enrollment growth in 2017. But the innovative strategies behind higher education finance reform in California and elsewhere have typically been advanced first by associations and civic advocates for those most affected by rising student debt and financier power: low-income communities and communities of color. I turn next to the story of these groups who are reimagining finance from below.

7. Reimagining (Higher Education) Finance from Below

On November 9, 2011, thousands of students walked out of classes at UC Berkeley and marched on a nearby Bank of America branch chanting, "Hey hey! Ho ho! Wall Street regents got to go!"[1] The chant referred to members of the University of California (UC) Board of Regents with Wall Street ties, such as Monica Lozano, who also served on the board of Bank of America, and private equity manager Dick Blum, who we met in chapter 6. UC had doubled tuition over the previous eight years, and the 2008 financial crisis had devastated the state higher education budget. Angered by the threat of further increases in tuition and student debt, the protesters launched the largest sustained campus-based political mobilization in California since the state ended affirmative action at its public universities in the 1990s.

The leaders of the 2011 mobilization were everything that America's Ivy League financiers are not. They included UC Santa Cruz sociology student Claudia Magaña, UC Berkeley gardener Kathryn Lybarger, and Los Angeles high school teacher Josh Pechthalt. I also helped lead the effort as a graduate student at UC Berkeley. Each of us had been elected to lead one of California's statewide associations representing hundreds of thousands of students and education workers. We collaborated with leaders of community organizations like Amy Schur and Christina Livingston of the Association of Californians for Community Empowerment (ACCE), who sought to improve state social programs by increasing taxes on corporate property and top income earners.

On the eve of the November 9 protests, our ad hoc coalition called on the board members of California's public universities to endorse tax increases and other measures to make financiers and other millionaires pay for "refunding public education." By November 2012, the coalition defied elite expectations by successfully pushing the state to adopt the highest state income tax on millionaires in the United States and California's highest millionaire tax rate since 1942.[2] The millionaire tax arrested the continuous rise in financier tax avoidance in California for the first time since the 1980s. The state, in turn, used some of the tax to freeze tuition, reverse cuts to public universities, and increase spending on community colleges and grants to low-income students. In the process, the coalition won backing for the tax from California's public university board members, including Lozano and Blum. Over the next eight years, the tax increase helped California to increase higher education funding faster than almost any other US state.

The California mobilization employed one of two strategies that overlapping coalitions have developed to increase financial equity in higher education. I call these two strategies "bargaining with bankers" and a "financial big bang." The California mobilization pursued the more gradualist bargaining-with-bankers strategy. In addition to traditional advocacy for policy change, this bargaining strategy also bypasses lawmakers to put social pressure on financiers to support tax increases on themselves. In doing so, it pushes into the public sphere the distributional conflicts that finance typically obscures.[3]

The bargaining strategy succeeded in California because the state's public universities weave an unusually broad and powerful network of intimate ties among civic leaders. Public university ties paradoxically mirror the intimacy of Ivy League ties between financiers and other elites. In California, public university social ties likewise extend to financiers like Blum and Lozano. But California public universities create a more universal shared identity and social ties that also connect civic leaders of socially diverse communities. Just as financiers needed intimate ties to pursue risky new investment strategies, university ties helped California civic leaders to carry out an untested strategy that broke with political and social norms.

The big bang strategy seeks a more immediate transformation that resets the rules of finance with minimal negotiation with financiers. Key big bang proposals include the cancellation of all student debt and federally funded, free college for all. The distributional implications of these proposals are comparable to the creation of America's Social Security and Medicare systems, shifts that welfare-state scholars have referred to as policy big bangs that transformed the politics of old age insurance and health care.[4] Those earlier big bangs occurred during large-scale breakdowns in the nation's social and economic order.

The vanguard of the big bang strategy has harnessed an even broader new identity shared by more than forty million Americans: that of student loan borrower. This new identity is captured by the "you are not a loan" slogan popularized by the Debt Collective offshoot of Occupy Wall Street in 2012.[5] The Debt Collective and a loose alliance of other organizations has invoked the debtor identity to build intimate ties between public, private, and for-profit college students. In doing so, this new alliance united more fragmented individuals than the stakeholders and alumni of California's public universities. As with the California coalition, intimate ties have helped Debt Collective members to undertake risky strategies such as debt strikes. With these dramatic tactics, they opened up the mainstream of American politics to their calls to cancel student debt and make higher education free. These proposals gained further support from politicians and citizens as the COVID-19 pandemic and recession made it harder for even broader legions of borrowers to repay their debts.

In this final chapter, I first explain why diverse coalitions typically produce more innovative and successful strategies for change among nonelite social groups. I note how public universities and student debt both offer powerful shared identities to convene such coalitions. Second, I show that the California coalition creatively combined the varied knowledge of its members to develop a bargaining-with-bankers strategy. Third, I discuss how the convening of diverse debtors similarly helped debt cancellation advocates to forge a big bang strategy. Last, I discuss the prospects for bargaining and big bangs in the connected domains of US higher education policy, tax policy, and financial regulation.

Coalitions, Borderland Actors, and Strategic Innovation

Even with big bangs, new policy regimes are never built from scratch. Change makers always imagine something new in reference to what came before. When socioeconomic orders break down, the possibilities for a new order are still constrained by the existing cultural frameworks and resource distributions of a society. Sociologists Fernando Enrique Cardoso and Enzo Faletto proposed that movements then must imagine the "barely structurally possible" in order to achieve deep and lasting transformations.[6] Change agents are strategic when, in the words of historian Perry Anderson, they use awareness of such structural constraints to take collective actions that "produce a premeditated future."[7] This leads to a question: When and how do subordinated social groups develop effective strategies of collective action?

The sociology of innovation suggests that diverse coalitions are more likely to develop creative new strategies for their empowerment objectives than are nondiverse coalitions. Coalition participants bring varied perspectives and practices to the table. Their efforts to combine these perspectives and practices into a unified plan of action then produces creative new strategies. The early twentieth-century women's movement, the civil rights movement, and the 1960s farmworker movement all benefited from this creative dynamic of coalitions.[8] But coalition participants need sufficient shared culture to understand each other's varied experiences when developing a new strategy. A common identity can similarly facilitate this sensemaking process. For example, farmworker leaders built a multiracial and cross-class coalition by mobilizing Catholic churches and identity.

Public universities are a wellspring of shared culture and identity for coalition building. As we have seen with financiers, universities inculcate students with a common culture and identity. California civic leaders are equivalently connected by college friendships, collegiate sports fandom, and alumni identities. Public universities, however, do this at an exponentially larger scale than do private universities. In states like California, more selective schools like UC Berkeley are also organizationally and symbolically tied to less-selective schools like UC Riverside and the California State University campuses. Public universities—even selective ones—further enroll students from a wider variety of class backgrounds.[9] Less-selective public universities in states like California are unparalleled by private institutions in their racial and class diversity.[10] Civic leaders can unite their respective communities by drawing on the resulting friendship networks and experiences to reach across social boundaries.

Universities also create what sociologist Marshall Ganz calls borderland actors. Borderland actors play a critical translational role for coalition participants to increase their mutual understanding and trust. They have experiences of "straddling cultural or institutional worlds" that equip them for this connective role. As an example, Ganz points to how many United Farm Workers leaders had gained experiences across multiple worlds as clergy, World War II soldiers, and university students.[11] They used their ties to the civil rights movement and to students to help build the United Farm Workers coalition and to develop its unorthodox strategies like boycotts and disciplined nonviolence during strikes.

We shall see that borderland actors play critical roles in both the banker bargaining and big bang coalitions for higher education finance reform. Their translational and connective work has been especially critical to the development of the big bang strategies for debt cancellation and free college. The banker bargaining coalitions primarily drew on the socially valorized identity of public university alumni. To mobilize fragmented student loan borrowers from for-profit and private schools, groups like the Debt

Collective had to subvert the stigmatization of the borrower identity. Borderland actors also have helped enlist elites—including lawmakers and their staff—in support of both the bargaining and big bang strategies.

Public University Ties and Bargaining with Bankers in California

Prior to 2012, California voters had only approved one small income tax increase since the 1970s. But persistent erosion of tax revenue as a share of GDP had been amplified by a slow economic recovery from the great recession. To stop further tuition increases or education funding cuts, a much larger tax increase was necessary. The loose alliance of civic groups in California coalesced around a policy strategy of an unusually large tax increase on millionaires. They developed an equally unorthodox political strategy for winning the tax increase—nonviolent protest directed at financiers tied to public universities and a ballot initiative campaign in defiance of state Democratic Party leaders. Together, the policy and political strategy amounted to bargaining with bankers via political intermediaries in state government. We can see public university ties in action in the development and successful implementation of both the policy proposal and the political strategy.

The millionaire tax policy strategy sought to minimize organized opposition by using a broader but smaller tax increase on all millionaires. As the largest group of high-income Americans (see chapter 2), financiers would pay a disproportionate share of the millionaire tax. But by targeting millionaires more broadly, proponents hoped to raise more revenue while minimizing organized opposition by a smaller and more unified group of financiers. Early versions of this plan were distributed in the summer of 2011 by California Calls, an alliance of racial and economic justice organizations; the California Federation of Teachers (CFT); and the liberal Courage Campaign—an online organization that emerged from California LGBTQ mobilizations for marriage rights. These plans drew on research I discussed in chapter 6 that showed private equity tax avoidance had particularly undercut state property tax revenue.[12] The plans were shared at statewide coalition meetings of dozens of community organizations, labor unions, and student groups in Los Angeles and Burbank that I attended on July 19 and August 8, 2011.

California Calls played a key role in enlisting the participation of the UC Student Association in developing and campaigning for the millionaire tax plan from July 2011 onward. California Calls founder, Anthony Thigpen, had been a student activist at California State University (CSU) Northridge. It was natural for California Calls leaders to invite UC Student Association (UCSA) President Claudia Magaña and other student leaders to their June 2011 strategy because California Calls Deputy Director Sabrina Smith had attended UCLA and helped lead campaigns for affirmative action as the organizing director of the UCSA.

Parallel to the development of the millionaire tax initiative, community and labor organizers worked with students to develop a plan to put pressure on university-affiliated financiers. The plan also aimed to garner public support for a millionaire tax. Service Employees International Union (SEIU) organizer Jono Shaffer referenced his experience as a UC Santa Cruz student activist when reaching out to UC and California State University graduate student leaders in June 2011. He shared a plan developed with the Alliance of Californians for Community Empowerment. The plan called for choosing "Bank of America, Chase or Wells Fargo—as a primary corporate target to . . . 'put a face' on the culprits, and expose the people behind the corporations" that did not "pay their fair share."[13] The plan reflected past SEIU strategies to pressure the financial backers of real estate companies to win union recognition for workers.

After three months of deliberation and planning, on November 11, 2011, the leaders of nineteen statewide unions, community associations, and student organizations sent a joint letter to every member of the governing boards of the UC, CSU, and state community college systems. The signers together represented nearly 250,000 students and over 500,000 teachers and school employees. In anticipation of each board's November meeting, the letter called on each board member to pledge their support for "specific measures . . . making Wall Street and the super-rich pay their fair share."[14] The top measure was "increasing income taxes on California's wealthiest."

Over the next ten days, the union and student leaders coordinated walkouts, protests, and occupations of campus greens involving thousands of students at ten different UC and CSU campuses. The protests garnered national media attention. Student and union leaders planned for the mobilization to culminate with a protest at the UC Board of Regents meeting at UC San Francisco on November 16. Unions had donated $60,000 for students to take buses to the protest. Citing unnamed "rogue elements" among the protesters, UC President Mark Yudof announced on November 11 that the regents would cancel their meeting for the first time in memory. Two thousand students assembled in San Francisco on November 16 anyway and marched on the flagship branch of Bank of America.

Following the protests, Governor Jerry Brown proposed a tax increase on December 1, 2011. But his proposal relied mostly on a sales tax increase and increased income taxes on millionaires by just 1 percent from 10.3 percent to 11.3 percent.[15] The millionaire tax coalition decided to proceed with its own measure and launched its own ballot initiative on December 4 to increase millionaire income taxes by 5 percentage points to 15.3 percent.

Student, community, and labor leaders also continued to coordinate beyond the protests. Students launched signature-gathering efforts in support of the millionaire tax ballot initiative. Student and labor leaders also coordinated their lobbying of state lawmakers, asking them to support the millionaire tax and a freeze on tuition. Students backed additional financial aid proposals by the Institute for College Access and Success. And UC Student Association and UC graduate student employee union leaders engaged in direct talks with Yudof and UC regents, including Lozano and Board Chair Sherry Lansing. With more labor financial backing, ten thousand students descended on the state legislative building in Sacramento to nonviolently "occupy the capitol" on March 5, 2012.

On April 4, 2012, the leaders of the CFT teacher union, California Calls, ACCE, and the Courage Campaign announced that they had reached an agreement with Governor Brown to merge their respective tax proposals. The merged tax proposal, Proposition 30, included an increase from 10.3 percent to 13.3 percent on dual income households with earnings over $1 million annually.[16] The governor and the coalition agreed that they would campaign together to get voters to approve the tax increase in a referendum on the November 2012 ballot.

Following the tax initiative agreement, the millionaire tax coalition turned its attention to the 2012 state budget to ensure that their constituencies would benefit from the tax increase. The labor and community leaders cosigned an April 10 letter with UC Student Association President Magaña and other student leaders. The letter called on Governor Brown to use some of the proposed tax increase to "refund students—not Wall Street" in the 2012 state budget. The letter specifically called for reversing tuition increases and state higher education funding cuts.[17]

As the millionaire tax coalition turned to lobbying around the state budget, its leaders tapped their public university ties to lawmakers and higher education experts. Governor Brown was himself a graduate of UC Berkeley. But State Assembly Speaker John A. Pérez and his chief higher education consultant Max Espinoza had the strongest social links to students. Pérez had participated in UCSA and protests for faculty and student diversity as the chair of the CalSERVE student political party at UC Berkeley in the 1980s. Pérez also worked with the Movimiento Estudiantil Chicanx de Aztlán and other groups to build multiracial coalitions on campus. Like many UCSA leaders (including Magaña), Pérez became a union representative after college before running for public office. Espinoza had led protests to preserve affirmative action as a leader with Movimiento Estudiantil Chicanx de Aztlán at UCLA. UCSA nominated Espinoza to represent students on the Board of Regents. Espinoza had also entered UC in 1994 in one of the first cohorts to borrow heavily using federal student loans following a doubling of UC tuition from 1991 to 1994.

In an interview, Espinoza told me that he understood what was at stake for students and low-wage education employees because of his own experience as a financial aid recipient and student loan borrower. Espinoza added that he felt a sense of common purpose with student, community, and labor leaders. He attributed this to a shared "California dream" bolstered by the state's historic ideal of affordable higher education for all.

Espinoza provided the millionaire tax allies with critical technical insights about the state budget. Even with support from labor lobbyists and analysts, the coalition lacked the capacity to track and understand the consequential minutia of a byzantine state budget that topped $100 billion. In contrast, the governor's Department of Finance and the administrations of the state's college and university systems had dozens of staff devoted to this task. The coalition was also advised by analysts with the Institute for College Access and Success, which UC Berkeley alumnus Bob Shireman had founded a decade earlier. For example, the Institute for College Access and Success and Espinoza directed the coalition's attention to proposed changes in the state budget that would have reduced Cal Grant awards to low-income students but maintained awards to predatory for-profit colleges.

Throughout the events of 2011 and 2012, millionaire tax coalition leaders exchanged confidential information on strategies and internal deliberations. This definitive sign of intimacy enabled them to take risks and break with political norms. Community, student, and labor leaders shared private plans for illicit collective actions such as nonviolent civil disobedience and walkouts. They also routinely reported to each other on the content of private meetings with UC regents and lawmakers. Through this intimacy, they were able to learn if enough allies would support their strategy for it to work. The risks of political blowback were real if allies did not follow through. Students could suffer school discipline or legal sanction.

Intimate ties helped a core of union leaders hang together in support of the millionaire tax despite real risks of a falling-out with Democratic Party patrons in state government. UC Regent Blum (who was married to Democratic US Senator Dianne Feinstein and was a close friend of Governor Brown) already blamed UC's low-wage service workers union AFSCME 3299 for student protests in 2009 and 2010, telling an interviewer, "90 percent of the demonstrations, maybe more, that you see on this campus or other campuses is AFSCME."[18] UC Berkeley gardener and AFSCME 3299 President Kathryn Lybarger nevertheless refused to back down from her members' vote to endorse the millionaire tax. In a further testimony to the risks for union backers of the millionaire tax, Governor Brown convinced leaders of the state's largest union organizations—including the California Federation of Labor, California Teachers Association, SEIU State Council, and AFSCME 3299's parent federation—to support the governor's more regressive sales tax proposal. At a December 6, 2012, community-labor coalition meeting to celebrate the passage of Proposition 30, California Teachers Association President Dean Vogel publicly thanked CFT President Josh Pechthalt for standing against others in organized labor, including Vogel's own union, to force Governor Brown to compromise.

In an interview, Pérez told me that his background in building coalitions at UC and in the labor movement helped him as state assembly speaker to broker an agreement between Governor Brown and the millionaire tax backers to merge their respective ballot initiatives.[19] Pérez and others worried that both ballot initiatives would fail if they went on the November 2012 ballot together. To help avert this, Pérez engaged in "shuttle diplomacy" between Brown, a fellow Berkeley alum, and labor leaders backing the millionaire tax. The new merged initiative, however, bore a much closer resemblance to the millionaire tax with 79 percent of new revenue projected to come from income tax increases on the top 2 percent of earners.[20] Even after Brown agreed to back the new compromise initiative, the governor delayed withdrawing his own initiative until the new initiative gathered enough voter petition signatures to be placed on the ballot. This resistance by Brown reflects the delicacy of the relational work in negotiations over the tax.

But some of the most remarkable intimate relations occurred between Speaker Pérez, Espinoza, and UCSA President Magaña. Both directly and via Espinoza, Pérez routinely consulted with Magaña about how she and students would react to budget measures under negotiation with the governor and UC leaders. On July 24, 2012, Speaker Pérez took the extraordinary step of asking Espinoza to tell students before it was made public that a budget deal had been reached to freeze tuition with Proposition 30 tax funds.

The bargaining with bankers of the millionaire tax campaign came full circle when the governing boards of the UC and CSU systems both voted to endorse the Proposition 30 tax hike in July 2012. Regent Blum voted to endorse the measure on July 18 even though he likely would pay more in taxes on his private equity earnings than any other board member. Blum declared in a UC press release, "We should all support this. I personally will be supporting it vigorously."[21] Regent Lozano also endorsed the tax increase and tuition freeze. Espinoza said that Lozano privately had been an even fiercer advocate for the agreement. California voters went on to approve Proposition 30 in November 2012 by a 55 percent to 45 percent margin, establishing California's highest state income tax rate on millionaires since 1942. Undergraduate tuition remained effectively frozen at public universities and community colleges from 2011 to 2021.

The 2012 tax increase and budget deal fell far short of the millionaire tax coalition's goals. Accordingly, there have been quieter echoes of bargaining with bankers in California since 2012. The millionaire tax coalition reunited in 2016 to pass a twelve-year extension of Proposition 30's taxes on millionaires. Revenue growth from the tax expansion has helped coalition partners to make some progress in areas where the 2012 bargain was lacking.

For example, Governor Brown eliminated UC undergraduate enrollment targets from the 2012 state budget with a line-item veto requested by UC President Yudof. This permitted UC to keep in-state enrollments flat through 2016 despite growth in applications from qualified California high school graduates. UCSA and their labor allies had opposed the enrollment target elimination and continued to advocate for increasing in-state enrollments. Following the extension of Proposition 30 millionaire taxes, UC agreed to increase in-state undergraduate enrollments for the first time since 2007. Speaker Pérez also passed a new middle-class scholarship program in 2013 that helped UC and CSU to mostly reduce loan borrowing by low- and middle-income students. After leaving the state assembly, Pérez was appointed to the Board of Regents where he served a term as chair. In this new role, Pérez has called for expanding debt-free financial aid to more UC students.

Since 2011, similar education coalitions have sought to bargain with bankers in other cities and states with strong public university systems and established education labor unions. Leaders in the California coalition have formally and informally advised these mobilizations. Christina Livingston of ACCE and Liz Perlman of AFSCME 3299 helped to form Bargaining for the Common Good in 2014 and remain on its national advisory committee. UC Berkeley gardener and AFSCME 3299 President Kathryn Lybarger was elected president of the two million–member California Federation of Labor in 2015. ACCE leader Maurice Weeks left California to help community organizations and labor unions in other states to "go on offense against Wall Street to beat back their destruction of communities of color."[22] Weeks continues this work today as the coexecutive director of Action Center on Race and the Economy. Via these national networks, Livingston, Perlman, and Weeks have advised and learned from other deliberate efforts to bargain with bankers in Chicago,[23] Los Angeles,[24] Massachusetts, New Jersey,[25] New York,[26] Puerto Rico,[27] and Seattle.[28]

The coalitions that have sought to bargain with bankers have also backed big bang proposals to cancel student debt and make college free. But activists outside the dense civic networks of public universities played a key role in popularizing these ideas. The 2011 Occupy Wall Street protests brought together these individuals who otherwise would have stayed fragmented. We turn now to how they promoted debt cancellation by mobilizing evocative protests around the identity of student debtor.

Debtor Ties and Imagining Big Bangs

Private nonprofit and for-profit colleges award 38 percent of US bachelor's degrees. Unlike public universities, they are not governed by state-appointed boards or state governments. While they receive large federal subsidies, private institutions also have much less dependence on state funding. Without these links to state government, stakeholders in private colleges lack equivalent mechanisms for bargaining with bankers. Alumni with student debt additionally lack a comparable way to bargain via state policy. Federal tax and student aid policy offer a more plausible venue for private-sector education stakeholders and borrowers to change inequalities in who pays for and who benefits from US higher education.

Major federal policies to reduce inequality in the twentieth century tended to begin in big bang waves of legislation. The 1930s New Deal and the 1960s Great Society were the nation's seminal policy big bangs of the twentieth century. These big bangs changed the institutional framework for further social policy expansion. The New Deal created Social Security, unemployment insurance, the Glass-Steagall restrictions on financial speculation, the modern Federal Reserve system,[29] and a 79 percent "wealth tax" on all income above $5 million. The Great Society created Medicare, Medicaid, Head Start early education, food stamps, the Department of Housing and Urban Development, and the precursors to Pell Grants and federal student loans. These bursts of redistributive policy change occurred during the national crises of the Great Depression and the civil rights movement, respectively. Wealthy elites and their conservative allies normally can block redistributive state interventions via the checks and balances of US federalism.[30] But the 1930s and 1960s breakdowns in social order briefly made it possible for nonelites and their elite allies to assemble large enough political coalitions to push through new regimes for redistribution.

Ideas for major policy changes do not spontaneously emerge during the crises that usher them into law. For example, labor union leaders and social reformers had debated the creation of a federal old age insurance program modeled after the British system for decades prior to the creation of US Social Security.[31] But during crises, diverse political outsiders can look at previously marginal ideas in new ways and adapt them to the present. For example, the Great Depression fueled the creation of 3,400 grassroots Townsend Clubs in support of old age pensions. Their proposal for a more generous proposal eventually pushed Congress to pass Social Security.[32]

The Occupy Wall Street protests brought together tens of thousands of diffuse political outsiders, analogous to members of the Townsend movement. New York was the eponymous epicenter that began this protest wave on September 17, 2011. The New York protesters and their counterparts in one hundred other cities set up encampments in squares and public places, often in cities' financial districts. For many protesters, student debt had made a slow economic recovery feel more like a Great Depression.[33] In addition to their economic hardship, Occupiers expressed moral outrage at the persistent wealth of the bankers they blamed for the 2008 crisis. But many of the Occupiers came from outside of the labor unions, community organizations, and public university student groups that were central to the California millionaire tax campaign.

A subgroup of Occupiers instead developed a dual strategy of calling for radical national policy changes while providing each other with mutual assistance. This subgroup operated first within the organization Strike Debt and since 2014 as the Debt Collective. A central component of their mutual assistance involved the sharing of their private struggles with debt. For example, they helped to produce *The Debt Resistor's Operations Manual* in September 2012. The preface of the manual reads,

> Because there is so much shame, frustration and fear surrounding our debt, we seldom talk about it openly with others. An initial step in building a debt resistance movement involves sharing the myriad ways debt affects us, both directly and indirectly.[34]

The manual includes an entire chapter about student loans. The student loan chapter ranges from tips on how to rehabilitate debts to arguments for collective political action to make college free and to cancel student debts.

The founders of the Debt Collective developed their mutual support programs as they reconciled the worldviews of radical academics and critically minded financial-sector workers. Many of these academics and veterans of finance had attended or even taught at elite private universities in the Northeast Corridor.[35] Anthropologist Hannah Appel, a Debt Collective cofounder, attributes their innovations to interactions between these otherwise siloed groups. For example, Debt Collective members participated in the Occupy Alternative Banking Working Group that met at Columbia University from 2011 through at least 2014. Appel describes the group as follows:

> Many of its early core participants had industry backgrounds . . . current and former mortgage-backed securities traders; financial accounting and risk-management experts; bankers, bank analysts and data crunchers; a bevy of economists and economics professors; securities and tax lawyers; and so on. Between them they have worked for Arthur Anderson, Banker's Trust, Chase Manhattan, CitiBank, Deutsche Bank, DE Shaw, Drexel Burnham, Goldman Sachs, HSBC, Moody's Investor Services, Salomon Smith Barney, Riskmetrics, Société Générale, Swiss Bank, and a variety of private equity firms, law firms, universities, and colleges. Of course there are others of us in the group too—the curious anthropologist ever-willing to take minutes, small business owners, labor activists, retirees, freelance writers and journalists, a credit union activist, educators and students, an architect, a professional figure skater, quite a few unemployed folks.[36]

From this milieu, leaders of Strike Debt, the Debt Collective precursor, developed the Rolling Jubilee program to buy consumer debts that were in default and cancel those debts. Because debt collectors are only able to collect a fraction of defaulted consumer debts, banks routinely sell them for pennies on the dollar. Rolling Jubilee exploited the low price of defaulted consumer loans through grassroots fundraising to purchase and cancel such debts. Between 2012 and 2014, Rolling Jubilee raised $701,137 to purchase and cancel almost $32 million in debt, including $17 million in student debt for 12,199 former students.[37] Rolling Jubilee generated extensive social media participation and legacy media coverage.[38] Those touched by Rolling Jubilee learned that it is not only possible to cancel unpayable student debts; it is relatively cheap.

Through Rolling Jubilee, Strike Debt organizers began to talk with a heavily indebted group who were rarely part of their initial conversations: for-profit college students. In 2014, the investor-owned Corinthian Colleges collapsed after regulatory scrutiny for dismal student outcomes and alleged fraud. Corinthian is the chain that sought to avoid reputational damage from scandals by operating sixteen different brands at once, twelve of which provided the same health degrees with the same curriculum. After Corinthian's collapse, Rolling Jubilee purchased and cancelled the debts of students from its Everest-branded campuses. They notified the borrowers with a letter reading, "Jubilant Greetings! . . . We are writing to you with good news. We just got rid of some of your Everest College debt!"[39] The letter also provided a phone number for borrowers to contact Rolling Jubilee organizers.

Expanding on the Rolling Jubilee, Debt Collective organizers went on to talk with hundreds of Corinthian borrowers about engaging in a debt strike as a way to pressure the US Department of Education to cancel all their student loans. Individually, many of these students could not repay their debts anyway. Why not refuse to pay collectively? On February 14, 2015, fourteen former Corinthian students published a letter to the US Department of Education to announce their debt strike.[40] The debt strike again garnered sustained national media coverage, with Corinthian nursing student Mallory Heiney speaking for the strikers in an op-ed in the *Washington Post*.[41] More than one hundred other Corinthian, EDMC, and ITT Tech students joined the strike in the coming year.[42] Organizers set up Facebook groups for former students, membership in which grew to more than twenty thousand.[43] The debt strike also rallied growing media attention and support from consumer advocacy organizations and US Senator Elizabeth Warren to make the US Department of Education cancel debts for hundreds of thousands of for-profit college borrowers. Warren and twelve other senators wrote to US Secretary of Education Arnie Duncan on June 26 and December 9, 2014, to call for the secretary to cancel the student loans of Corinthian and other for-profit college students. The senators proposed that Duncan use a provision of the Higher Education Act known as "borrower defense" that makes student loans unenforceable if "acts or omissions" of a college have harmed a student.[44] On May 19 of 2015, the National Consumer Law Center (NCLC) bolstered the strikers' and Warren's case by filing a formal petition to Department of Education outlining the legal basis for Duncan to cancel Corinthian borrowers' debts en masse.[45]

Further organizational backing was marshaled by Higher Education Not Debt (HEND), a coalition formed in 2013 with backing from the national parent organizations for the groups that led the California campaign, including ACCE, AFSCME, AFT, SEIU, and the US Student Association. HEND was founded with staffing and fiscal sponsorship from the Generation Progress youth arm of the liberal Center for American Progress think tank. With dozens of other labor, think tank, and consumer rights "campaign partners," HEND provided research capacity, technical expertise, political access, and new forums in which support for debt cancellation would grow. HEND, Generation Progress, AFT, SEIU, and forty-five other consumer and civil rights groups backed NCLC petition for class-wide cancellation of student debt.[46]

Duncan and the Obama administration, however, resisted cancelling student debt automatically for all former Corinthian students. Despite Duncan's dubious belief in technology as a solution for educational inequality, the Department of Education required Corinthian students to apply individually for debt cancellation via paper forms or via a PDF form that worked only on personal computers with Adobe Acrobat. As a result, volunteer coders with the Debt Collective had to design a PDF generator and web front end to let Corinthian borrowers apply for cancellation via smartphones.[47] Following pressure from advocates, the department created its own mobile-compatible web form by 2016 and implemented a postal and digital media outreach campaign to solicit applications for debt cancellation from borrowers who attended Corinthian or other closed for-profit college chains.[48] As of October 2016, the department had received eighty-two thousand claims for debt cancellation. The department initially cancelled the debt of 47,942 borrowers, or 84 percent of claimants.[49]

While the initial debt cancellations were an unprecedented victory, resistance by Duncan and the Department of Education left hundreds of thousands of defrauded for-profit college borrowers without relief. The department had the legal authority to cancel debts automatically for all borrowers who attended for-profit colleges shut down by regulators. Requiring individual applications slowed debt cancellation to a crawl and let countless borrowers fall through the cracks. Then in 2017, newly elected President Donald Trump appointed Betsy DeVos, the wife of a private equity financier, to lead the US Department of Education. DeVos effectively ended borrower defense debt cancellation until Trump's reelection defeat in 2020. Under DeVos, borrower defense cancellation claims grew to exceed 300,000.[50] The department cancelled $2.6 billion in debt for 188,000 of these borrowers within the first nine months of Joe Biden's presidency.

The push for borrower defense further expanded a valuable web of intimate ties between debt cancellation advocates and a set of underappreciated potential elite allies: Democratic congressional staffers. Representative Maxine Waters, the ranking Democrat on the House Finance committee had endorsed the Corinthian debt strike on March 3, 2015.[51] Former Deutsche Bank and Merrill Lynch vice president turned Occupy Wall Street veteran Alexis Goldstein then worked with early congressional allies like Waters to organize a briefing for Democratic congressional staffers. In the briefing, borrowers and debt strikers directly shared their stories of hardship. Goldstein told me in a written correspondence that "staff told me after what a difference it made to make them get it." A year later, Goldstein and other allies organized another briefing for Senate staff.

Amid growing media and congressional attention to calls for debt cancellation, Democratic politicians embraced even more radical proposals for free college and debt cancellation during the 2016 and 2020 presidential elections. In February 2015, Senator Warren was joined by future Senate Majority Leader Charles Schumer and Senator Brian Schatz in introducing a bill to make college debt-free. The legislation promised to ensure students leave school "having no debt upon graduation from all public institutions."[52] A month later, Senator Bernie Sanders introduced his own proposal to make public higher education "tuition-free." Sanders proposed to pay for his program through a "Wall Street speculation" fee of up to 0.5 percent on financial transactions.[53] As the 2016 Democratic nominee for president, Hillary Clinton adopted a platform with components of both the Warren and Sanders plans. The Clinton plan promised to make public universities both tuition- and debt-free for all students from households with less than $125,000 in income.[54]

During the 2020 presidential campaign, Warren and Sanders added mass student loan debt cancellation to the political mainstream. On April 22, 2019, Warren called for cancelling debts of up to $50,000 for forty-two million student loan borrowers.[55] Two months later, Sanders and congressional representatives Ilhan Omar and Pramila Jayapal introduced legislation to cancel all $1.6 trillion in federal student debt. After introducing her own legislation with House Majority Whip James Clyburn, Warren announced on January 14, 2020, that she would use executive authority under the Higher Education Act to "cancel student debt on day one of my presidency."[56]

Neither Sanders nor Warren won the Democratic nomination for president, but Democrat Joe Biden incorporated major elements of their proposals in his own successful campaign for the presidency. In May 2020, Biden endorsed cancelling at least $10,000 in student debt and making public colleges tuition-free for low- and middle-income households.[57] Biden also agreed with Sanders to appoint prominent supporters of free college and debt cancellation to unity task forces charged with fleshing out the details of his policy agenda. These appointees to his economic and education policy task forces included Ohio State University economist Darrick Hamilton, AFT President Randi Weingarten, and former Generation Progress executive director Maggie Thompson.[58] Biden made further appointments of free college and debt cancellation advocates to key Department of Education and White House posts, including former Roosevelt Institute leaders Julie Margetta Morgan and Joelle Gamble.

Political support for debt cancellation expanded further in 2020 as researchers and activists focused new attention on racial inequalities in student debt. After helping to found the HEND coalition, researchers with the Demos think tank partnered in 2015 with academics at Brandeis University's

Institute on Assets and Social Policy to produce some of the first major studies of racial inequality in student debt.[59] In 2016, dozens of leaders and major organizations in the Black Lives Matter movement bolstered the case for student debt cancellation and free college by endorsing both as necessary elements of a comprehensive push to close the racial wealth gap.[60]

A focus on racial inequality in student debt came even more into the mainstream after the National Association for the Advancement of Colored People (NAACP) appointed Tiffany Loftin as its youth and college director in 2018. Loftin had both led resistance to student debt as the chair of the UC Santa Cruz student government in 2011 and had helped to form HEND as the president of the US Student Association in 2013. With leadership from Loftin, the NAACP broadened mainstream support for debt cancellation against the backdrop of the historic 2020 uprisings in response to police brutality. Between November of 2020 and January 2021, the NAACP and 325 other major labor, liberal, and racial justice groups signed on to a letter calling for President-Elect Biden to cancel student debt on day one of his presidency.[61] Goldstein, now with Americans for Financial Reform, was a key organizer of the letter, helping to unite support for a debt cancellation big bang from both racial justice organizers and groups behind the California bargaining approach. Inspired by the letter from civic groups, I joined prominent academics who study education debt, higher education, and racial inequality and organized a letter in support of debt cancellation signed by more than 1,100 scholars.[62]

Amid this civic agitation and economic turmoil from the pandemic, Democrats in the House of Representatives passed legislation in 2020 for the first mass student debt cancellation in US history. The Republican majority in the US Senate shelved the House's relief bill that included mass debt cancellation. After becoming Senate majority leader in 2021, however, Chuck Schumer reiterated his support for cancelling $50,000 in student debt per borrower via executive action or legislation. Ten Republican senators also joined with Democrats to pass a separate bill to restore and strengthen the borrower defense debt cancellation program that DeVos eviscerated. Advocates for veterans who had been targeted by for-profit colleges helped to convince Republican senators to back the bill. Trump vetoed the borrower defense bill, but it will almost certainly be revived and signed by Biden. Congress and the Trump administration also took another step toward debt cancellation in March 2020 by freezing all payments and interest accrual for federal student loans as part of relief programs for COVID-19. As this book went to press, federal student loan interest and payments were set to remain frozen through January 2022. These developments reflected how breakdowns in social order can make possible new coalitions for big bang policy changes.

A Connected Future

While proposals for free college and student debt cancellation have rapidly gained support, much remains uncertain about the futures of US financiers and US higher education. The prior chapters have documented that the potent combinations of deregulation and tax cuts were critical to the resurgence of US financiers in society and higher education since the 1980s. Similarly, major federal regulatory and tax policy shifts would be necessary for any abrupt reversal in the power of financiers.

Sometimes, major social crises such as the COVID-19 pandemic can briefly destabilize and reorder political coalitions in ways that allow for such policy big bangs. But the political coalitions behind the big bangs of the New Deal and the war on poverty also leveraged Democratic Party super majorities in Congress and Democratic control of the presidency. As the United States recovered from COVID-19, Democrats had gained only the barest majority in Congress. Republican leaders meanwhile remain committed to thwarting any major policy achievements that Democrats could use to win more decisive control over Congress and the levers of the federal government.

In this context, the status quo is untenable for the US student loan system. With every generation, more Americans gain a shared identity and experience as student debtors. Student debts now hang over these borrowers for far longer than for previous generations. The average borrower in the 1990s paid off their debt within seven years.[63] Today, even the median white borrower still owes 65 percent of their original debt twelve years later.[64] The median Black borrower still owes 113 percent of their original debt after twelve years, while the median Latinx borrower still owes 83 percent. An increasing share of borrowers enroll in income-based repayment programs that reduce their payment obligation. But even low-income borrowers with zero repayment obligation experience adverse impacts from student loans in their credit scores and their ability to obtain consumer credit.[65]

In short, calls to eliminate educational debt have become politically popular because the burden of student loans has become so widespread. For Democrats' Black and Latinx political base, student debt has become a disaster. But student loans also weigh on large segments of the white working and middle classes to which both major US political parties are more attentive. As a result, polls have found that as many as 67 percent of voters support at least some form of debt cancellation, including strong majorities of Black, white, Democratic, Republican, and independent respondents.[66]

Cancelling student debt is also good policy for those interested in reducing economic and educational inequality. Some critics argue that universal debt cancellation would be wasteful and regressive because it would help even wealthy students with student loans.[67] But these critics have their facts wrong. Debt cancellation would be highly progressive. As my collaborators and I write in our academic letter in support of debt cancellation, the reason is simple: "Poor students borrow and rich students do not."[68] We elaborate in the letter:

> Among the students who began college in 2012, 55 percent of those with incomes below $30,000 in 2017 had debt compared to just 28 percent of those with incomes above $125,000 that year.[69] Similarly, one survey found that 49 percent of retail workers have student debt.[70] We lack comparable data for investment bankers or hedge fund managers. But we do know that high earners in those professions graduate disproportionately from top private universities where an average of just 18 percent of all undergraduates borrow at all. This disparity in student debt is why debt cancellation is supported by SEIU, the nation's largest service workers union, but not the American Bankers Association.

Economists Andre M. Perry and Carl Romer have shown that it is better to evaluate the progressivity of debt cancellation in relationship to household wealth than in terms of household income.[71] They find that 51 percent of all student debt is held by households with zero or negative total net worth. As a result, debt cancellation substantially boosts wealth for the bottom 20 percent of all households for initial household wealth. Debt cancellation boosts wealth even more for the bottom 30 percent of Black households for initial household wealth. But there is no discernible impact on household wealth for the disproportionately white top 50 percent of households. Consequently, student debt cancellation would take an initial step toward closing the racial wealth gap in the US.

Consistent with its progressive benefit structure, broad debt cancellation tends to be more popular with lower-income respondents and respondents who have not attended college.[72] With the expansion of other social benefits and economic equity programs blocked by Democratic Party caution and Republican Party opposition, cancelling the loans of some wealthy borrowers may be a small price to pay for wiping out the debts of tens of millions of less-advantaged borrowers. And compared to student loan and financial aid policy, progressive taxation is a more equitable, popular, and effective way to redistribute some of the private returns that have accrued to the well-off from the public subsidies for their higher educations.[73] In fact, one policy option for debt cancellation would be to pass separate tax reform legislation to "claw-back" income gains for borrowers with high incomes at the time or in the future.

As mainstream pressure to cancel student debt expands, a virtuous cycle of student debt cancellation appears increasingly likely. Biden has hesitated to broadly exercise his executive authority to cancel student debts early in his presidency, but the US Department of Education is moving forward to expand student debt cancellation for teachers, public employees, and for-profit college students who claim they were misled by recruiters. Consistent with the bargaining-with-bankers strategy, advocates will likely target areas of student loan failure, such as the racial student debt gap, to push large-scale, if not wholesale, debt cancellation. The cancellation of these debts will lay the groundwork for further student debt relief. When the next recession arrives, for example, student debt opponents would no doubt ask why any remaining student debt payments cannot be paused again as they were during the COVID-19 pandemic and recession.

Rent seeking by financiers, such as the expansion of predatory for-profit colleges, is also likely to persist until the federal student loan system is radically reformed. The recurrence of scandals from such predatory rent seeking will provide regular opportunities for new political pushes for broader student debt cancellation. Financiers will probably adapt their strategies for rent seeking each time that regulators expose boondoggles such as predation by investor-owned for-profit colleges. For example, investors have shifted from backing stand-alone for-profit colleges to financing firms that subcontract with public and nonprofit institutions to offer online-only degree programs.[74] As of 2018, such programs enrolled 1.9 million students, equivalent to the entire for-profit college sector at its peak. At Arizona State University Online, the most heralded of these schools, its most recent reported graduation rate was just 4 percent.[75] But 45 percent of Arizona State University Online students borrowed during their first year of enrollment, taking on about $5,000 in debt each year they were enrolled. The regulation of these public-private online programs may be the next theater of bargaining with bankers in US higher education.

The longer that federal student loan programs do survive, the less likely they are to resemble their current form. A decade after the Obama administration ended private banks' involvement in federal student loan financing, it is clear that private banks are out of the federal system for good. If private loan originators ever had a chance to force their way back in, it would have been during the first period of unified Republican control of both houses of Congress and the presidency from 2017 through 2018. That period passed without even an attempt to restore private loan originators' participation in federal student loans. With private banks out of the system, federal student loans have lost a critical political backer for keeping student loans nondischargeable and high-cost for students. This political shift has made it easier for advocates to expand income-based repayment programs and other borrower relief policies such as the 2020 universal pause in interest accrual and repayment. This political dynamic will help shift policy further to reduce interest rates closer to zero and make income-based repayment relief and cancellation more automatic—common features of student loans in European social democracies.

We are also likely to see incremental progress toward federal funding of debt-free college. State governments have already taken incremental steps to make community college at least nominally free. President Biden also prioritized free community college in his first-year legislative agenda. A debt-free arms race has meanwhile begun among elite universities, with Harvard having increased financial aid to the point that only 2 percent of its undergrads had any federal loan borrowing at all in 2019. Advocates can point to the recurrence of rent seeking in forms like public-private online degree programs in pushing to expand debt-free public programs as an alternative.

The virtuous cycle of debt cancellation is also likely to bolster the case for federally funding debt-free higher education. If the federal government is going to lose money by reducing student loan interest rates and routinely cancelling debts, why not just pay for students to attend college debt-free in the first place? A bipartisan majority in Congress moved in this direction by increasing Pell Grant awards and expanding eligibility to previously incarcerated students at the end of 2020. Biden and Democratic leaders in Congress subsequently said they intend to double the value of Pell Grants, a move that would make college debt-free for millions.

While incremental movement toward debt cancellation and debt-free college seems likely, it is difficult to imagine a more equitable higher education financial system if financiers' power and wealth go unchecked in America at large. Even if the federal government establishes debt-free higher education for all, financiers and the very wealthy will still seek to set themselves and their children apart via elite private universities. Taxes on university endowments might check the extent to which wealthy private universities can hoard investment returns mostly for the benefit of elites. Varied proposals for taxing endowments have gained support among lawmakers, including Republicans who included an endowment tax in their 2017 tax bill. But revenue from the endowment tax was primarily used to offset other tax cuts for wealthy investors by the tax bill. Meanwhile, the Ivy League remains flush with cash, and their students are still overwhelmingly well-off.

Lawmakers could use confiscatory levels of endowment taxes to redistribute endowments from schools that continue to hoard returns. Such taxes could offer exemptions to those wealthy schools that use their endowments to dramatically increase their overall enrollments and their admissions of less-advantaged students. But if financiers retain their current concentration of wealth, they are likely to find new and creative ways to pool resources with other elites for reproducing themselves and their social status at exclusive universities. Untaxed private wealth effectively lets the very rich secede from tax-financed systems of social provision such as public higher education.

The success of bargaining with bankers or big bang alternatives, then, may depend on the extent to which university social ties are leveraged beyond elite circles to reorganize the entire US financial system—not just higher education finance. The case of California illustrates the potential of university social ties for forging a consensus around broader transformations, with the vast majority of Proposition 30 millionaire tax revenue going to school and health programs outside of higher education. Many of the most ambitious proposals for reducing inequality via tax reform were likewise developed by academic economists and law professors in conversation with civic and political leaders. Senator Warren herself was a bankruptcy law professor before she became a political crusader for consumer finance protection, reregulating private equity, and taxing Wall Street. Her efforts are buttressed by an academic law network. To push executive actions or congressional legislation for higher tax rates and stronger tax enforcement, advocates will need to mobilize such networks to publicly and privately pressure both policy makers and financiers themselves.

In other words, higher education finance cannot be made more equitable without a broader move toward equity in US financial regulation and tax policy. At the same time, proponents of greater financial equity cannot succeed without grappling with the cross-pressures of university social ties. In addition to scrambling political coalitions, social crises like the COVID-19 pandemic and the financial crisis of 2008 can remind Americans that individual welfare for many still depends on the welfare of the collective. Universities have the ability to foster a collective (and sociological) imagination that moves beyond these intuitions with new ideas for placing financiers in service of the common good. But we have seen that universities also can be insular ivory towers, connecting financiers and other elites by defining who is in and who is out. With this duality, one thing is certain in these uncertain times: the future of US higher education and the future of the nation's larger financial system will be socially connected.

METHODOLOGICAL APPENDIX

A Comparative, Qualitative, and Quantitative Study of Elites

Social scientists categorize many of the analytic methods in this book as quantitative or statistical methodologies. Indeed, I use computer programs to count the characteristics and social ties of many people and organizations. I include linear regression statistics about the relationships between these people and organizations in four of the book's seven chapters.

But statistics alone cannot explain a social transformation as large and complex as the rise of financiers in US higher education and society. Big data is not a stand-alone solution for understanding big change. In fact, social scientists always employ methods of observation and analysis that are nonquantitative, even when estimating statistics. This is because the social world is organized around meaning. Meaning—in social ties, identities, and inequalities—is complex but intelligible in ways that are uncountable. Statistical analyses go awry when the quantitative researcher is insufficiently explicit with themselves or their audience about the qualitative observation and thinking that led them to count something.

I try to do one thing in common in both my qualitative and quantitative observation and thinking: use explicit comparisons. I arrived at this approach to linking the qualitative and quantitative in my own work by studying comparative and historical methodologies. But a variety of social science traditions offer the same key insights that people, including researchers, understand the meaning of a thing via comparison both to what it resembles and what it does not. The most essential comparison to explain the rise of financiers is to compare their qualities and their social position over time. As a result, every chapter chronicles differing extents of change and stasis in the roles and impacts of financiers, their ideas, and their social relationships.

At one level, the book approaches the US higher education and financial sectors as a single case. This lens views elite private schools, federal student loan policy, hedge fund managers, for-profit colleges, public universities, and students of different social stations as all part of the same stratified system. Changes in one corner of the system, such as federal student loan policy, are then expected to reverberate across other parts of the system, like for-profit colleges, public universities, and low-income college students. With only a single case, I am limited in what I can say about how financier social ties may have transformed higher education outside the United States or prior to the 1970s.

At another level, I treat the different strata and social groupings within the system as cases within the case to be compared. For example, we can only fully understand the impact of student loan expansion at public universities facing funding cuts by comparing student loan borrowing by public university students to loan borrowing by students at highly endowed private universities and investor-owned for-profit colleges. These analyses of cases within the case resemble what sociologist Theda Skocpol has called a comparatively informed case study.[1]

I decided what qualitative and quantitative data to gather for this study via Du Boisian triangulation and what Skocpol and sociologist Sarah Quinn have called the targeted primary approach.[2] These approaches use theories and evidence from existing journalistic and scholarly studies and supplements them with new data gathering to fill in gaps. The targeted primary approach is promising for studying elites because they are few in number and unusually motivated to protect their privacy from social scientific study.

In research for this book, I particularly draw on qualitative ethnographic and interview evidence from studies by Tressie McMillan Cottom, Megan Neely, Lauren Rivera, Hannah Appel, Caitlin Zaloom, Karen Ho, Amy Binder, Andrea Abel, Daniel Davis, Nick Bloom, Laura Hamilton, and Kelly Nielsen.[3] I draw similar evidence from financier interviews in major newspapers and in books by journalists like Michael Lewis, Sebastian Mallaby, and Steven Waldman.[4] Their combined observations of hundreds of elite university students, financial-sector elites, and investor-owned for-profit colleges provide indispensable data for the book. These data helped me begin to see how financiers used higher education social ties to amass their fortunes, and to identify where I needed more data.

Between 2016 and 2020, I assembled three broad categories of data to complement the secondary data discussed above. I elaborate on each category of data below. First, I conducted twenty-one in-depth interviews with people in key parts of finance and the higher education system at transformative moments in time. One purpose of these interviews was to consult "people who were there" to make sure that I was not missing something in my reading of secondary sources regarding how financiers, university leaders, or students understood the meanings of their actions. Second, I gathered historical documents ranging from influential endowment investing studies and congressional hearing minutes to campaign plans and statements by student, labor, and community leaders. I selected which documents to review based on the secondary record regarding turning points in the expansion of student loans, endowments, and for-profit colleges. Finally, I linked original data and ten quantitative data sets covering the four hundred richest Americans; 5,162 university board members; and 14,759 federal aid–eligible public, private, and for-profit universities. The data go as far back as 1973.

In the book, I have tried to primarily use data visualizations and regression analyses that are relatively simple and transparent. I do so to make the argument and narrative easier to digest. I have tried to redress any oversimplifications by referring readers to related academic papers that conduct more robust statistical tests. The code and results for some of these tests is published in a Git repository for the book at https://github.com/HigherEdData/bankersintheivorytower. One of the most common statistical modeling techniques I employ as more robust tests are longitudinal fixed effects models.[5] These models exploit the structure of much of my data by testing for within-school change over time in relationship to shifts in ownership, state funding, bond borrowing, and governing board composition involving financiers.

I note sources of data as they are presented throughout the book. I provide an overview of all the data here to help others who I hope will fill the gaps that I myself have left.

In-Depth Interviews

I conducted twenty-one in-depth interviews via phone, written correspondence, and in person between March 2017 and March 2021. I selected interviewees who participated in key transformations of federal student loans and of schools within each of the three major higher education strata. The interviewees include a private equity adviser, an endowment adviser, a university financial manager, a university chancellor, a university system board chair and former state assembly speaker, a liberal arts college president, lobbyists, high-level for-profit college managers, for-profit college students, two US Department of Education officials, legislative staffers, and policy advocates. Ten of the interviewees agreed to be identified by name. Eleven interviewees spoke on the condition of anonymity, including all those involved in private university and for-profit college finance and management.

I conducted a first wave of interviews in March 2017 as I formulated initial theses for the book. This also helped me identify where I needed to gather historical documents and quantitative data to validate the recollections and representations by interviewees—and to fill gaps left after the interviews. I then did the inverse and conducted another wave of interviews in 2018, 2019, and 2021 to validate and flesh out discoveries from my analyses of historical documents and quantitative data. The particular roles and affiliations of the interviewees follow.

Interviews that were particularly relevant for chapter 2 on financier ties to private schools and chapter 4 on endowments include one high-level endowment adviser for a major asset management corporation, one former president of a highly selective and prestigious liberal arts college, one top financial manager at one of the oldest and most prestigious universities in the United Kingdom, and former UC Berkeley chancellor Robert Birgeneau.

I conducted particularly relevant interviews for chapter 3's analysis of financiers' political role in student loan expansion with the following participants in the early 1990s federal reform process: Charlie Kolb, US Department of Education undersecretary and deputy assistant to the president for domestic policy for George H. W. Bush; an anonymous lobbyist for Sallie Mae; an anonymous lobbyist for other consumer lenders; Jane Wellman, executive director for National Association of Independent Colleges and Universities (NAICU); an anonymous former NAICU lobbyist; and Becky Timmons, lobbyist for the American Council on Education, the umbrella organization for college and university industry associations.

The particularly relevant interviewees for chapter 5 on the Wall Street takeover of for-profit colleges (and for the chapter 7 discussion of debt cancellation activism) are an anonymous former vice president with Corinthian Colleges; an anonymous adviser to private equity funds with postsecondary education investments; a former employee of the Association of Private Sector Colleges and Universities; a former high-level manager with Florida Career Colleges; Alyssa Brock, former New England Institute of Art (NEIA) student and We Are AI activist; Don Quijada, former NEIA student and We Are AI activist; and Kim Tran, former NEIA student and We Are AI activist.

Particularly relevant interviews for chapter 6 and chapter 7 analyses of the financial squeeze on the University of California are Chancellor Birgeneau (see above), former California State Assembly Speaker and current UC Board of Regents Chair John A. Pérez, and Max Espinoza, former UCLA student leader and senior adviser to California State Assembly speakers. Former Deutsche Bank and Merrill Lynch vice president turned Occupy Wall Street veteran Alexis Goldstein was a key interviewee regarding the push for debt cancellation in chapter 7.

Historical Primary Documents

Prior scholarship and my first wave of in-depth interviews steered me to various historical primary documents detailing the relationships between financiers and universities. While financiers carefully guard their private lives and their business secrets, they are not shy about their university affiliations. This extends the long tradition of universities as publishers of social rank. Throughout the book, financiers' curated media profiles and biographical statements from company websites provide qualitative details of how financiers reference university ties in their presentation of self. The most extreme instance of this is the transcripts of private equity financier Dick Blum's dozens of hours of interviews for a University of California oral history project (Blum served as a UC regent from 2002 through the publication of this book). Such primary documents were especially helpful in chapters 2, 4, and 6. I often recovered financiers' company biographies and other media profiles using the internet Web Archive.

For chapter 3, I reviewed minutes from congressional hearings surrounding the renewals of the US Higher Education Act in 1979 and in 1992.[6] These minutes provided essential contemporaneous documentation of shifts in how financiers and university leaders thought and spoke about student loans versus grant-based federal financing of US higher education. Scholarship by Elizabeth Popp Berman and Abby Stivers also helped me identify contemporaneous newspaper articles with relevant statements by financiers, university leaders, and their lobbyists.[7]

For chapter 4, the 1969 "Law and the Lore of Endowment Funds" report helped me define the dominant cultural beliefs among financiers and university leaders regarding endowments before they became hedge funds.[8] Newspaper reportage on endowment investment also provided informative first-person accounts of the relationship between endowments and social ties involving private equity managers, hedge fund managers, and university leaders. The *New York Times* and *Detroit Free Press* published investigative reports with particularly candid self-representations.[9]

For chapter 6, in addition to transcripts of the Blum interview, I reviewed University of California Board of Regents meeting minutes from 2003 onward around key decisions regarding tuition and bond borrowing. I also draw from minutes in 2007 and the Affordability Working Group commissioned by the regents. Together, these documents helped me to compare the social orientations and applications of financial logics of financiers at public universities to their counterparts at private universities.

For chapter 7, my own participation in bargaining with bankers over the millionaire tax from 2011 to 2013 in California made me aware of an array of relevant public and private documents. These documents included meeting agendas; campaign plans; and open letters crafted by community, labor, and student leaders to "make banks pay." I provide links to these documents when they were public and web archived. I also engaged in ongoing informal conversations with national student loan advocates from 2013 through 2021. This directed me to public documents that chronicle the development of multiple plans for debt-free higher education and debt cancellation by consumer advocates, liberal think tanks, student organizations, veteran groups, and labor unions.

Quantitative Data on Elites and Universities

I have built quantitative data sets that advance the study of higher education and elites in two important ways. First, I use an open-source "data carpentry" approach to social and financial data on universities and elites from ten different data sets and supplement them with original data gathering. This is an initial step toward solving a problem of higher education data fragmentation that Kenneth Green refers to as "data babel." Second, I provide a model for how to gather large-scale social data on elites. This builds on recent innovations in using web scraping and campaign finance data to observe elite political action.

The problem of higher education data babel is really two problems. To begin with, social scientists for decades neglected to collect good measures of the university-level policy choices or resource allocations that might influence educational inequality. Instead, they focused on gathering individual-level data on college students' social and economic backgrounds and characteristics. These data sets, such as the National Longitudinal Survey of Youth and the Beginning Postsecondary Students survey helped scholars learn about the role of social background in college success. But the surveys did not gather sufficient information about universities as organizations to identify which policy or resource shifts could shift the needle toward greater educational equity. The part of the babel problem here is that these data cannot speak to policy interventions.

There is a solution to the lack of social scientific data on universities as organizations: obtain measures of university policies and finances from administrative and private-sector data sources. But this solution has to overcome a second data babel problem: these data sets are highly fragmented in their structure across the different organizations that collect them. Henry Brady, Adam Goldstein, Laura Hamilton, Mitchell Stevens, Frederick Wherry, and I have begun to build an online Higher Education DataHub to publish open-source statistical software code at https://github.com/HigherEdData for linking these fragmented data sets. Similar to the Open Tree of Life synthesis of all published phylogenetic data,[10] we aim not only to publish code for analyzing data; we also hope to publish code for processing and linking data from different sources. Our code might contain errors or choices not appropriate for some research questions, but publishing the code will allow future researchers to modify data-processing and linking procedures without reinventing the wheel.

Code for assembling and analyzing data used in this book are published in the book's Git repository together with the additional analyses and robustness checks that exceeded what I could include in the book itself. The replication code in the repository is accompanied by source data when data are not proprietary or privacy restricted. In such cases, I hope my code will still be of use to researchers who can obtain the restricted data through appropriate channels.

Paradoxically, linking university data relevant to social equity has become easier because of the early 1990s federal student loan expansion. The 1993 student loan amendments to the US Higher Education Act required all colleges and universities using the loans to report organizational data to the US Department of Education's Integrated Postsecondary Education Data System (IPEDS).[11] Changes to the act also created the National Student Loan Data System. As a result, all federally qualified public, private, and for-profit postsecondary institutions have had to report data on financial expenditures, counts of instructors, graduation rates, enrollment counts by race and gender, and more since 1994. IPEDS thus provides a time-constant unique identifier and annual data for almost all accredited US postsecondary institutions ever since. The annual IPEDS directory of schools thus provides a nearly comprehensive scaffold for linking data on universities and affiliated elites from an array of other sources. Education scholar Ozan Jaquette provides an indispensable guide to overcoming challenges in processing IPEDS data for such linkages.[12]

Analyses in the book use both school- and person-level data that I have linked to the IPEDS scaffold. I will review them here as they appear chronologically in the book. Chapter 2 uses two person-level data sets linked to IPEDS data. For a parallel study, geographer Albina Gibadullina and I gathered data on the postsecondary education affiliations and firm-level financial- and technology-sector affiliations for the four hundred richest Americans in 1989, 2003, and 2017. We gathered the data from a variety of sources ranging from company websites to news articles and obituaries. We specifically coded whether each Forbes 400 member was affiliated with a hedge fund or private equity fund. We also coded the schools from which Forbes 400 individuals had bachelor's, MBA, and law degrees using the IPEDS unique identifier.

Chapter 2 also uses data on all 5,162 individuals who served between 2003 and 2017 on the governing boards of the top thirty private and top thirty public universities in the 2017 Times Higher Education (THE) rankings. The schools are listed in table A.1. The individual board members for each year were identified using archived university web pages (http://web

TABLE A.1 List of universities in the top thirty Times Higher Education by sector

Private	*Public*
Boston University	Florida State University
Brandeis University	Indiana University
Brown University	Michigan State University
California Institute of Technology	North Carolina State University System
Carnegie Mellon University	Ohio State University System
Case Western Reserve University	Pennsylvania State University System
Columbia University	Purdue University
Cornell University	Rutgers University
Dartmouth College	State University of New York System
Duke University	Texas A&M University System
Emory University	The University of Texas System
Georgetown University	University of Arizona
Harvard University	University of California System
Johns Hopkins University	University of Cincinnati
MIT	University of Colorado System
New York University	University of Delaware
Northeastern University	University of Florida
Northwestern University	University System of Georgia
Princeton University	University of Hawaii
Rice University	University of Illinois System
Stanford University	Board of Regents, State of Iowa
Tufts University	University of Maryland System
University of Chicago	University of Massachusetts System
University of Notre Dame	University of Michigan
University of Pennsylvania	University of Minnesota System
University of Pittsburgh	University of North Carolina System
University of Rochester	University of South Florida
University of Southern California	University of Utah
Vanderbilt University	University of Virginia
Washington University	University of Washington
Yale University	University of Wisconsin System

.archive.org/) and direct inquiries to university archivists and board staff. We again used IPEDS unique identifiers to link each of these individuals to data for the school whose board they served on for every year they served. We further matched the data on all the top thirty board members to our Forbes 400 data by name. Overall, 13 percent of Forbes 400 members served on top thirty private boards during the year they were on the Forbes 400 in our three years of Forbes 400 data. We used the same procedure to code the financial firm affiliations of each board member as described above for Forbes 400 coding.

The schools for which we gathered board data include all thirty private institutions in the top two hundred of the THE World University Rankings and all thirty public university *systems* that included a university in the top 250 of the THE World University Rankings for 2016–2017 (see appendix table A.1 for a full list).[13] Public university boards sometimes govern multiple institutions in the top 250, such as the University of California. We use all schools within the top two hundred and top 250 rankings as natural cutoff points because THE does not assign specific rankings to schools above the ranking of two hundred. Rather, THE groups schools into brackets of fifty for rankings above two hundred, such as 201 to 250 and 251 to 300. We include all public systems with schools in the 201 to 250 bracket in order to have an equal number of boards for public and private institutions in the sample. We use the THE over other rankings so that analysis could easily be extended to institutions from outside of the United States in future studies. One drawback of our sample is that it does not include elite liberal arts colleges. Reassuringly, replications of our analyses using Gary Jenkins's data on the boards of the top twenty-nine liberal arts colleges in 2014 yield equivalent results to those for the THE top thirty private universities (see Git repository).

For chapter 4, I linked endowment and donation data from two sources to IPEDS data and our board data. I use a proprietary data set purchased from the Voluntary Support of Education survey for total endowment assets by school and total donations by school annually from 1973 onward. I also use proprietary data provided to me by the National Association of College and University Business Officers (NACUBO). The NACUBO Endowment Survey data includes data from 2000 through 2013 for endowment annual rates of return and annual rates of endowment allocation to different types of investment assets. The NACUBO investment asset categories include private equity funds, hedge funds, and endowment funds managed internally as private equity and hedge funds. I supplemented the analyses of the linked data with analyses of data I purchased from the Chronicle of Philanthropy on the fifty largest donations by Americans annually from 2000 onward. The Chronicle of Philanthropy codes the industry affiliation of each donor. Future research could link the Chronicle 50 data to our Forbes 400 and university board member data.

For chapter 5, I linked IPEDS data on student outcomes and schools' organizational characteristics to an original data set on for-profit college ownership and two other data sets measuring student outcomes. The data cover the full population of 7,904 for-profit colleges that were eligible to enroll students with Title IV federal financial aid in a degree or certificate program from 1990 through 2015. Nonaccredited entities such as the former Trump University are not included. Data are from IPEDS for total enrollments; enrollment counts by gender, race, and need-based aid eligibility; loan borrowing rates; and graduation rates. Data on loan repayment and wages after school are National Student Loan Data System and IRS data published by College Scorecard. Data on law enforcement actions are original data assembled for my study on private equity in higher education with Sabrina Howell and Constantine Yannelis.[14] I also linked data on borrower defense claims published by the Century Foundation.

Ownership data for chapter 5 was assembled with Howell and Yannelis through manual searches of the ownership history of all for-profit colleges to match each school to its parent company. One way that we identify parent firm ownership is by matching schools to firms based on the employer ID number reported in IPEDS. Two other sources were especially useful: First, schools have been required since 2008 to describe their ownership history in online course catalogues, which we obtained via web archives. Second, we use unpublished documents from the 2012 Senate HELP Committee report of for-profit colleges and 10-K statements for publicly traded firms. We identify private equity buyouts of parent firms by searching the ThomsonOne and Preqin databases.

Finally, chapter 6 uses data from IPEDS on in-state enrollments, student loan borrowing, net tuition revenue, and state appropriations from 2001 through 2016. Chapter 6 also uses descriptive statistics published by the University of California and the California State University systems on their websites for in-state enrollments and student debt over time. Chapter 6 similarly uses descriptive statistics on state tax revenue from the California Legislative Analyst Office and on state GDP from the Bureau of Economic Analysis.[15] Chapter 4 likewise uses descriptive statistics over time on total federal student loan borrowing and total federal student aid grant and work-study spending from College Board Trends in Student Aid. Chapter 4 also uses descriptive statistics from the State Higher Education Officers state appropriation data and federal budget outlay data from 1964 to 1970.

NOTES

Chapter 1

1. For example, see Fabrikant 2018.

2. For example, see Miller 2018.

3. Amounts are in 2016 constant dollars from my calculations using data from the Integrated Postsecondary Education Data System. This trend is also documented in Clotfelter 2017.

4. Chetty et al. 2017; Aisch et al. 2017.

5. Best and Best 2014, 48.

6. Only 40 percent of all college students in the 2007–2008 entering cohort with household income above $100,000 left school with any debt. Students with higher incomes are even less likely to leave school with debt. At the top ten private schools in the US News rankings, only 18 to 19 percent of first-year undergrads have borrowed at all in recent years, according to data from the Integrated Postsecondary Education Data System. The parents of these students may borrow separately to pay for their children's college costs, but data on this borrowing is limited. For more, see Eaton 2018.

7. See https://web.archive.org/web/20210218004453/https://nces.ed.gov/ipeds/datacenter/institutionprofile.aspx?unitId=166027&goToReportId=6.

8. For some important but partial explanations for the rise of student loans, see Berman and Stivers 2016; Best and Best 2014; Looney and Yannelis 2015.

9. For a canonical version of this from economists, see Jensen and Meckling 1976.

10. Data from Forbes 400 and an original database from Eaton and Gibadullina 2020. See chapter 2 and figure 2.1 for more details.

11. Rivera 2016; Binder and Wood 2012; Neely 2018; Ho 2009; Binder, Davis, and Bloom 2016; Stevens 2009.

12. Mizruchi 2013; Berger et al. 1995; Ivashina and Sun 2011; Mallaby 2010; Gao and Huang 2016.

13. Mallaby 2010, 4587; Fabrikant 2007.

14. Epstein 2005.

15. Zelizer 2009; Zelizer 2013, 306; Wherry 2012.

16. Fligstein and Roehrkasse 2016; Fligstein and Goldstein 2010.

17. OECD 2020, https://doi.org/10.1787/889e8641-en.

18. *Indicators of Higher Education Equity in the United States* 2016.

19. See OECD 2018, https://doi.org/10.1787/9789264301085-en.

20. New York Times 2017.

21. Torche 2011.

22. Deming et al. 2016; Deming, Goldin, and Katz 2012; Cottom 2017.

23. Garritzmann 2016; Schulze-Cleven et al. 2017.

24. Close 2016.

25. Looney and Yannelis 2015.

26. Miller 2017.

27. Figure 1.1 includes only data from institutions offering four-year degrees.

28. Jung 2015; Goldstein 2012; Lin and Tomaskovic-Devey 2013; Lin and Neely 2020; Fligstein and Shin 2007.

29. Cottom 2017; Seamster and Charron-Chénier 2017; Goldrick-Rab 2016.

30. OECD 2019, 287.

31. OECD 2019, 315.

32. OECD 2019, 299.

33. A new wave of scholarship has approached US higher education as an organizational ecology. I seek to add clarity on the role of the federal fiscal state in this ecology's emergence. For related recent work, see Stevens and Gebre-Medhin 2016; Eaton and Stevens 2020.

34. Sociologists of education may be surprised to learn that Marshall developed much of his theory of the welfare state through a discussion of educational provision. See Marshall 1950.

35. Katznelson and Weir 1988.

36. Stevens and Kirst 2015; Scott and Kirst 2017.

37. Collins 1979.

38. Contrary to conventional wisdom, total US expenditures on social goods are well above average for industrialized nations at 30 percent of GDP. The high share of GDP going to social goods in the United States is in large part a function of the United States having the highest share of private expenditures on social goods. See Weir, Orloff, and Skocpol 1988; K. J. Morgan and Campbell 2011; Pierson 1993; Hacker 2002; Gottschalk 2000; Fishback 2010; "Social Expenditure Update 2019 Public Social Spending Is High in Many OECD Countries" 2019.

39. Starr 1982.

40. Harvard Crimson 1945; Hutt and Stevens 2017.

41. Hutchins 1945.

42. Mettler 2005.

43. Geiger 2004; Geiger 2002.

44. Brint and Karabel 1989.

45. Loss 2011.

46. US Census Bureau 2017.

47. Davies and Zarifa 2012.

48. At the top 10 percent of private schools for admissions selectivity in 1972, over 65 percent of students' fathers were college graduates, and the average household earnings of students' parents was over $150,000 in 2017 dollars. Even at the top 10 percent of public universities, just 48 percent of students' fathers had college degrees, and average household earnings were just $102,000. At the bottom 50 percent of public universities, just 29 percent of students' fathers had college degrees. Clotfelter 2017.

49. In 1980, the shares of first-year undergraduates who were African American were below the African American share of the college-age population in the Ivy League, top liberal arts colleges, and top public universities by 5 percentage points, 7 percentage points, and 6 percentage points, respectively. For details, see Ashkenas, Park, and Pearce 2017. Enrollment shares for Hispanics were 2 percentage points to 4 percentage points below the Hispanic share of the college-age population. African American and Hispanic enrollment shares only matched or exceeded their share of the college-age population in the bottom 50 percent of public universities and at community colleges. For details, see Clotfelter 2017; National Center for Education Statistics 2016.

50. The earliest year with comprehensive data on such spending is 1990. In that year, private nonprofit schools above the ninety-ninth percentile for admissions selectivity spent $40,000 per

student on educational support, while private schools below the twenty-fifth percentile for selectivity spent just $15,000. Even at the most selective public universities, spending per student was just $22,000. In the bottom 50 percent of public universities, spending per student was just $11,000. These spending inequalities were paralleled by inequalities in student-faculty ratios and faculty compensation. See Clotfelter 2017.

51. Fligstein and Shin 2007; Goldstein 2012; Fligstein 1993.

52. The federal tax revenue lost to exemptions related to endowments totaled $19.5 billion in 2010, almost half the total federal expenditure on Pell Grants. See Eaton 2017a. Predatory for-profit colleges meanwhile not only saddled students with debt under expanded loan programs but also sucked up a growing share of federal grant aid dollars that could have otherwise helped students attend more effective public or nonprofit schools. For-profit college enrollment as a share of all postsecondary enrollment grew from just 5 percent in the 1990s to a peak of 11 percent in 2011, but the share of Pell Grant funds going to for-profits increased from 13 percent to 25 percent in the same period. See Mettler 2014.

53. See Eaton et al. 2016. Between 2003 and 2003, overall, interest for state and nonprofit colleges' institutional borrowing nearly doubled from $6 billion to $11 billion.

54. Ginder, Kelly, and Mann 2019.

55. Chetty et al. 2017.

56. These analyses of cases within the case resembles what sociologist Theda Skocpol has called a comparatively informed case study. See Skocpol 1995.

57. Du Bois 1899, 1903, 1935; Morris 2017.

58. Quinn 2019.

59. Page, Seawright, and Lacombe 2018.

60. Cottom 2017; Neely 2018; Appel 2014; Zallom 2019; Ho 2009; Binder, Davis, and Bloom 2016; Binder and Abel 2019; Hamilton and Nielsen 2021; Rivera 2016.

61. Lewis 2010; Lewis 2011; Mallaby 2010; Waldman 1996.

62. https://github.com/HigherEdData/bankersintheivorytower.

63. Eaton and Gibadullina 2020.

Chapter 2

1. Mark Mizruchi and a number of other scholars have validated Brandeis's assessment of early twentieth-century finance led by J. P. Morgan, George F. Baker, James Stillman, and Jacob Schiff. See Mizruchi and Bunting 1981; Corey 1930; Cochran and Miller 1942.

2. Mizruchi 2013; Davis and Mizruchi 1999.

3. Karabel 2005.

4. Mills 2000, 106–7.

5. Allen 1935.

6. Binder, Davis, and Bloom 2016; Neely 2018; Ho 2009; Rivera 2016.

7. Lin and Tomaskovic-Devey 2013; Tomaskovic-Devey and Lin 2011; Piketty 2014.

8. Davis and Binder 2016.

9. Evans 1995; Polanyi 2001; Granovetter 1985.

10. Swidler 1986; Granovetter 1973.

11. Mills wrote, "The elite are simply those who have the most of what there is to have, which is generally held to include money, power, and prestige—as well as all the ways of life to which these lead." Mills 2000, 9.

12. Mills 2000, 114–15.

13. Mills 2000, 112; https://www.cambridge.org/core/services/aop-cambridge-core/

content/view/28176F04814FBFCB807A83FF419696F7/S000768050002290Xa.pdf/charles-copeland-1867-1944.pdf.

14. Mills 2000, 106–7.
15. Allen 1935.
16. Krippner 2005, 179–80.
17. Tomaskovic-Devey and Lin 2011.
18. Lin and Tomaskovic-Devey 2013.
19. Lin and Tomaskovic-Devey 2013; Gordon and Dew-Becker 2008, 203; Hacker and Pierson 2010.
20. Mizruchi 2013; Stearns 1986.
21. Lin and Tomaskovic-Devey 2013.
22. Davis 2008.
23. Mizruchi 2013; Pardo-Guerra 2019.
24. Gordon and Dew-Becker 2008.
25. Hacker and Pierson 2011, 2041.
26. Ganz 2000.
27. Hacker and Pierson 2011, 2196.
28. Piketty 2014.
29. Krippner 2011.
30. Hacker and Pierson 2010; Fligstein and Goldstein 2012; Lin and Tomaskovic-Devey 2013.
31. See Kaplan and Rauh 2009. Growing inequality in pretax and posttax income, moreover, has almost entirely been driven by increasing shares of income going to the richest 1 percent of Americans per table 10 from Congressional Budget Office 2015. See also Alvaredo et al. 2013.
32. Lin and Tomaskovic-Devey 2013.
33. Quinn 2017; Quinn 2012.
34. Eaton et al. 2016.
35. US Department of Education 2009.
36. US Department of Education 2017.
37. Weitzman 2019.
38. Investment Company Institute 2018.
39. Steinbaum, Bernstein, and Sturm 2018.
40. Steinbaum, Bernstein, and Sturm 2018.
41. Son and Roux 2015; Kaplan and Rauh 2009.
42. Kaplan and Rauh 2009.
43. Jensen and Meckling 1976.
44. Appelbaum and Batt 2014.
45. Appelbaum and Batt 2014.
46. Gompers and Lerner 2001.
47. Mallaby 2010.
48. Konczal 2009.
49. Appelbaum and Batt 2014.
50. Black 2017; Steinbaum, Bernstein, and Sturm 2018; Selby-Green 2018.
51. Kaplan and Rauh 2009.
52. Korom, Lutter, and Beckert 2017.
53. Eaton and Gibadullina 2020.
54. Eaton and Gibadullina 2020.
55. Uzzi 1999.
56. DiMaggio and Garip 2012.

57. Mills 2000, 68.

58. Ashkenas, Park, and Pearce 2017. For further details, see Clotfelter 2017.

59. Chetty et al. 2017.

60. Karabel 2005.

61. https://www.history.com/news/harvard-yale-admissions-social-rank.

62. Binder, Davis, and Bloom 2016; Binder and Abel 2019.

63. Mills 2000, 49.

64. Gompers and Lerner 2001; Mallaby 2010; Appelbaum and Batt 2014.

65. Appelbaum and Batt 2014, 61.

66. Gao and Huang 2016.

67. Lewis 2011, 105.

68. Lerner, Schoar, and Wang 2008; Mallaby 2010, 176.

69. Neely 2018.

70. Lewis 2011; Rivera 2016.

71. Mallaby 2010, 4556; Fabrikant 2016.

72. Lerner, Schoar, and Wang 2008, 221; Mallaby 2010, 190.

73. Mallaby 2010, 4587.

74. The thirty schools are the top thirty US private universities in the 2016 rankings by Times Higher Education. For the full list, see appendix table A.1.

75. Goldin and Katz 2009; Lerner, Schoar, and Wang 2008.

76. Eaton and Gibadullina 2020.

77. Stevens, Armstrong, and Arum 2008; Stevens and Gebre-Medhin 2016; Eaton and Stevens 2020.

78. For example, see organizational accounts of the role of universities in solving New Deal, World War II, and postwar administrative and social problems in Loss 2011; Hutt and Stevens 2017.

79. Pusser, Slaughter, and Thomas 2006; Jenkins 2015; Toutsi 2010; Kerr and Gade 1989; Madsen 1997.

80. Jenkins 2015.

81. Eaton and Gibadullina 2020.

82. Eaton and Gibadullina 2020.

83. Eaton and Gibadullina 2020.

84. Ostrower 1995; Barman 2017.

85. Rivera 2016; Binder, Davis, and Bloom 2016.

86. Lewis 2010.

87. Rivera 2016.

Chapter 3

1. This is the combined outstanding loan amounts for Direct Loans and Perkins Loans, which are both directly owned by the Department of Education in its loan portfolio. See https://studentaid.gov/sites/default/files/fsawg/datacenter/library/PortfolioSummary.xls.

2. See https://www.forbes.com/sites/greatspeculations/2018/06/27/a-breakdown-of-the-loan-portfolios-of-the-largest-u-s-banks-2.

3. Cellini and Goldin 2014.

4. Quinn 2017; Krippner 2011.

5. Fligstein and McAdam 2012; Ganz 2000; Jacobs and Dirlam 2016; Wilson and Aponte 2009.

6. Quinn 2019; Krippner 2011.

7. Hacker and Pierson 2010; Walker and Rea 2014; Martin 2008.

8. For source data, see Table 2 in College Board 2020.

9. Hout 2012; Torche 2011; Neckerman and Torche 2007.

10. Eaton et al. 2019; Webber 2017; Weerts, Sanfordeah, and Reinert 2012; Quinterno 2012; Goldrick-Rab 2016; Goldrick-Rab et al. 2009.

11. "Reauthorization of the Higher Education Act of 1965" 1991.

12. Fligstein and Goldstein 2012; Fligstein 2001; Fligstein 1993; Quinn 2019; Quinn 2017.

13. Zelizer 2009; Zelizer 2013.

14. Shireman 2017.

15. Best and Best 2014.

16. State spending is from Grapevine historical data and national tables at https://education.illinoisstate.edu/grapevine/tables/. Spending on the precursors to federal Pell Grants and work study from 1964 to 1970 is estimated using "Table 3.2: Outlays by Function and Subfunction" from the Office of Management and Budget here: https://obamawhitehouse.archives.gov/omb/budget/Historicals. Data on Pell Grant and work-study spending since 1991 is from table 2 in *Trends in Student Aid* from College Board 2020.

17. "Reauthorization of the Higher Education Act of 1965" 1991.

18. "Higher Education Amendments of 1979" 1979.

19. "Higher Education Amendments of 1979" 1979.

20. Hacker and Pierson 2011.

21. Morgan and Campbell 2011.

22. "Reauthorization of the Higher Education Act of 1965" 1991.

23. "Reauthorization of the Higher Education Act of 1965" 1991.

24. Martin 2008.

25. Mizruchi 2013.

26. Mizruchi 2013.

27. Hacker and Pierson 2011; Mizruchi 2013.

28. Fourcade 2009.

29. Page, Bartels, and Seawright 2013.

30. Johnson and Kwak 2011.

31. Robert Weissman et al. 2009.

32. Cioffi 2006; Hacker and Pierson 2011.

33. Tomaskovic-Devey and Lin 2011; Krippner 2011.

34. Lin and Tomaskovic-Devey 2013; Fligstein and Shin 2007; Goldstein 2012; Gordon 1996; Kalleberg 2011.

35. Jensen 1989.

36. Tilly 1991.

37. Cottom 2017.

38. "Reauthorization of the Higher Education Act of 1965" 1991.

39. "Reauthorization of the Higher Education Act of 1965" 1991.

40. "Reauthorization of the Higher Education Act of 1965" 1991.

41. March 15, 2017, interview.

42. "Reauthorization of the Higher Education Act of 1965" 1991.

43. Quinn 2017, 2019.

44. Berman and Stivers 2016; Shireman 2017.

45. Berman and Stivers 2016.

46. R. Wilson 1987; Berman and Stivers 2016.

47. "Reauthorization of the Higher Education Act of 1965" 1991.

48. Kantrowitz 2019

49. "Reauthorization of the Higher Education Act of 1965" 1991.

50. Berman and Stivers 2016.

51. Shireman 2017.

52. March 9, 2017, interview.

53. "Reauthorization of the Higher Education Act of 1965" 1991.

54. "Reauthorization of the Higher Education Act of 1965" 1991.

55. "Reauthorization of the Higher Education Act of 1965" 1991.

56. "Reauthorization of the Higher Education Act of 1965" 1991.

57. Berman 2011.

58. Shireman 2017.

59. "Hearing on S.1845 of the Committee on Labor and Human Resources, United States Senate, One Hundred Second Congress, First Session," October 29, 1991, https://files.eric.ed.gov/fulltext/ED341354.pdf.

60. Waldman 1996.

61. Miller and Burd 2007. The plan is available at https://s3.amazonaws.com/new-america-composer/attachments_archive/SLM_Strategy_Document.pdf.

62. Rivera 2016.

63. Waldman 1996; https://www.chronicle.com/article/William-Blakey-Lawyer-Who/125364.

64. Volden, Wai, and Wiseman 2020.

65. Krippner 2011.

66. Quinn 2017.

67. Tomaskovic-Devey and Lin 2011.

68. My calculations using IPEDS data.

69. Eaton 2017b; Eaton, Howell, and Yannelis 2020.

70. Eaton et al. 2019.

71. National Center for Education Statistics 2017. https://nces.ed.gov/programs/digest/d17/tables/dt17_104.20.asp.

72. Eaton 2017b.

73. Addo, Houle, and Simon 2016; California State Student Association and The Institute for College Access & Success 2017; Houle 2013; Eaton 2018.

74. Quinterno 2012; Weerts, Sanfordeah, and Reinert 2012.

75. Eaton et al. 2019; Webber 2017.

76. My calculations using IPEDS data.

77. Bound and Turner 2007.

78. Akers and Chingos 2016; Avery and Turner 2012.

79. Dwyer, McCloud, and Hodson 2012; Dwyer, Hodson, and McCloud 2013.

80. Close 2016.

81. Looney and Yannelis 2015.

82. Eaton 2018.

83. Fligstein 2001.

84. Lin and Neely 2020; Tomaskovic-Devey and Lin 2011; Lin and Tomaskovic-Devey 2013.

85. Goldstein and Fligstein 2014; Fligstein and Goldstein 2010; Fligstein and Roehrkasse 2016.

86. Fligstein and Habinek 2014.

87. A former US Department of Education official told me this in an anonymous interview on October 11, 2016.

88. Shireman 2017.

89. Fox 2010.

90. Shireman 2017.

91. See figure 12A College Board 2020.

92. Office of Inspector General 2018.

Chapter 4

1. Lewin 2015.

2. "Harvard Business School Announces Fundraising Campaign" 2014; Harvard Business School September 2016 Campaign Update, https://www.alumni.hbs.edu/Documents/giving/HBS_Campaign_Update_Sep2016.pdf.

3. "Harvard Business School to Create New Convening Center" 2014.

4. Harvard Magazine 2012.

5. "Hedge Papers No. 54: Hurricane Harvard and the Damage Done to Puerto Rico" 2018.

6. "Seth Klarman, MBA 1982." 2011. *Harvard Business School Alumni Stories*, January 1, 2011, https://www.alumni.hbs.edu/stories/Pages/story-bulletin.aspx?num=1978.

7. Schools' percentiles for endowment wealth are assigned based on the percentile they fell in during the first year for which they reported endowment data to the Voluntary Support of Education survey from 1973 onward for private institutions and for 1986 onward for public institutions. Data for earlier years from each sector is not included because it is incomplete, leading to an unbalanced panel and shifts in the composition of percentiles over time. Over this period, the number of schools in the panel ranges from 846 in 1976 to 1,143 in 2011. Data on endowment asset wealth from the National Association of College and University Business Offers Endowment Survey is used for years in which Voluntary Support of Education data is missing.

8. Clotfelter 2017.

9. Most of these other elite, well-endowed schools, including Rockefeller University, Mayo Medical School, and Rensselaer Polytechnic Institute, were not included in Gary Jenkins's data gathering on board membership because they do not enroll undergraduates.

10. "In Elite Schools' Vast Endowments, Malcolm Gladwell Sees 'Obscene' Inequity" 2015.

11. Eaton 2017a.

12. Unz 2012.

13. Eaton 2017a.

14. Chetty et al. 2017.

15. See chapter 2 for further details on differences and similarities among private equity funds, hedge funds, and venture capital funds.

16. Cary and Bright 1969.

17. Tobin 1974.

18. Lerner, Schoar, and Wang 2008.

19. MacKenzie and Millo 2003.

20. Goodkin 2012.

21. Jensen and Meckling 1976; Fligstein 1993.

22. Davis and Stout 1992; Appelbaum and Batt 2014.

23. Mizruchi 2013; Pardo-Guerra 2019; Gordon and Dew-Becker 2008; Hacker and Pierson 2011, 750.

24. Tomaskovic-Devey and Lin 2011; Krippner 2011.

25. Hacker and Pierson 2010; Appelbaum and Batt 2014.

26. Will 2017; IRS Definition of Private Operating Foundation, https://www.irs.gov/charities-non-profits/private-foundations/definition-of-private-operating-foundation; IRS Tax

on Net Investment Income of Private Foundations: Reduction in Tax, https://www.irs.gov/charities-non-profits/private-foundations/tax-on-net-investment-income.

27. Lerner, Schoar, and Wang 2008.

28. Appelbaum and Batt 2014.

29. Lerner, Schoar, and Wang 2008.

30. Fabrikant 2016.

31. Lerner, Schoar, and Wang 2008.

32. Jenkins 2015.

33. For an excellent ethnography regarding the importance of wealthy patrons to hedge funds, see Neely 2018.

34. See Poorvu's faculty website: https://www.hbs.edu/faculty/Pages/profile.aspx?facId=6531.

35. "Jordan Baruch" 2012.

36. "In Elite Schools' Vast Endowments, Malcolm Gladwell Sees 'Obscene' Inequity" 2015.

37. Mallaby 2010; Fabrikant 2007.

38. Appelbaum and Batt 2014.

39. Ritter 2014.

40. As was mentioned, private equity has famously used junk bonds as a high-risk source of leverage for buyouts. Hedge funds tend to use credit lines, buying on margin, and derivatives as vehicles for leverage in their investments in more liquid assets such as publicly traded stocks, derivatives, and currencies. Fung and Hsieh 2016.

41. Neely 2018.

42. Neely 2018.

43. Smith 2013.

44. Smith 2013.

45. Smith 2013.

46. Dolan and Jesse 2018.

47. Kumar 2016.

48. Gompers and Lerner 2001; Kaplan and Schoar 2005; Ljungqvist, Persson, and Tag 2016; Lerner, Schoar, and Wang 2008.

49. McClintock 2006; Stiglitz 2000.

50. Piketty 2014, 447–49.

51. Piketty 2014.

52. Lerner, Schoar, and Wang 2008.

53. See methods appendix for data details.

54. Further regression models in the online replication files show that the relationship weakens to a 1.6 percentage point positive association after controlling schools' total endowment assets the prior year. The positive association between returns and board ties also persists after controlling for the share of endowment invested in private equity and hedge funds (with a *p*-value of 0.07). In other words, financiers' board ties were positively associated with higher returns on top of higher returns from investing with private equity and hedge funds in general. But this positive association vanishes after 2008, even in years after 2009 when equity markets posted large gains. Regression models in the appendix also show that the positive association between returns and private equity and hedge fund investments reverses after 2009 for both the top thirty schools and for all 678 schools that reported this data.

55. Further regression models in the appendix show that there is no consistent association between returns and admissions selectivity for either public or private universities. This casts doubt on the conjecture that more elite schools have better returns because they can recruit more talented financial managers. Prior endowment size, financier board ties, and early investments

with private equity and hedge funds appear far more central to elite universities' outsized investment returns.

56. Taylor 2016.

57. "Hedge Papers No. 25—Endangered Endowments: How Hedge Funds Are Bankrupting Higher Education."

58. New York Times 2016.

59. See Lerner, Schoar, and Wang 2008.

60. Douglas and Bleemer 2018.

61. Eaton 2017c.

62. Eaton 2017c.

63. This has been shown previously in Clotfelter 2017.

64. My calculations using Voluntary Support of Education data.

65. For an overview of each of these factors in gift giving, see Barman 2017. Regarding reciprocity, see Polanyi 2001. Regarding status and exchange, see Blau 2017. Regarding altruism, see Richard 1970.

66. Barman 2017.

67. Ostrower 1995.

68. Khan 2010; 2012; Cousin, Khan, and Mears 2018.

69. Auten, Clotfelter, and Schmalbeck 2000; Keltner 2016.

70. For the long literature on universities in social reproduction, see Karabel 2005; Stevens 2009; Bourdieu and Passeron 1990.

71. Sullivan 2013.

72. Los Angeles Times 1991.

73. Golden 2003.

74. Golden 2007.

75. My calculations using Philanthropy 50 data.

76. After controlling for confounding factors, the positive association accounts for donations being only 2 percent higher. Larger endowments also are associated with higher donations. This may reflect that endowment wealth helps pay for larger fundraising operations. The association of donations with both financier board membership and endowment size is consistent across a variety of regression models included in the online replication files.

77. Eaton 2017a.

78. Eaton et al. 2019.

79. Brady 2015.

80. Chetty et al. 2017.

81. For a detailed discussion, see Clotfelter 2017.

82. Ashkenas, Park, and Pearce 2017.

83. Stewart 2018.

84. Piketty 2014.

85. Stewart 2018.

86. Vandevelde and Fortado 2018.

87. Whyte 2018; Lorin 2016. See Harvey 2005 regarding accumulation by dispossession.

Chapter 5

1. Harvard Business Review 2014.

2. Harvard Business Review 2014.

3. Budros 2002; Fligstein and Shin 2007; Appelbaum and Batt 2014; Lin and Neely 2020; Lin and Tomaskovic-Devey 2013.

4. Zelizer 2009, 2013.

5. Polanyi 2001; Quinn 2019; Krippner 2011; Lin and Neely 2020.

6. Berman and Stivers 2016; US Senate Committee on Health Education Labor and Pensions 2012; Mettler 2014.

7. Collins 1979.

8. Hansmann 1980.

9. Grubb and Lazerson 2009; Du Bois 1903, 1935.

10. Kinser 2006.

11. Horvath and Powell 2016; Ostrower 1995; Barman 2017.

12. Deming, Goldin, and Katz 2012.

13. "New England Institute of Art History" 2012.

14. Berle and Means 1932; Jensen and Meckling 1976.

15. Goldin and Margo 1992.

16. Davis and Stout 1992; Davis and Thompson 1994; Appelbaum and Batt 2014.

17. Shleifer and Summers 1988; Appelbaum and Batt 2014.

18. Useem 1993.

19. Davis 2009; Davis and Thompson 1994.

20. Kahan and Rock 2007; Jiao, Massa, and Zhang 2016; Mallaby 2010.

21. Klein and Zur 2016; Davis and Thompson 1994.

22. Tomaskovic-Devey and Lin 2011.

23. Dealbook 2007.

24. Eaton 2020; Eaton, Howell, and Yannelis 2020; Gupta et al. 2021; Zhu, Hua, and Polsky 2020.

25. Jensen and Ruback 1983; Jensen 1986; Harvey 2005.

26. Neely 2018; Lerner, Sorensen, and Strömberg 2011; Lin and Neely 2020; Mallaby 2010.

27. Rosen 2010.

28. Dealbook 2007.

29. Creswell 2015.

30. Creswell 2015.

31. Kosman 2014.

32. "New England Institute of Art History" 2012.

33. All statistics relating to NEIA are from the College Scorecard Database unless otherwise noted.

34. Kirkham 2011.

35. Regarding fraudulent recruitment, see Halperin 2017; Fisher 2018; Saul 2015.

36. Cao and Habash 2017.

37. Wherry 2012; Zelizer 2009; Zelizer 2013.

38. This saying echoes sociologist Mark Granovetter's famous meditation on the role of social embeddedness in malfeasance. See Granovetter 1985.

39. Anonymous March 27, 2017, interview.

40. Similarly, Career Education Corporation President Gary McCullough built his career in marketing at Procter and Gamble Corp.'s Home Products division before transitioning to Wrigley Corporation, where "he was responsible for the successful re-launches of the Juicy Fruit, Doublemint, Spearmint and Eclipse® brands, and for launching the Orbit® brand of chewing gum in the United States." https://www.higheredjobs.com/HigherEdCareers/authorBio.cfm?authorID=42&articleID=224.

41. Eaton, Howell, and Yannelis 2020.

42. Anonymous March 27, 2017, interview.

43. Anonymous March 27, 2017, interview.

44. Anonymous March 27, 2017, interview.

45. Goldstein and Eaton 2020.

46. Anonymous March 9, 2018, email correspondence.

47. Anonymous March 27, 2017, interview.

48. Burd 2011.

49. Eaton 2020; Eaton, Howell, and Yannelis 2020; Goldstein and Eaton 2020; https://github.com/HigherEdData/bankersintheivorytower.

50. Deming et al. 2016.

51. Cellini, Darolia, and Turner 2020; Liu and Belfield 2020; Cellini and Chaudhary 2014; Armona, Chakrabarti, and Lovenheim 2017; Cellini and Turner 2018; Deming, Goldin, and Katz 2012; Deming et al. 2016.

52. Bound and Turner 2007; Eaton, Howell, and Yannelis 2020.

53. Anonymous March 27, 2017, interview.

54. Cottom 2017, 2897.

55. Crenshaw 1990.

56. Addo, Houle, and Simon 2016.

57. Miller 2017.

58. Miller 2019.

59. Oliver and Shapiro 2006; Shapiro 2004; Thurston 2018.

60. "Hedge Papers No. 54 Hurricane Harvard and the Damage Done to Puerto Rico: How the University's Endowment Investment Harms the Island" 2018; Eaton 2017a; Saul 2017; Urbi 2019.

61. Legum and Mclean 2017; Ripan 2013.

62. Rosen 2010.

63. The 2006 NACUBO Endowment Survey reported the following investments in the private equity funds that bought out EDMC: Providence Equity capital had funds from Michigan State, Purdue, Swarthmore, University of Wisconsin (0, III, V), and Washington University. Goldman Sachs had capital from College of Holy Cross, Elizabethtown vintage III, Illinois Wesleyan, Medical College of Georgia, Miami U of Ohio, Oberlin, Penn State, Santa Clara University, Syracuse University (capital partners 2000), University of New Hampshire, West Virginia University (PEP), and Wittenberg University.

64. "CPUC Resources Committee Annual Report for the Academic Year 2017–2018" 2018.

65. Meyer and Rowan 1977; Dobbin and Zorn 2005; Polanyi 2001.

66. Gupta et al. 2021; Zhu, Hua, and Polsky 2020; Morgenson 2008; Goldstein 2015; Dmitrieva et al. 2019.

67. Mettler 2014.

68. Friedman 2019; Saul 2015; Cowley 2021; Morgenson 2016.

Chapter 6

1. "Major Features of the 2003 California Budget" 2003.

2. Geraci, Lage, and Rubens 2015.

3. Hamilton and Nielsen 2021.

4. Eaton et al. 2019.

5. Chetty et al. 2017.

6. "The TWLF Marching on Sproul Plaza" 1969; "Campus Commemorates 1968 Student-Led Strike" 2008.

7. Cottom 2017.

8. Fleischer 2015.

9. Badertscher, Katz, and Rego 2013; Cheng et al. 2012.

10. Sarin and Summers 2020.

11. Quackenbush 2019.

12. Goldberg and Kersten 2010.

13. Martin 2008.

14. Saul 2017.

15. Eaton 2017a.

16. Bureau of Economic Analyis 2018; California Legislative Analyst's Office 2017.

17. Douglass and Bleemer 2018; Eaton et al. 2013; Parker 2015.

18. Geraci, Lage, and Rubens 2015.

19. Geraci, Lage, and Rubens 2015, 131.

20. Eaton et al. 2013; Geraci, Lage, and Rubens 2015, 136.

21. Geraci, Lage, and Rubens 2015, 143.

22. Geraci, Lage, and Rubens 2015, 121–22.

23. Eaton et al. 2013; Yan 2009.

24. Geraci, Lage, and Rubens 2015, 121–22.

25. Eaton et al. 2013; Moody's Investor Service 2012.

26. Geraci, Lage, and Rubens 2015, 247.

27. Geraci, Lage, and Rubens 2015, 162.

28. Douglas and Bleemer 2018.

29. Bound and Turner 2007.

30. Eaton et al. 2019; "Pell Grant Recipients as a Peer Metric" 2018.

31. Eaton 2018; Eaton et al. 2019.

32. "First Comes Diploma, Then Comes Debt" 2019.

33. Fligstein 2001; McClure, Barringer, and Brown 2019.

34. Interview on March 13, 2020.

35. Hamilton and Nielsen 2021; "Rating Action: Moody's Downgrades University of California to Aa2 and Assigns Aa2 to $950M of GRBs; Outlook Stable" 2014.

36. Hall and Dudley 2019.

37. Shireman 2019.

38. This is the 150 percent normative time graduation rate for the 2013 entering cohort. Borrowing statistics are for the most recent cohort. See https://web.archive.org/web/20201124215517/https://nces.ed.gov/ipeds/datacenter/institutionprofile.aspx?unitId=483124&goToReportId=6.

39. Birgeneau 2015.

Chapter 7

1. Asimov and Berton 2011.

2. Young 2017; Varner and Young 2012.

3. Quinn 2019; Krippner 2011.

4. Weir, Orloff, and Skocpol 1988.

5. Prupis 2014.

6. Cardoso and Faletto 1979.

7. Anderson 2016.

8. Ganz 2000; Clemens 1993.

9. Chetty et al. 2017.

10. Hamilton and Nielsen 2021.

11. Ganz 2000, 1052.

12. Goldberg and Kersten 2010.

13. Unpublished "Setting the Stage for 2012" memo. Jono Shaffer shared the memo with me in 2011.

14. The signers of the letter were Rich Anderson, president, UAW 4123—CSU student employees; Xiaoqing Cao, PhD, president, UAW 5810—UC postdoctoral researcher; Zenei Cortez, RN, co-president, CNA/NNU—Registered Nurses at UC; Cheryl Deutsch, president, UAW 2865—UC student employees; Carl Friedlander, president, Community College Council of the California Federation of Teachers; Pat Gantt, president, CSU Employees Union—SEIU Local 2579; Mike Garcia, president—SEIU United Service Workers West; Rick Jacobs, founder and chair, Courage Campaign; Katherine Lybarger, president, AFSCME 3299—UC service and patient care workers; Jelger Kalmijn, president, UPTE-CWA 9119—UC professional and technical employees; Claudia Magaña, president, UC Student Association; Dean Murakami, vice president of the California Federation of Teachers—Los Rios Community College faculty member; Marcos Perez, California regional organizer—United Students Against Sweatshops; Pablo Rodriguez, executive director—Communities for a New California; Bob Samuels, president, UC-AFT—UC lecturers and librarians; Bob Schoonover, president, SEIU 721—Southern California public and school employees; Amy Schur, executive director—Alliance of Californians for Community Empowerment; Dean Vogel, president—California Teachers Association.

15. See https://web.archive.org/web/20120217134546/http://ag.ca.gov/cms_attachments/initiatives/pdfs/i1035_11-0090.pdf.

16. Varner and Young 2012.

17. See https://cucfa.org/news/2012_apr11.php.

18. Geraci, Lage, and Rubens 2015.

19. I interviewed Pérez by phone on March 11, 2021.

20. https://web.archive.org/web/20160304193049/http://www.dof.ca.gov/documents/FullBudgetSummary_web2013.pdf.

21. UC News Room 2012.

22. https://www.acreinstitute.org/staff.

23. McCartin et al. 2018.

24. "Forum on 'Bargaining for the Common Good: Lessons from L.A. and Beyond'" 2016.

25. "Rutgers' Center for Innovation in Worker Organization at SMLR Hosts 'Bargaining for the Common Good' Convening" 2019.

26. Lerner and Bhatti 2016.

27. Lerner and Bhatti 2016.

28. https://smlr.rutgers.edu/content/bargaining-common-good.

29. Romer 1992.

30. Weir, Orloff, and Skocpol 1988.

31. Skocpol 1995.

32. Amenta 2008; Amenta 2000.

33. Johnson 2011.

34. Strike Debt 2012.

35. For a list of the founders of Strike Debt's successor organization, The Debt Collective, see https://debtcollective.org. For the board of the Collective's Rolling Jubilee nonprofit, see https://rollingjubilee.org/transparency/.

36. Appel 2014.

37. For details, see https://rollingjubilee.org/transparency/#debtbuys.

38. For example, see Kaminer 2012.

39. Vara 2017.

40. The original letter is at https://web.archive.org/web/20150331024305/https://debt collective.org/studentstrike.

41. Heiney 2015.

42. For a full list, see http://stage.debtcollective.org/studentstrike#undefined.

43. You can find the Facebook groups at https://www.facebook.com/groups/everestaven gers/, https://www.facebook.com/groups/aistudents/, and https://www.facebook.com/groups/ITTTechnicalInstituteLawsuitWarriors/.

44. You can see the senators' letter making the proposal at https://www.warren.senate.gov/files/documents/2014%2012%209%20Corinthian%20Letter.pdf.

45. https://www.studentloanborrowerassistance.org/wp-content/uploads/2015/04/corin thian-petition.pdf.

46. https://www.studentloanborrowerassistance.org/wp-content/uploads/2015/04/corin thian-petition.pdf.

47. See https://civichall.org/civicist/what-the-dept-of-education-should-have-done-years -ago/.

48. https://www2.ed.gov/documents/press-releases/borrower-defense-report.pdf.

49. Statistics on borrower defense claims are published at https://studentaid.gov/data -center/student/loan-forgiveness/borrower-defense-data.

50. Statistics on borrower defense claims are published at https://studentaid.gov/data -center/student/loan-forgiveness/borrower-defense-data.

51. http://www.huffingtonpost.com/2015/03/03/maxine-waters-corinthian-15-_n _6796246.html.

52. The Warren Schatz letter is at https://www.schatz.senate.gov/imo/media/doc/DebtFree College.pdf.

53. Sanders 2015.

54. "Making College Debt-Free and Taking on Student Debt" 2016; Saul and Flegenheimer 2016; Rappeport 2016.

55. Herndon 2019.

56. Warren 2020.

57. Biden 2020.

58. Golshan 2020.

59. Huelsman et al. 2015.

60. See https://web.archive.org/web/20161021140249/https://policy.m4bl.org/about/, https://web.archive.org/web/20161020092536/https://policy.m4bl.org/reparations/, and https://www.thenation.com/article/archive/black-lives-matter-group-issues-a-concrete-list-of -demands/.

61. https://ourfinancialsecurity.org/2020/11/sign-on-letter-over-230-orgs-call-on-president -elect-biden-to-cancel-federal-student-debt-on-day-one-using-executive-action/.

62. https://www.dignityanddebt.org/projects/an-open-letter-to-president-biden-scholars -support-your-promise-to-cancel-student-debt/.

63. Eaton et al. 2016.

64. Miller 2017.

65. Wherry, Seefeldt, and Alvarez 2019.

66. https://filesforprogress.org/datasets/2020/12/dfp_vox_student_debt.pdf.

67. Catherine and Yannelis 2020.

68. https://www.dignityanddebt.org/projects/an-open-letter-to-president-biden-scholars -support-your-promise-to-cancel-student-debt/.

69. Data from US Department of Education, National Center for Education Statistics, 2012/17 Beginning Postsecondary Students Longitudinal Study (BPS:12/17).

70. www.commonbond.co/post/retail-employees-need-student-loan-benefits-but-companies-have-been-slow-to-act.

71. Perry and Romer 2021.

72. https://filesforprogress.org/datasets/2020/12/dfp_vox_student_debt.pdf.

73. Piketty 2014.

74. Hall and Dudley 2019.

75. https://web.archive.org/web/20201124215517/https://nces.ed.gov/ipeds/datacenter/institutionprofile.aspx?unitId=483124&goToReportId=6.

Appendix

1. Skocpol 1995.

2. Du Bois 1899; 1935; Morris 2017; Quinn 2019.

3. Cottom 2017; Neely 2018; Appel 2014; Zaloom 2019; Ho 2009; Binder, Davis, and Bloom 2016; Binder and Abel 2019; Hamilton and Nielsen 2021; Rivera 2016.

4. Lewis 2010, 2011; Mallaby 2010; Waldman 1996.

5. Morgan and Winship 2007; Vaisey and Miles 2014; Jaquette and Parra 2014; Eaton 2020.

6. "Reauthorization of the Higher Education Act of 1965" 1991; "Higher Education Amendments of 1979" 1979.

7. Berman and Stivers 2016.

8. Cary and Bright 1969.

9. Dolan and Jesse 2018; Lewin 2015.

10. Hinchliff et al. 2015; McTavish et al. 2017.

11. "Higher Education Amendments of 1992 Conference Report to Acompany S. 1150. House of Representatives, 102nd Congres, 2nd Session" 1992.

12. Jaquette and Parra 2014.

13. Though it is sometimes considered to be a "public related" institution, we consider University of Pittsburg to be a private institution because it has a self-selecting board that originated prior to the formalization of the school's relationship with the state of Pennsylvania.

14. Eaton, Howell, and Yannelis 2020.

15. Bureau of Economic Analyis 2018; California Legislative Analyst's Office 2017.

REFERENCES

Addo, Fenaba R., Jason N. Houle, and Daniel Simon. 2016. "Young, Black, and (Still) in the Red: Parental Wealth, Race, and Student Loan Debt." *Race and Social Problems* 8 (1): 64–76.

Aisch, Gregor, Larry Buchanan, Amanda Cox, and Kevin Quealy. 2017. "Some Colleges Have More Students from the Top 1 Percent than the Bottom 60." *New York Times*, January 18, 2017.

Akers, Beth, and Matthew M. Chingos. 2016. *Game of Loans: The Rhetoric and Reality of Student Debt*. Princeton, NJ: Princeton University Press.

Allen, Frederick Lewis. 1935. *The Lords of Creation*. New York: Quadrangle.

Alvaredo, Facundo, Anthony B. Atkinson, Thomas Piketty, and Emmanuel Saez. 2013. "The Top 1 Percent in International and Historical Perspective." *Journal of Economic Perspectives* 27 (3): 3–20.

Amenta, Edwin. 2000. *Bold Relief: Institutional Politics and the Origins of Modern American Social Policy*. Princeton, NJ: Princeton University Press.

———. 2008. *When Movements Matter: The Townsend Plan and the Rise of Social Security*. Princeton, NJ: Princeton University Press.

Anderson, Perry. 2016. *Arguments within English Marxism*. New York: Verso.

Appel, Hannah. 2014. "Occupy Wall Street and the Economic Imagination." *Cultural Anthropology*, 29 (4): 602–25.

Appelbaum, Eileen, and Rosemary Batt. 2014. *Private Equity at Work: When Wall Street Manages Main Street*. New York: Russell Sage Foundation.

Armona, Luis, Rajashri Chakrabarti, and Michael F. Lovenheim. 2017. "How Does For-Profit College Attendance Affect Student Loans, Defaults and Earnings?" NBER Working Paper No. 25042, National Bureau of Economic Research, Cambridge, MA.

Ashkenas, Jeremy, Haeyoun Park, and Adam Pearce. 2017. "Even with Affirmitive Action, Blacks and Hispanics Are More Underrepresented at Top Colleges than 35 Years Ago." *New York Times*, August 24, 2017.

Asimov, Nanette, and Justin Berton. 2011. "UC Campus Police Move in on Student Protesters." *San Francisco Chronicle*, November 9, 2011.

Auten, Gerald E., Charles T. Clotfelter, and Richard L. Schmalbeck. 2000. "Taxes and Philanthropy among the Wealthy." Office of Tax Policy Research Working Paper No. 1998-1, Ross School of Business, University of Michigan, Ann Arbor.

Avery, Christopher, and Sarah Turner. 2012. "Student Loans: Do College Students Borrow Too Much—Or Not Enough?" *Journal of Economic Perspectives* 26 (1): 165–92.

Badertscher, Brad A., Sharon P. Katz, and Sonja O. Rego. 2013. "The Separation of Ownership and Control and Corporate Tax Avoidance." *Journal of Accounting and Economics* 56 (2): 228–50.

Barman, Emily. 2017. "The Social Bases of Philanthropy." *Annual Review of Sociology* 43 (1): 271–90.

Berger, Allen N., Anil K. Kashyap, Joseph M. Scalise, Mark Gertler, and Benjamin M. Friedman.

1995. "The Transformation of the US Banking Industry: What a Long, Strange Trip It's Been." *Brookings Papers on Economic Activity* 1995 (2): 55–218.

Berle, Adolf, and Gardiner Means. 1932. *The Modern Corporate and Private Property*. New York: Macmillan.

Berman, Elizabeth Popp. 2011. *Creating the Market University: How Academic Science Became an Economic Engine*. Princeton, NJ: Princeton University Press.

Berman, Elizabeth Popp, and Abby Stivers. 2016. "Student Loans as a Pressure on US Higher Education." *Research in the Sociology of Organizations* 46 (1): 129–60.

Best, Joel, and Eric Best. 2014. *The Student Loan Mess: How Good Intentions Created a Trillion-Dollar Problem*. Berkeley: University of California Press.

Biden, Joe. 2020. "Joe Biden Outlines New Steps to Ease Economic Burden on Working People." *Medium*, April 9, 2020. https://medium.com/@JoeBiden/joe-biden-outlines-new-steps-to-ease-economic-burden-on-working-people-e3e121037322.

Binder, Amy J., and Andrea R. Abel. 2019. "Symbolically Maintained Inequality: How Harvard and Stanford Students Construct Boundaries among Elite Universities." *Sociology of Education* 92 (1): 41–58.

Binder, Amy J., Daniel B. Davis, and Nick Bloom. 2016. "Career Funneling: How Elite Students Learn to Define and Desire 'Prestigious' Jobs." *Sociology of Education* 89 (1): 20–39.

Binder, Amy J., and Kate Wood. 2012. *Becoming Right: How Campuses Shape Young Conservatives*. Princeton, NJ: Princeton University Press.

Birgeneau, Robert. 2015. "Op-Ed: To Fix California's Colleges, Reform Prop. 13 by Taxing Corporations More." *Los Angeles Times*, November 1, 2015.

Black, Garrett James. 2017. "The Current US Private Equity Scene in 11 Charts." *PitchBook*, August 1, 2017. https://pitchbook.com/news/articles/the-current-us-private-equity-scene-in-11-charts.

Blau, Peter. 2017. *Exchange and Power in Social Life*. New York: Routledge.

Bound, John, and Sarah Turner. 2007. "Cohort Crowding: How Resources Affect Collegiate Attainment." *Journal of Public Economics* 91 (5): 877–99.

Bourdieu, Pierre, and Jean-Claude Passeron. 1990. *Reproduction in Education, Society and Culture*. New York: SAGE.

Brady, Henry. 2015. "UC Education: Cadillac Product, Chevy Price." *Berkeley Blog*. September 1, 2015. https://blogs.berkeley.edu/2015/09/01/uc-education-cadillac-product-chevy-price/.

Brint, Steven, and Jerome Karabel. 1989. *The Diverted Dream: Community Colleges and the Promise of Educational Opportunity in America, 1900–1985*. New York: Oxford University Press.

Budros, Art. 2002. "The Mean and Lean Firm and Downsizing: Causes of Involuntary and Voluntary Downsizing Strategies." *Sociological Forum* 17 (2): 307–42.

Burd, Stephen. 2011. "The Transformation of EDMC." *New America*, October 12, 2011. https://www.newamerica.org/education-policy/higher-education/higher-ed-watch/the-transformation-of-edmc/.

Bureau of Economic Analyis. 2018. "Real Personal Income by State and Metropolitan Area, 2018." Suitland, MD. https://www.bea.gov/tools/.

California Legislative Analyst's Office. 2017. "State of California Revenues, 1950–51 to 2017–18." Sacramento, CA. https://lao.ca.gov/PolicyAreas/state-budget/historical-data.

California State Student Association and the Institute for College Access and Success. 2017. "Where Debt Comes Due at CSU: Unequal Debt Burdens among California State University Graduates." Oakland, CA. https://ticas.org/wp-content/uploads/legacy-files/pub_files/where_debt_comes_due_at_csu.pdf.

"Campus Commemorates 1968 Student-Led Strike." 2008. *SF State News*, September 22, 2008. https://www.sfsu.edu/news/2008/fall/8.html.

Cao, Yan, and Tariq Habash. 2017. "College Complaints Unmasked." Century Foundation, Washington, DC, November 8, 2017. https://tcf.org/content/report/college-complaints-unmasked.

Cardoso, Fernando Henrique, and Enzo Faletto. 1979. *Dependency and Development in Latin America*. Berkeley: University of California Press.

Cary, William Lucius, and Craig B. Bright. 1969. *The Law and the Lore of Endowment Funds: Report to the Ford Foundation*. New York. Ford Foundation.

Catherine, Sylvain, and Constantine Yannelis. 2020. "The Distributional Effects of Student Loan Forgiveness." NBER Working Paper No. 28175, National Bureau of Economic Research, Cambridge, MA.

Cellini, Stephanie, Rajeev Darolia, and Lesley Turner. 2020. "Where Do Students Go When For-Profit Colleges Lose Federal Aid?" *American Economic Journal* 12 (2): 46–83.

Cellini, Stephanie Riegg, and Latika Chaudhary. 2014. "The Labor Market Returns to a For-Profit College Education." *Economics of Education Review* 43:125–40.

Cellini, Stephanie Riegg, and Claudia Goldin. 2014. "Does Federal Student Aid Raise Tuition? New Evidence on For-Profit Colleges." *American Economic Journal* 6 (4): 174–206.

Cellini, Stephanie Riegg, and Nicholas Turner. 2018. "Gainfully Employed? Assessing the Employment and Earnings of For-Profit College Students Using Administrative Data." NBER Working Paper No. 22287, National Bureau of Economic Research, Cambridge, MA.

Cheng, C. S. Agnes, Henry He Huang, Yinghua Li, and Jason Stanfield. 2012. "The Effect of Hedge Fund Activism on Corporate Tax Avoidance." *Accounting Review* 87 (5): 493–1526.

Chetty, Raj, John N. Friedman, Emmanuel Saez, Nicholas Turner, and Danny Yagan. 2017. "Mobility Report Cards: The Role of Colleges in Intergenerational Mobility." NBER Working Paper No. 23618, National Bureau of Economic Research, Cambridge, MA.

Cioffi, John W. 2006. "Building Finance Capitalism: The Regulatory Politics of Corporate Governance Reform in the United States and Germany." In *The State after Statism: New State Activities in the Age of Liberalization*, edited by Jonah Levy, 111–30. Cambridge, MA: Harvard University Press.

Clemens, Elisabeth S. 1993. "Organizational Repertoires and Institutional Change: Women's Groups and the Transformation of US Politics, 1890–1920." *American Journal of Sociology* 98 (4): 755–98.

Close, Kerry. 2016. "The Number of People Behind on Student Loan Payments Is Staggering." *Time*, April 7, 2016. http://web.archive.org/web/20180417101311/http://time.com/money/4284940/student-loan-payments-debt-college/.

Clotfelter, Charles T. 2017. *Unequal Colleges in the Age of Disparity*. Cambridge, MA: Harvard University Press.

Cochran, Thomas Childs, and William Miller. 1942. *The Age of Enterprise: A Social History of Industrial America*. New York: Macmillan.

College Board. 2020. *Trends in Student Aid: 2020*. https://trends.collegeboard.org/student-aid.

Collins, Randall. 1979. *The Credential Society: An Historical Sociology of Education and Stratification*. New York: Academic Press.

Congressional Budget Office. 2015. "The Distribution of Household Income, 2014." Washington, DC. https://www.cbo.gov/publication/53597.

Corey, Lewis. 1930. *The House of Morgan: A Social Biography of the Masters of Money*. New York: G. Howard Watt.

Cottom, Tressie McMillan. 2017. *Lower Ed: The Troubling Rise of For-Profit Colleges in the New Economy*. New York: New Press.

Cousin, Bruno, Shamus Khan, and Ashley Mears. 2018. "Theoretical and Methodological Pathways for Research on Elites." *Socio-Economic Review* 16 (2): 225–49.

Cowley, Stacy. 2021. "$10 Billion in Student Debt Erased Under Biden, but Calls Grow for More." *New York Times*, September 10, 2021.

"CPUC Resources Committee Annual Report for the Academic Year 2017–2018." 2018. Princeton, NJ. https://cpucresources.princeton.edu/sites/cpucresources/files/cpuc_resources_committee_report_2017-2018.pdf.

Crenshaw, Kimberle. 1990. "Mapping the Margins: Intersectionality, Identity Politics, and Violence against Women of Color." *Stanford Law Review* 43:1241.

Creswell, Julie. 2015. "The Private Equity Firm That Grew Too Fast." *New York Times*, April 5, 2015.

Davies, Scott, and David Zarifa. 2012. "The Stratification of Universities: Structural Inequality in Canada and the United States." *Research in Social Stratification and Mobility* 30:143–58.

Davis, Daniel, and Amy Binder. 2016. "Selling Students: The Rise of Corporate Partnership Programs in University Career Centers." *Research in the Sociology of Organizations* 46 (1): 395–422.

Davis, Gerald F. 2008. "A New Finance Capitalism? Mutual Funds and Ownership Re-concentration in the United States." *European Management Review* 5 (1): 11–21.

———. 2009. *Managed by the Markets: How Finance Re-Shaped America*. Oxford: Oxford University Press.

Davis, Gerald F., and Mark S. Mizruchi. 1999. "The Money Center Cannot Hold: Commercial Banks in the U.S. System of Corporate Governance." *Administrative Science Quarterly* 44 (2): 215–39.

Davis, Gerald F., and Suzanne K. Stout. 1992. "Organization Theory and the Market for Corporate Control: A Dynamic Analysis of the Characteristics of Large Takeover Targets, 1980–1990." *Administrative Science Quarterly* 37:605–33.

Davis, Gerald F., and Tracy A. Thompson. 1994. "A Social Movement Perspective on Corporate Control." *Administrative Science Quarterly* 39: 141–73.

Dealbook. 2007. "Providence Equity Raises $12 Billion Buyout Fund." *New York Times*, February 21, 2007.

Deming, David J., Claudia Goldin, and Lawrence F. Katz. 2012. "The For-Profit Postsecondary School Sector: Nimble Critters or Agile Predators?" *Journal of Economic Perspectives* 26 (1): 139–64.

Deming, David J., Noam Yuchtman, Amira Abulafi, Claudia Goldin, and Lawrence F. Katz. 2016. "The Value of Postsecondary Credentials in the Labor Market: An Experimental Study." *American Economic Review* 106 (3): 778–806.

DiMaggio, Paul, and Filiz Garip. 2012. "Network Effects and Social Inequality." *Annual Review of Sociology* 38 (1): 93–118.

Dmitrieva, Katia, Davide Scigliuzzo, Kelsey Butler, and Sally Bakewell. 2019. "Everything Is Private Equity Now." *Bloomberg*, October 8, 2019.

Dobbin, Frank, and Dirk Zorn. 2005. "Corporate Malfeasance and the Myth of Shareholder Value." *Political Power and Social Theory* 17:179–98.

Dolan, Matthew, and David Jesse. 2018. "University of Michigan Pours Billions into Funds Run by Contributors' Firms." *Detroit Free Press*, February 1, 2018.

Douglas, John Aubrey, and Zachary Bleemer. 2018. "Approaching a Tipping Point? A History and Prospectus of Funding for the University of California." UC Berkeley Center for Studies in Higher Education, Berkeley, CA. douglassbleemer.tipping_point_report.august_20_2018.pdf.

Du Bois, William Edward Burghardt. 1899. *The Philadelphia Negro: A Social Study*. Philadelphia: University of Pennsylvania Press.

———. 1903. *Souls of Black Folk*. Chicago: A. C. McClurg & Co.

———. 1935. *Black Reconstruction in America: Toward a History of the Part Which Black Folk Played in the Attempt to Reconstruct Democracy in America, 1860–1880*. New York: Harcourt, Brace, and Howe.

Dwyer, Rachel E., Randy Hodson, and Laura McCloud. 2013. "Gender, Debt, and Dropping Out of College." *Gender and Society* 27 (1): 30–55.

Dwyer, Rachel E., Laura McCloud, and Randy Hodson. 2012. "Debt and Graduation from American Universities." *Social Forces* 90 (4): 1133–55.

Eaton, Charlie. 2017a. "The Ivory Tower Tax Haven: The State, Financialization, and the Growth of Wealthy College Endowments." Public Finance Research Series, Berkeley: Haas Institute for a Fair and Inclusive Society, University of California, Berkeley.

———. 2017b. "The Student Loan Mess: How Good Intentions Created a Trillion-Dollar Problem." *Contemporary Sociology: A Journal of Reviews* 46 (6): 659–61.

———. 2017c. "How Colleges Lost Billions to Hedge Funds in 2016." *Chronicle of Higher Education*, February 20, 2017.

———. 2018. "Debt Free College and Student Out-of-Pocket Costs: The Case of California." In *Designing Financial Aid for California's Future*, 22–39. Washington, DC: Institute for College Access and Success.

———. 2020. "Agile Predators: Private Equity and the Spread of Shareholder Value Strategies to U.S. For-Profit Colleges." *Socio-Economic Review* (February 2020): 1-25.

Eaton, Charlie, and Albina Gibadullina. 2020. "The Social Circuitry of High Finance: Universities and Intimate Ties among Economic Elites." Research and Occational Paper Series 11.20, UC Berkeley Center for Studies in Higher Education, Berkeley, CA.

Eaton, Charlie, Adam Goldstein, Jacob Habinek, Mukul Kumar, Tamera Lee Stover, and Alex Roehrkasse. 2013. "Bankers in the Ivory Tower: The Financialization of Governance at the University of California." UC Berkeley Center on Culture, Organizations, and Politics Working Paper, Institute for Research on Labor and Employment, Berkeley, CA.

Eaton, Charlie, Jacob Habinek, Adam Goldstein, Cyrus Dioun, and Daniela García Santibáñez Godoy. 2016. "The Financialization of U.S. Higher Education." *Socio-Economic Review* 14 (3): 507–35.

Eaton, Charlie, Sabrina Howell, and Constantine Yannelis. 2020. "When Investor Incentives and Consumer Interests Diverge: Private Equity in Higher Education." *Review of Financial Studies* 33 (9): 4024–4060.

Eaton, Charlie, Sheisha Kulkarni, Robert Birgeneau, Henry Brady, and Michael Hout. 2019. "The Organizational Ecology of College Affordability: Research Activity, State Grant Aid Policies, and Student Debt at U.S. Public Universities." *Socius* (January 2019):1–19.

Eaton, Charlie, and Mitchell L. Stevens. 2020. "Universities as Peculiar Organizations." *Sociology Compass* 14:e12768.

Epstein, Gerald A. 2005. *Financialization and the World Economy*. Northhampton, MA: Edward Elgar.

Evans, Peter B. 1995. *Embedded Autonomy: States and Industrial Transformation*. Princeton, NJ: Princeton University Press.

Fabrikant, Geraldine. 2007. "For Yale's Money Man, a Higher Calling." *New York Times*, February 18, 2007.

———. 2016. "The Money Management Gospel of Yale's Endowment Guru." *New York Times*, November 8, 2016.

———. 2018. "Harvard's Endowment Grew 10% Last Year, but Some Rivals Did Better." *New York Times*, September 28, 2018.

"First Comes Diploma, Then Comes Debt." 2019. University of California Student Association (UCSA) and the Institute for College Access & Success (TICAS). https://ticas.org/wp-content/uploads/legacy-files/pub_files/first_comes_diploma_then_comes_debt.pdf.

Fishback, Price V. 2010. "Social Welfare Expenditures in the United States and the Nordic Countries: 1900–2003." NBER Working Paper No. 15982, National Bureau of Economic Research, Cambridge, MA.

Fisher, Jenna. 2018. "AG Healey Accuses Brookline Art College of Fraud in Lawsuit." *Patch*, July 31, 2018. https://patch.com/massachusetts/brookline/ag-healey-accuses-brookline-art-college-fraud-lawsuit.

Fleischer, Victor. 2015. "How a Carried Interest Tax Could Raise $180 Billion." *New York Times*, June 5, 2015.

Fligstein, Neil. 1993. *The Transformation of Corporate Control*. Cambridge, MA: Harvard University Press.

———. 2001. *The Architecture of Markets: An Economic Sociology of Twenty-First-Century Capitalist Societies*. Princeton, NJ: Princeton University Press.

Fligstein, Neil, and Adam Goldstein. 2010. "The Anatomy of the Mortgage Securitization Crisis." *Research in the Sociology of Organizations* 30:27–68.

———. 2012. "A Long Strange Trip: The State and Mortgage Securitization, 1968–2010." In *The Oxford Handbook of the Sociology of Finance*, edited by Karin Knorr Cetina and Alex Preda, 339–56. Oxford: Oxford University Press.

Fligstein, Neil, and Jacob Habinek. 2014. "Sucker Punched by the Invisible Hand: The World Financial Markets and the Globalization of the US Mortgage Crisis." *Socio-Economic Review* 12 (4): 637–65.

Fligstein, Neil, and Doug McAdam. 2012. *A Theory of Fields*. New York: Oxford University Press.

Fligstein, Neil, and Alexander F. Roehrkasse. 2016. "The Causes of Fraud in the Financial Crisis of 2007 to 2009: Evidence from the Mortgage-Backed Securities Industry." *American Sociological Review* 81 (4): 617–43.

Fligstein, Neil, and Taekjin Shin. 2007. "Shareholder Value and the Transformation of the US Economy, 1984–2001." *Sociological Forum* 22 (4): 399–424.

"Forum on 'Bargaining for the Common Good: Lessons from L.A. and Beyond.'" 2016. Rutgers School of Management and Labor Relations, New Brunswick, NJ. https://smlr.rutgers.edu/news/forum%C2%A0%C2%A0'bargaining%C2%A0%C2%A0-common-good-lessons%C2%A0%C2%A0la-and-beyond.

Fourcade, Marion. 2009. *Economists and Societies: Discipline and Profession in the United States, Britain, and France, 1890s to 1990s*. Princeton, NJ: Princeton University Press.

Fox, Gene. 2010. "The Government Takeover of Student Lending." *Forbes*, May 2, 2010.

Friedman, Zack. 2019. "Why This For-Profit College Will Cancel $500 Million of Student Loans." *Forbes*, January 7, 2019.

Fung, William, and David A. Hsieh. 2016. "Empirical Characteristics of Dynamic Trading Strategies : The Case of Hedge Funds." *Review of Financial Studies* 10 (2): 275–302.

Ganz, Marshall. 2000. "Resources and Resourcefulness: Strategic Capacity in the Unionization of California Agriculture, 1959–1966." *American Journal of Sociology* 105 (4): 1003–62.

Gao, Meng, and Jiekun Huang. 2016. "Capitalizing on Capitol Hill: Informed Trading by Hedge Fund Managers." *Journal of Financial Economics* 121 (3): 521–45.

Garritzmann, Julian L. 2016. *The Political Economy of Higher Education Finance: The Politics of Tuition Fees and Subsidies in OECD Countries, 1945–2015*. New York: Palgrave Macmillan.

Geiger, Roger L. 2002. "The Competition for High-Ability Students: Universities in a Key Marketplace." In *The Future of the City of Intellect: The Changing American University*, edited by Steven Brint, 82–106. Stanford, CA: Stanford University Press.

———. 2004. *Knowledge and Money: Research Universities and the Paradox of the Marketplace*. Stanford, CA: Stanford University Press.

Geraci, Victor, Ann Lage, and Lisa Rubens. 2015. "Conversations with Richard C. Blum: Businessman, Philanthropist, President Emeritus Board of Regents University of California. Conversations Conducted by Victor Geraci, Ann Lage, and Lisa Rubens." Regional Oral History Office, Bancroft Library, UC Berkeley, Berkeley, CA. https://bancroft.berkeley.edu/ROHO///narrators/blum_richard.html.

Ginder, Scott A., Janice E. Kelly-Reid, and Farrah B. Mann. 2019. "Enrollment and Employees in Postsecondary Institutions, Fall 2017; and Financial Statistics and Academic Libraries, Fiscal Year 2017: First Look (Provisional Data)." NCES 2019-021rev, National Center for Education Statistics, Washington, DC. https://files.eric.ed.gov/fulltext/ED591907.pdf.

Goldberg, Lenny, and David Kersten. 2010. "System Failure: California's Loophole-Ridden Commercial Property Tax." California Tax Reform Association. http://www.mikemcmahon.info/Prop13TaxAnalysis2010.pdf.

Golden, Daniel. 2003. "For Groton Grads, Academics Aren't Only Keys to Ivy Schools." *Wall Street Journal*, April 3, 2003.

———. 2007. *The Price of Admission: How America's Ruling Class Buys Its Way into Elite Colleges and Who Gets Left Outside the Gates*. New York: Broadway.

Goldin, Claudia, and Lawrence F. Katz. 2009. *The Race between Education and Technology*. Cambridge, MA: Harvard University Press.

Goldin, Claudia, and Robert A. Margo. 1992. "The Great Compression: The Wage Structure in the United States at Mid-Century." *Quarterly Journal of Economics* 107 (1): 1–34. https://doi.org/10.2307/2118322.

Goldrick-Rab, Sara. 2016. *Paying the Price: College Costs, Financial Aid, and the Betrayal of the American Dream*. Chicago: University of Chicago Press.

Goldrick-Rab, Sara, Douglas N. Harris, Christopher Mazzeo, and Gregory Kienzl. 2009. *Transforming America's Community Colleges: A Federal Policy Proposal to Expand Opportunity and Promote Economic Prosperity*. Washington, DC: Metropolitan Policy Program at Brookings. https://www.brookings.edu/research/transforming-americas-community-colleges-a-federal-policy-proposal-to-expand-opportunity-and-promote-economic-prosperity/.

Goldstein, Adam. 2012. "Revenge of the Managers: Labor Cost-Cutting and the Paradoxical Resurgence of Managerialism in the Shareholder Value Era, 1984 to 2001." *American Sociological Review* 77 (2): 268–94.

Goldstein, Adam, and Charlie Eaton. 2020. "Asymmetry by Design? Identity Obfuscation, Reputational Pressure, and Consumer Predation in U.S. For-Profit Higher Education." *American Sociological Review* (September 2021): 1–38. https://doi.org/10.1177/00031224211043223.

Goldstein, Adam, and Neil Fligstein. 2014. "The Transformation of Mortgage Finance and the Industrial Roots of the Mortgage Meltdown." UC Berkeley Center on Culture, Organizations, and Politics Working Paper, Institute for Research on Labor and Employment, Berkeley, CA. https://escholarship.org/uc/item/2zx8r7fb.

Goldstein, Matthew. 2015. "Equity Firms Are Lending to Landlords, Signaling a Shift." *New York Times*, March 3, 2015.

Golshan, Tara. 2020. "Joe Biden and Bernie Sanders Unveil Names for Joint Policy Task Forces."

HuffPost, May 12, 2020. https://www.huffpost.com/entry/joe-biden-bernie-sanders-climate-task-force-ocasio-cortez_n_5ebb5b87c5b6ae915a8be292.

Gompers, Paul, and Josh Lerner. 2001. "The Venture Capital Revolution." *Journal of Economic Perspectives* 15 (2): 145–68.

Goodkin, Michael. 2012. *The Wrong Answer Faster: The Inside Story of Making the Machine That Trades Trillions*. Hoboken, NJ: Wiley.

Gordon, David M. 1996. *Fat and Mean: The Corporate Squeeze of Working Americans and the Myth of Managerial "Downsizing."* New York: Free Press.

Gordon, Robert J., and Ian Dew-Becker. 2008. "Controversies about the Rise of American Inequality: A Survey." NBER Working Paper No. 13982, National Bureau of Economic Research, Cambridge, MA.

Gottschalk, Marie. 2000. *The Shadow Welfare State: Labor, Business, and the Politics of Health-Care in the United States*. Ithaca, NY: Cornell University Press.

Granovetter, Mark S. 1973. "The Strength of Weak Ties." *American Journal of Sociology* 78 (6): 1360–80.

———. 1985. "Economic Action and the Problem of Embeddedness." *American Journal of Sociology* 91:481–510.

Grubb, W. Norton, and Marvin Lazerson. 2009. *The Education Gospel*. Cambridge, MA: Harvard University Press.

Gupta, Atul, Sabrina Howell, Constantine Yannelis, and Abhinav Gupta. 2021. "Does Private Equity Investment in Healthcare Benefit Patients? Evidence from Nursing Homes." NBER Working Paper No. 28474, National Bureau of Economic Research, Cambridge, MA.

Hacker, Jacob S. 2002. *The Divided Welfare State: The Battle over Public and Private Social Benefits in the United States*. New York: Cambridge University Press.

Hacker, Jacob S., and Paul Pierson. 2010. "Winner-Take-All Politics: Public Policy, Political Organization, and the Precipitous Rise of Top Incomes in the United States." *Politics and Society* 38 (2): 152–204.

———. 2011. *Winner-Take-All Politics: How Washington Made the Rich Richer—and Turned Its Back on the Middle Class*. New York: Simon and Schuster.

Hall, Stephanie, and Taela Dudley. 2019. "Dear Colleges: Take Control of Your Online Courses." Century Foundation, Washington, DC, September 12, 2019. https://tcf.org/content/report/dear-colleges-take-control-online-courses/.

Halperin, David. 2017. "Strip Mall For-Profit College Owners Locked Up; Wall Street Owners Walk Away." *HuffPost*, November 25, 2015. https://www.huffpost.com/entry/strip-mall-for-profit-col_b_8648574.

Hamilton, Laura, and Kelly Nielsen. 2021. *Broke: The Racial Consequences of Underfunding the New University*. Chicago: University of Chicago Press.

Hansmann, Henry B. 1980. "The Role of Nonprofit Enterprise." *Yale Law Journal* 89 (5): 835–901.

Harvard Business Review. 2014. "Jonathan M. Nelson MBA 1983." https://www.alumni.hbs.edu/Documents/Awards/2014_HBS_AAA_Nelson.pdf.

"Harvard Business School Announces Fundraising Campaign." 2014. *Harvard Business School Newsroom*, April 25, 2014. https://www.hbs.edu/news/releases/Pages/default.aspx?year=2014&month=04.

"Harvard Business School to Create New Convening Center." 2014. *Harvard Business School Newsroom*, June 15, 2014. https://www.hbs.edu/news/releases/Pages/harvard-business-school-create-new-convening-center.aspx.

Harvard Crimson. 1945. "Conant Suggests GI Bill Revision." January 23, 1945. https://www.thecrimson.com/article/1945/1/23/conant-suggests-gi-bill-revision-pentering/.

Harvard Magazine. 2012. "The Harvard Corporation's Committees." February 6, 2012.

Harvey, David. 2005. *A Brief History of Neoliberalism*. New York: Oxford University Press.

"Hedge Papers No. 25—Endangered Endowments: How Hedge Funds Are Bankrupting Higher Education." 2016. *Hedge Clippers*, February 7, 2016. https://hedgeclippers.org/endangered-endowments/.

"Hedge Papers No. 54: Hurricane Harvard and the Damage Done to Puerto Rico: How the University's Endowment Investment Harms the Island." 2018. *Hedge Clippers*, January 23, 2018. http://hedgeclippers.org/report-no-54-hurricane-harvard-and-the-damage-done-to-puerto-rico-how-the-universitys-endowment-investment-harms-the-island/.

Heiney, Mallory. 2015. "My For-Profit University Folded. I Refuse to Pay Back My Student Loans." *Washington Post*, March 16, 2015.

Herndon, Astead W. 2019. "Elizabeth Warren's Higher Education Plan: Cancel Student Debt and Eliminate Tuition." *New York Times*, April 22, 2019. https://www.nytimes.com/2019/04/22/us/politics/elizabeth-warren-student-debt.html.

"Higher Education Amendments of 1979: Hearings Before the Subcommittee on Education, Arts and Humanities, Part 1." 1980. Washington, DC: US Government Printing Office. https://files.eric.ed.gov/fulltext/ED191414.pdf.

"Higher Education Amendments of 1992 Conference Report to Acompany S. 1150. House of Representatives, 102nd Congress, 2nd Session." 1992. Washington, DC: US House of Representatives. http://files.eric.ed.gov/fulltext/ED351985.pdf.

Hinchcliff, Cody E., Stephen A. Smith, James F. Allman, J. Gordon Burleigh, Ruchi Chaudhary, Lyndon M. Coghill, Keith A. Crandall, Jiabin Deng, Bryan T. Drew, Romina Gazis, Karl Gude, David S. Hibbett, Laura A. Katz, H. Dail Laughinghouse IV, Emily Jane McTavish, Peter E. Midford, Christopher L. Owen, Richard H. Ree, Jonathan A. Rees, Douglas E. Soltis, Tiffani Williams, and Karen A. Cranston. 2015. "Synthesis of Phylogeny and Taxonomy into a Comprehensive Tree of Life." *Proceedings of the National Academy of Sciences* 112 (41): 12,764–12,769.

Ho, Karen. 2009. *Liquidated: An Ethnography of Wall Street*. Durham, NC: Duke University Press.

Horvath, Aaron, and Walter W. Powell. 2016. "Contributory or Disruptive: Do New Forms of Philanthropy Erode Democracy?" In *Philanthropy in Democratic Societies*, edited by Rob Reich, Lucy Bernholz, and Chiara Cordelli, 87–122. Chicago: University of Chicago Press.

Houle, Jason N. 2013. "Disparities in Debt: Parents' Socioeconomic Resources and Young Adult Student Loan Debt." *Sociology of Education* 87 (1): 53–69.

Hout, Michael. 2012. "Social and Economic Returns to College Education in the United States." *Annual Review of Sociology* 38:379–400.

Huelsman, Mark, Tamara Draut, Tatjana Meschede, Lars Dietrich, Thomas Shapiro, and Laura Sullivan. 2015. *Less Debt, More Equity: Lowering Student Debt While Closing the Black-White Wealth Gap*. New York: Demos. https://www.demos.org/research/less-debt-more-equity-lowering-student-debt-while-closing-black-white-wealth-gap.

Hutchins, Robert M. 1945. "The Threat to American Education." *Collier's*, January 20–22, 1945.

Hutt, Ethan, and Mitchell Stevens. 2017. "From Soldiers to Students: The Tests of General Educational Development (GED) as Diplomatic Measurement." *Social Science History* 24 (4).

"In Elite Schools' Vast Endowments, Malcolm Gladwell Sees 'Obscene' Inequity." 2015. *NPR*, August 22, 2015. https://www.npr.org/2015/08/22/433735934/in-elite-schools-vast-war-chests-malcolm-gladwell-sees-obscene-inequity.

Indicators of Higher Education Equity in the United States. 2016. Washington, DC: Pell Institute. http://www.pellinstitute.org/downloads/publications-Indicators_of_Higher_Education_Equity_in_the_US_2016_Historical_Trend_Report.pdf.

Investment Company Institute. 2018. "2018 Investment Company Fact Book." Washington, DC. https://www.icifactbook.org.

Ivashina, Victoria, and Zheng Sun. 2011. "Institutional Stock Trading on Loan Market Information." *Journal of Financial Economics* 100 (2): 284–303.

Jacobs, David, and Jonathan C. Dirlam. 2016. "Politics and Economic Stratification: Power Resources and Income Inequality in the United States." *American Journal of Sociology* 122 (2): 469–500.

Jaquette, Ozan, and Edna E. Parra. 2014. "Using IPEDS for Panel Analyses: Core Concepts, Data Challenges, and Empirical Applications." In *Higher Education: Handbook of Theory and Research*, edited by Michael B. Paulsen, 467–533. New York: Springer.

Jenkins, Gary W. 2015. "The Wall Street Takeover of Nonprofit Boards." *Stanford Social Innovation Review* 13 (3): 46–52.

Jensen, Michael C. 1986. "Agency Cost of Free Cash Flow, Corporate Finance, and Takeovers." *Corporate Finance and Takeovers. American Economic Review* 76 (2): 323–329.

———. 1989. "Eclipse of the Public Corporation." *Harvard Business Review* 67 (September–October): 61–74.

Jensen, Michael C., and William H. Meckling. 1976. "Theory of the Firm: Managerial Behavior, Agency Costs and Ownership Structure." *Journal of Financial Economics* 3 (4): 305–60.

Jensen, Michael C., and Richard S. Ruback. 1983. "The Market for Corporate Control: The Scientific Evidence." *Journal of Financial Economics* 11 (1): 5–50.

Jiao, Yawen, Massimo Massa, and Hong Zhang. 2016. "Short Selling Meets Hedge Fund 13F: An Anatomy of Informed Demand." *Journal of Financial Economics* 122 (3): 544–67.

Johnson, Jenna. 2011. "At Occupy Wall Street Protests, Student Loan Frustration." *Washington Post*, October 10, 2011. https://www.washingtonpost.com/blogs/campus-overload/post/at-occupy-wall-street-protests-student-loan-frustration/2011/10/10/gIQAV5CHaL_blog.html.

Johnson, Simon, and James Kwak. 2011. *13 Bankers: The Wall Street Takeover and the Next Financial Meltdown*. New York: Random House.

"Jordan Baruch." 2012. In *Memorial Tributes Volume 16: National Academy of Engineering*. Washington, DC: National Academies Press.

Jung, Jiwook. 2015. "Shareholder Value and Workforce Downsizing, 1981–2006." *Social Forces* 93 (4): 1335–1368.

Kahan, Marcel, and Edward B. Rock. 2007. "Hedge Funds in Corporate Governance and Corporate Control." *University of Pennsylvania Law Review* 155 (5): 1021–93.

Kalleberg, Arne L. 2011. *Good Jobs, Bad Jobs: The Rise of Polarized and Precarious Employment Systems in the United States, 1970s–2000s*. New York: Russell Sage.

Kaminer, Ariel. 2012. "Occupy Wall St. Offshoot Aims to Erase People's Debts." *New York Times*, November 13, 2012.

Kantrowitz, Mark. 2019. "Historical Federal Student Loan Limits." *Savingforcollege.com*, July 26, 2019. https://www.savingforcollege.com/article/historical-federal-student-loan-limits.

Kaplan, Steven N., and Joshua Rauh. 2009. "Wall Street and Main Street: What Contributes to the Rise in the Highest Incomes?" *Review of Financial Studies* 23 (3): 1004–50.

Kaplan, Steven N., and Antoinette Schoar. 2005. "Private Equity Performance: Returns, Persistence, and Capital Flows." *Journal of Finance* 60 (4): 1791–823.

Karabel, Jerome. 2005. *The Chosen: The Hidden History of Admission and Exclusion at Harvard, Yale, and Princeton*. Boston: Houghton Mifflin Harcourt.

Katznelson, Ira, and Margaret Weir. 1988. *Schooling for All: Class, Race, and the Decline of the Democratic Ideal*. Berkeley: University of California Press.

Keltner, Dacher. 2016. *The Power Paradox: How We Gain and Lose Influence.* New York: Penguin.

Kerr, Clark, and Marian L. Gade. 1989. *The Guardians: Boards of Trustees of American Colleges and Universities: What They Do and How Well They Do It.* Washington, DC: Association of Governing Boards of Universities and Colleges.

Khan, Shamus Rahman. 2010. *Privilege: The Making of an Adolescent Elite at St. Paul's School.* Princeton, NJ: Princeton University Press.

———. 2012. "The Sociology of Elites." *Annual Review of Sociology* 38: 361–77.

Kinser, Kevin. 2006. *From Main Street to Wall Street: The Transformation of For-Profit Education.* San Francisco: Jossey-Bass.

Kirkham, Chris. 2011. "With Goldman's Foray into Higher Education, a Predatory Pursuit of Students and Revenues." *HuffPost,* October 14, 2011. https://www.huffpost.com/entry/goldman-sachs-for-profit-college_n_997409.

Klein, April, and Emanuel Zur. 2016. "Entrepreneurial Shareholder Activism: Hedge Funds and Other Private Investors." *Journal of Finance* 64 (1): 187–229.

Konczal, Mike. 2009. "Shadow Banking: What It Is, How It Broke, and How to Fix It." *The Atlantic,* July 13, 2009. https://www.theatlantic.com/business/archive/2009/07/shadow-banking-what-it-is-how-it-broke-and-how-to-fix-it/21038/.

Korom, Philipp, Mark Lutter, and Jens Beckert. 2017. "The Enduring Importance of Family Wealth: Evidence from the Forbes 400, 1982 to 2013." *Social Science Research* 65:75–95.

Kosman, Josh. 2014. "Goldman Sachs, KKR Flunk in College Investment." *New York Post,* July 2, 2014.

Krippner, Greta R. 2005. "The Financialization of the American Economy." *Socio-Economic Review* 3 (2): 173–208.

———. 2011. *Capitalizing on Crisis.* Cambridge, MA: Harvard University Press.

Kumar, Nishant. 2016. "Past Perfect, Future Tense: Global Hedge-Fund Industry in Charts." *Bloomberg,* December 16, 2016.

Legum, Judd, and Danielle Mclean. 2017. "These Wealthy Institutions Are Quietly Financing White Nationalism." *Think Progress,* October 19, 2017. https://archive.thinkprogress.org/these-wealthy-institutions-are-quietly-financing-white-nationalism-5313db89b185/.

Lerner, Josh, Antoinette Schoar, and Jialan Wang. 2008. "Secrets of the Academy: The Drivers of University Endowment Success." *Journal of Economic Perspectives* 22 (3): 207–22.

Lerner, Josh, Morten Sorensen, and Per Strömberg. 2011. "Private Equity and Long-Run Investment: The Case of Innovation." *Journal of Finance* 66 (2): 445–77.

Lerner, Stephen, and Saqib Bhatti. 2016. "Organizing in a Brave New World." *New Labor Forum* 25 (3): 22–30.

Lewin, Tamar. 2015. "John Paulson Gives $400 Million to Harvard for Engineering School." *New York Times,* June 4, 2015.

Lewis, Michael. 2010. *Liar's Poker.* New York: Norton.

———. 2011. *The Big Short: Inside the Doomsday Machine.* New York: Norton.

Lin, Ken-Hou, and Megan Tobias Neely. 2020. *Divested: Inequality in Financialized America.* Oxford: Oxford University Press.

Lin, Ken-Hou, and Donald Tomaskovic-Devey. 2013. "Financialization and US Income Inequality, 1970–2008." *American Journal of Sociology* 118 (5): 1284–329.

Liu, Yuen Ting, and Clive Belfield. 2020. "The Labor Market Returns to For-Profit Higher Education: Evidence for Transfer Students. *Community College Review* 48 (2):133–155.

Ljungqvist, Alexander, Lars Persson, and Joachim Tag. 2016. "Private Equity's Unintended Dark Side: On the Economic Consequences of Excessive Delistings." NBER Working Paper No. 21909, National Bureau of Economic Research, Cambridge, MA.

Looney, Adam, and Constantine Yannelis. 2015. "A Crisis in Student Loans?" *Brookings Papers on Economic Activity* 2015 (Fall): 1–68.

Lorin, Janet. 2016. "Yale Finds Itself on Both Sides of Employee's Fight for a Home." *Hartford Courant*, June 5, 2016.

Los Angeles Times. 1991. "$25 Million Donated to Stanford." June 1, 1991.

Loss, Christopher P. 2011. *Between Citizens and the State: The Politics of American Higher Education in the 20th Century*. Princeton, NJ: Princeton University Press.

MacKenzie, Donald, and Yuval Millo. 2003. "Constructing a Market, Performing Theory: The Historical Sociology of a Financial Derivatives Exchange." *American Journal of Sociology* 109 (1): 107–45.

Madsen, H. 1997. *Composition of Governing Boards of Public Colleges and Universities*. Washington, DC: Association of Governing Boards of Universities and Colleges.

"Major Features of the 2003 California Budget." 2003. The Legislative Analyst's Office (LAO) Report, May 19, 2003, Sacramento, CA.

"Making College Debt-Free and Taking on Student Debt." 2016. The Office of Hillary Rodham Clinton. https://www.hillaryclinton.com/issues/college/.

Mallaby, Sebastian. 2010. *More Money than God: Hedge Funds and the Making of the New Elite*. New York: A&C Black.

Marshall, Thomas H. 1950. *Citizenship and Social Class*. Cambridge: Cambridge University Press.

Martin, Isaac William. 2008. *The Permanent Tax Revolt: How the Property Tax Transformed American Politics*. Stanford, CA: Stanford University Press.

McCartin, Joseph A., Marilyn Sneiderman, Stephen Lerner, and Maurice BP-Weeks. 2018. "Before the Chalk Dust Settles: Building on the 2018 Teachers' Mobilization." *American Prospect*, April 24, 2018.

McClintock, David. 2006. "How Harvard Lost Russia." *Institutional Investor* 40 (1): 62.

McClure, Kevin R., Sondra N. Barringer, and Joshua Travis Brown. 2019. "Privatization as the New Normal in Higher Education: Synthesizing Literature and Reinvigorating Research Through a Multilevel Framework." *Higher Education: Handbook of Theory and Research* 35:1–78.

McTavish, Emily Jane., Bryan T. Drew, Ben Redelings, and Karen A. Cranston. 2017. "How and Why to Build a Unified Tree of Life." *BioEssays* 39 (11).

Mettler, Suzanne. 2005. *Soldiers to Citizens: The G.I. Bill and the Making of the Greatest Generation*. New York: Oxford University Press.

———. 2014. *Degrees of Inequality: How Higher Education Politics Sabotaged the American Dream*. New York: Basic.

Meyer, John W., and Brian Rowan. 1977. "Institutionalized Organizations: Formal Structure as Myth and Ceremony." *American Journal of Sociology* 83 (2): 340–63.

Miller, Ben. 2017. "New Federal Data Show a Student Loan Crisis for African American Borrowers." Center for American Progress, October 16, 2016. https://www.americanprogress.org/issues/education-postsecondary/news/2017/10/16/440711/new-federal-data-show-student-loan-crisis-african-american-borrowers/.

———. 2018. "The Student Debt Problem Is Worse Than We Imagined." *New York Times*, August 25, 2018.

———. 2019. "The Continued Student Loan Crisis for Black Borrowers." Center for American Progress, December 2, 2019. https://www.americanprogress.org/issues/education-postsecondary/reports/2019/12/02/477929/continued-student-loan-crisis-black-borrowers/.

Miller, Ben, and Stephen Burd. 2007. "Sallie Mae's Plan of Attack." *New America*, July 9, 2007.

https://www.newamerica.org/education-policy/higher-education/higher-ed-watch/sallie-maes-plan-of-attack/.

Mills, C. Wright. 2000. *The Power Elite*. Oxford: Oxford University Press.

Mizruchi, Mark S. 2013. *The Fracturing of the American Corporate Elite*. Cambridge, MA: Harvard University Press.

Mizruchi, Mark S., and David Bunting. 1981. "Influence in Corporate Networks: An Examination of Four Measures." *Administrative Science Quarterly* 26 (3): 475–89.

Moody's Investor Service. 2012. "New Issue: Moody's Assigns Aa2 Rating to University of California's Approximately $96 Million Lease Revenue Refunding Bonds." *Global Credit Research*, September 6, 2012. https://www.moodys.com/research/Moodys-assigns-Aa2-rating-to-University-of-Californias-approximately-96--PR_254649.

Morgan, Kimberly J., and Andrea Louise Campbell. 2011. *The Delegated Welfare State: Medicare, Markets, and the Governance of Social Policy*. New York: Oxford University Press.

Morgan, Stephen L., and Christopher Winship. 2007. *Counterfactuals and Causal Inference: Methods and Principles for Social Research*. Cambridge: Cambridge University Press.

Morgenson, Gretchen. 2008. "Questions of Rent Tactics by Private Equity." *New York Times*, May 9, 2008.

———. 2016. "Corinthian Colleges Used Recruiting Incentives, Documents Show." *New York Times*, June 22, 2016.

Morris, Aldon. 2017. *The Scholar Denied: WEB Du Bois and the Birth of Modern Sociology*. Berkeley: University of California Press.

National Center for Education Statistics. 2016. "Table 306.20." *Digest of Education Statistics*. Washington, DC. https://nces.ed.gov/programs/digest/d16/tables/dt16_306.20.asp.

———. 2017. "Table 104.20." *Digest of Education Statistics*. Washington, DC. https://nces.ed.gov/programs/digest/d17/tables/dt17_104.20.asp.

Neckerman, Kathryn M., and Florencia Torche. 2007. "Inequality: Causes and Consequences." *Annual Review of Sociology* 33 (1): 335–57.

Neely, Megan Tobias. 2018. "Fit to Be King: How Patrimonialism on Wall Street Leads to Inequality." *Socio-Economic Review* 16 (2): 365–85.

"New England Institute of Art History." 2012. New England Institute of Art. http://web.archive.org/web/20120723193118/http://www.artinstitute.edu/boston/about/history.aspx.

New York Times. 2016. "Top 10 Hedge Fund Chiefs Took Home a Combined $10.07 Billion." *New York Times*, May 10, 2016.

———. 2017. "Some Colleges Have More Students from the Top 1 Percent Than the Bottom 60." *New York Times*, January 18, 2017.

OECD. 2018. "A Broken Social Elevator? How to Promote Social Mobility." *COPE Policy Brief*. Paris: OECD. https://www.oecd.org/social/broken-elevator-how-to-promote-social-mobility-9789264301085-en.htm.

———. 2019a. *Education at a Glance 2019*. Paris: OECD. http://www.oecd.org/education/EAG2014-Indicator%20A4%20(eng).pdf.

———. 2019b. *Social Expenditure Update 2019 Public Social Spending Is High in Many OECD Countries*. 2019. Paris: OECD. http://www.oecd.org/social/soc/OECD2019-Social-Expenditure-Update.pdf.

———. 2020. "Education at a Glance: Educational Attainment and Labour-force Status" *OECD Education Statistics* (database). https://doi.org/10.1787/889e8641-en.

Office of Inspector General. 2018. "The Department's Communication Regarding the Costs of Income-Driven Repayment Plans and Loan Forgiveness Programs." US Department of Education. https://www2.ed.gov/about/offices/list/oig/auditreports/fy2018/a09q0003.pdf.

Oliver, Melvin L., and Thomas M. Shapiro. 2006. *Black Wealth, White Wealth: A New Perspective on Racial Inequality*. New York: Taylor and Francis.

Ostrower, Francie. 1995. *Why the Wealthy Give: The Culture of Elite Philanthropy*. Princeton, NJ: Princeton University Press.

Page, Benjamin I., Larry M. Bartels, and Jason Seawright. 2013. "Democracy and the Policy Preferences of Wealthy Americans." *Perspectives on Politics* 11 (1): 51–73.

Page, Benjamin I., Jason Seawright, and Matthew J. Lacombe. 2018. *Billionaires and Stealth Politics*. Chicago: University of Chicago Press.

Pardo-Guerra, Juan Pablo. 2019. *Automating Finance: Infrastructures, Engineers, and the Making of Electronic Markets*. Cambridge: Cambridge University Press.

Parker, Phaelen. 2015. "State Spending per Student at CSU and UC Remains Near the Lowest Point in More Than 30 Years." March 2015. Sacramento, CA: California Budget Policy Center. https://calbudgetcenter.org/resources/state-spending-per-student-at-csu-and-uc-remains-near-the-lowest-point-in-more-than-30-years/.

"Pell Grant Recipients as a Peer Metric." 2018. *Topic in Brief*, December 2018. Berkeley, CA: UC Berkeley Office of Planning and Analysis. https://opa.berkeley.edu/sites/default/files/2016-17_pell_grant_ivy_compared.pdf.

Perry, Andre M. and Carl Romer. 2021. "Student Debt Cancellation Should Consider Wealth, Not Income." Washington, DC: Brookings Institution. https://www.brookings.edu/essay/student-debt-cancellation-should-consider-wealth-not-income/.

Pierson, Paul. 1993. "When Effect Becomes Cause: Policy Feedback and Political Change." *World Politics* 45 (4): 595–628.

Piketty, Thomas. 2014. *Capital in the Twenty-First Century*. Cambridge, MA: Harvard University Press.

Polanyi, Karl. 2001. *The Great Transformation: The Political and Economic Origins of Our Time*. Boston: Beacon.

Prupis, Nadia. 2014. "'You Are Not a Loan': Rolling Jubilee Abolishes Millions in Student Debt." *Common Dreams*, September 14, 2014. https://www.commondreams.org/news/2014/09/17/you-are-not-loan-rolling-jubilee-abolishes-millions-student-debt.

Pusser, Brian, Sheila Slaughter, and Scott L. Thomas. 2006. "Playing the Board Game: An Empirical Analysis of University Trustee and Corporate Board Interlocks." *Journal of Higher Education* 77 (5): 747–75.

Quackenbush, Jeff. 2019. "California Ballot Bid Seeks to Remove Prop. 13 Commercial Property Tax Cap to Fund Schools, Hospitals, Government." *North Bay Business Journal*, November 26, 2109.

Quinn, Sarah. 2012. "The Hidden Credit State: A Sociology of Federal Credit Programs in the United States." Unpublished paper, Department of Sociology, University of Washington.

———. 2017. "'The Miracles of Bookkeeping': How Budget Politics Link Fiscal Policies and Financial Markets." *American Journal of Sociology* 123 (1): 48–85.

———. 2019. *American Bonds: How Credit Markets Shaped a Nation*. Princeton, NJ: Princeton University Press.

Quinterno, John. 2012. *The Great Cost Shift: How Higher Education Cuts Undermine the Future of the Middle Class*. New York: Demos. https://www.demos.org/research/great-cost-shift-how-higher-education-cuts-undermine-future-middle-class.

Rappeport, Alan. 2016. "Hillary Clinton's College Plan Appeals to the Left, but Educators Have Doubts." *New York Times*, September 29, 2016.

"Rating Action: Moody's Downgrades University of California to Aa2 and Assigns Aa2 to $950M of GRBs; Outlook Stable." *Moody's Investor Service*, March 12, 2014. https://www.moodys.com/research/Moodys-downgrades-University-of-California-to-Aa2-and-assigns-Aa2--PR_294817.

"Reauthorization of the Higher Education Act of 1965: Hearings Before the Subcommittee on Education, Arts and Humanities of the Committee on Labor and Human Resources: United States Senate: One Hundred Second Congress, Part 1." 1991. Washington, DC: Government Printing Office. https://files.eric.ed.gov/fulltext/ED342332.pdf and https://files.eric.ed.gov/fulltext/ED340282.pdf.

Richard, Titmuss. 1970. *The Gift Relationship. From Human Blood to Social Policy*. New York: New Press.

Ripan, Obaidul Haque. 2013. "Do Hedge Funds and Insiders Love Education Management Corp (EDMC)?" *Insider Monkey*, April 19, 2013. https://www.insidermonkey.com/blog/do-hedge-funds-and-insiders-love-education-management-corp-edmc-122248/.

Ritter, Dan. 2014. "3 of the Biggest Hedge Fund Failures Ever." *USA Today*, June 4, 2014.

Rivera, Lauren A. 2016. *Pedigree: How Elite Students Get Elite Jobs*. Princeton, NJ: Princeton University Press.

Romer, Christina D. 1992. "What Ended the Great Depression?" *Journal of Economic History* 52 (4): 757–84.

Rosen, Michael. 2010. "Hedge Funds Target For-Profit Colleges." *Mid Coast Views*, June 9, 2010. http://midcoastviews.blogspot.com/2010/06/hedge-funds-target-for-profit-colleges.html.

"Rutgers' Center for Innovation in Worker Organization at SMLR Hosts 'Bargaining for the Common Good' Convening." 2019. Rutgers School of Management and Labor Relations, New_Brunswick, NJ. https://smlr.rutgers.edu/news/rutgers'-center-innovation-worker-organization-smlr-hosts-'bargaining-common-good'-convening.

Sanders, Bernard. 2015. "Statement by Senator Bernard Sanders on the College for All Act." May 19, 2015. https://www.sanders.senate.gov/wp-content/uploads/Sanders-statement-College-for-All-Act-2015.pdf.

Sarin, Natasha, and Larry Summers. 2020. "Understanding the Revenue Potential of Tax Compliance Investment." NBER Working Paper No. 27571, National Bureau of Economic Research, Cambridge, MA.

Saul, Stephanie. 2015. "For-Profit College Operator EDMC Will Forgive Student Loans." *New York Times*, November 17, 2015.

———. 2017. "The Paradise Papers: Endowments Boom as Colleges Bury Endowments Overseas." *New York Times*, November 8, 2017.

Saul, Stephanie, and Matt Flegenheimer. 2016. "Hillary Clinton Embraces Ideas from Bernie Sanders's College Tuition Plan." *New York Times*, July 6, 2016.

Schulze-Cleven, Tobias, Tilman Reitz, Jens Maesse, and Johannes Angermuller. 2017. "The New Political Economy of Higher Education: Between Distributional Conflicts and Discursive Stratification." *Higher Education* 73 (6): 795–812.

Scott, W. Richard, and Michael W. Kirst. 2017. *Higher Education and Silicon Valley: Connected but Conflicted*. Baltimore, MD: Johns Hopkins University Press.

Seamster, Louise, and Raphaël Charron-Chénier. 2017. "Predatory Inclusion and Education Debt: Rethinking the Racial Wealth Gap." *Social Currents* 4 (3): 199–207.

Selby-Green, Michael. 2018. "Ranked: The 10 Biggest Hedge Funds in the US." *Business Insider*, May 18, 2018.

Shapiro, Thomas M. 2004. *The Hidden Cost of Being African American: How Wealth Perpetuates Inequality*. New York: Oxford University Press.

Shireman, Robert. 2017. "Learn Now, Pay Later: A History of Income-Contingent Student Loans in the United States." *The Annals of the American Academy of Political and Social Science* 671 (1): 184–201.

———. 2019. "The Sketchy Legal Ground for Online Revenue Sharing." *Inside Higher Ed*, October 30, 2019. https://www.insidehighered.com/digital-learning/views/2019/10/30/shaky-legal-ground-revenue-sharing-agreements-student-recruitment.

Shleifer, Andrei, and Lawrence H. Summers. 1988. "Breach of Trust in Hostile Takeovers." In *Corporate Takeovers: Causes and Consequences*, edited by Alan J. Auerbach, 33–56. Chicago: University of Chicago Press.

Skocpol, Theda. 1995. *Protecting Soldiers and Mothers*. Cambridge, MA: Harvard University Press.

Smith, Randall. 2013. "Dartmouth Controversy Reflects Quandary for Endowments." *New York Times*, January 2, 2013.

Son, Hugh, and Pamela Roux. 2015. "Jaime Dimon Is Now a Billionaire and He Got There in an Unusual Way." *Bloomberg*, June 3, 2015.

Starr, Paul. 1982. *The Social Transformation of American Medicine*. New York: Basic.

Stearns, Linda Brewster. 1986. "Capital Market Effects on External Control of Corporations." *Theory and Society* 15 (1–2): 47–75.

Steinbaum, Marshall, Eric Harris Bernstein, and John Sturm. 2018. *Powerless: How Lax Antitrust and Concentrated Market Power Rig the Economy Against American Workers, Consumers, and Communities*. New York: Roosevelt Institute. https://rooseveltinstitute.org/publications/powerless-lax-antitrust-concentrated-market-power-rig-economy-workers-consumers-communities/.

Stevens, Mitchell L. 2009. *Creating a Class: College Admissions and the Education of Elites*. Cambridge, MA: Harvard University Press.

Stevens, Mitchell L., Elizabeth A. Armstrong, and Richard Arum. 2008. "Sieve, Incubator, Temple, Hub: Empirical and Theoretical Advances in the Sociology of Higher Education." *Annual Review of Sociology* 34:127–51.

Stevens, Mitchell L., and Ben Gebre-Medhin. 2016. "Association, Service, Market: Higher Education in American Political Development." *Annual Review of Sociology* 42:121–42.

Stevens, Mitchell L., and Michael Kirst. 2015. *Remaking College: The Changing Ecology of Higher Education*. Stanford, CA: Stanford University Press.

Stewart, James B. 2018. "College Endowments Opt for Alternative, and Less Lucrative, Route." *New York Times*, February 4, 2018.

Stiglitz, Joseph E. 2000. *Globalization and Its Discontents*. New York: Norton.

Strike Debt. 2012. "The Debt Resistors' Operations Manual." https://strikedebt.org/The-Debt-Resistors-Operations-Manual.pdf.

Sullivan, Kathleen J. 2013. "Robert M. Bass Returning to Stanford's Board of Trustees." *Stanford Report*, August 9, 2013. https://news.stanford.edu/news/2013/august/trustee-robert-bass-080913.html.

Swidler, Ann. 1986. "Culture in Action: Symbols and Strategies." *American Sociological Review* 51 (2): 273–86.

Taylor, Astra. 2016. "Universities Are Becoming Billion-Dollar Hedge Funds with Schools Attached." *The Nation*, March 4, 2016.

Thurston, Chloe N. 2018. *At the Boundaries of Homeownership: Credit, Discrimination, and the American State*. New York: Cambridge University Press.

Tilly, Chris. 1991. "Understanding Income Inequality." *Sociological Forum* 6 (4): 739–56.

Tobin, James. 1974. "What Is Permanent Endowment Income?" *American Economic Review* 64 (2): 427–32.

Tomaskovic-Devey, Donald, and Ken-Hou Lin. 2011. "Income Dynamics, Economic Rents, and the Financialization of the US Economy." *American Sociological Review* 76 (4): 538–59.

Torche, Florencia. 2011. "Is a College Degree Still the Great Equalizer? Intergenerational Mobility across Levels of Schooling in the United States." *American Journal of Sociology* 117 (3): 763–807.

Toutsi, Cristin. 2010. *2010 Policies, Practices, and Composition of Higher Education Coordinating Boards and Commissions.* Washington, DC: Association of Governing Boards of Colleges and Universities. https://agb.org/sites/default/files/legacy/2010CompositionSurvey_Report.pdf.

"The TWLF Marching on Sproul Plaza." 1969. *The Berkeley Revolution.* https://revolution.berkeley.edu/manuel-delgado-leading-twlf-sproul/.

UC News Room. 2012. "Regents Endorse Gov. Brown's Tax Initiative." July 18, 2012. https://link.ucop.edu/2012/07/24/uc-regents-endorse-prop-30-gov-brown's-tax-initiative/.

Unz, Ron. 2012. "Paying Tuition to a Giant Hedge Fund." *American Conservative.* December 4, 2012. https://www.theamericanconservative.com/articles/paying-tuition-to-a-giant-hedge-fund/.

Urbi, Jaden. 2019. "How the Ivy League Stays So Rich: College Endowments." *CNBC*, March 30, 2019. https://www.cnbc.com/2019/03/29/how-the-ivy-league-stays-so-rich-college-endowments.html.

US Census Bureau. 2017. "Educational Attainment in the United States: 2017." Washington, DC. https://www.census.gov/data/tables/2017/demo/education-attainment/cps-detailed-tables.html.

US Department of Education. 2009. "Top 100 Originators of FFELP Loans—FY08 and FY07." Washington, DC. https://ifap.ed.gov/sites/default/files/attachments/2019-05/2008Top100originatorspublicreport.xls.

———. 2017. "Servicer Portfolio by Loan Status." Washington, DC. https://studentaid.gov/sites/default/files/ServicerPortfoliobyLoanStatus123117.xls.

US Senate Committee on Health Education Labor and Pensions. 2012. *For Profit Higher Education: The Failure to Safeguard the Federal Investment and Ensure Student Success, Majority Committee Staff Report.* July 30, 2012. Washington, DC: Government Printing Office.

Useem, Michael. 1993. *Executive Defense: Shareholder Power and Corporate Reorganization.* Cambridge, MA: Harvard University Press.

Uzzi, Brian. 1999. "Embeddedness in the Making of Financial Capital: How Social Relations and Networks Benefit Firms Seeking Financing." *American Sociological Review* 64 (4): 481–505.

Vaisey, Stephen, and Andrew Miles. 2014. "What You Can—and Can't—Do with Three-Wave Panel Data." *Sociological Methods and Research* 46 (1): 44–67.

Vandevelde, Mark, and Lindsay Fortado. 2018. "US States Move to Close Carried Interest Loophole." *Financial Times*, May 2, 2018.

Vara, Vauhini. 2017. "The Occupy Movement Takes on Student Debt." *New Yorker*, September 17, 2017.

Varner, Charles, and Cristobal Young. 2012. "Millionaire Migration in California: The Impact of Top Tax Rates." *National Tax Journal* 64 (2): 255–84.

Volden, Craig, Jonathan Wai, and Alan E. Wiseman. 2020. "Elite Education, Liberalism, and Effective Lawmaking in the U.S. Congress." Association for Public Policy Analysis and Management Annual Meeting, Center for Effective Lawmaking Working Paper, Charlottesville, VA. https://thelawmakers.org/wp-content/uploads/2020/05/Working-Paper-CEL-Elite-Education-and-Legislative-Effectiveness-1.pdf.

Waldman, Steven. 1996. *The Bill: How Legislation Really Becomes Law: A Case Study of the National Service Bill.* New York: Penguin.

Walker, Edward T., and Christopher M. Rea. 2014. "The Political Mobilization of Firms and Industries." *Annual Review of Sociology* 40 (1): 281–304.

Warren, Elizabeth. 2020. "My Plan to Cancel Student Loan Debt on Day One of My Presidency." *Medium,* January 14, 2020. https://medium.com/@teamwarren/my-plan-to-cancel-student-loan-debt-on-day-one-of-my-presidency-fd12c3f5ebb5.

Webber, Douglas A. 2017. "State Divestment and Tuition at Public Institutions." *Economics of Education Review* 60:1–4.

Weerts, David, Thomas Sanfordeah, and Leah Reinert. 2012. *College Funding in Context: Understanding the Difference in Higher Education Appropriations across the States.* New York: Demos. https://www.demos.org/research/college-funding-context-understanding-difference-higher-education-appropriations-across.

Weir, Margaret, Ann Shola Orloff, and Theda Skocpol. 1988. *The Politics of Social Policy in the United States.* New York: Taylor and Francis.

Weissman, Robert, James Donahue, Harvey Rosenfield, Jennifer Wedekind, Marcia Carroll, Charlie Cray, Peter Maybarduk, Tom Bollier, and Paulo Barbone. 2009. *Sold Out: How Wall Street and Washington Betrayed America.* Washington, DC: Essential Information. http://wallstreetwatch.org/reports/sold_out.pdf.

Weitzman, Aaron. 2019. "Top 25 Muni Underwriters of 2018." *The Bond Buyer,* January 16, 2019. https://www.bondbuyer.com/list/top-25-municipal-underwriters-of-2018.

Wherry, Frederick F. 2012. *The Culture of Markets.* Malden, MA: Polity.

Wherry, Frederick F., Kristin S. Seefeldt, and Anthony S. Alvarez. 2019. *Credit Where It's Due: Rethinking Financial Citizenship.* New York: Russell Sage.

Whyte, Amy. 2018. "David Swensen Wrote an Angry Email. Then He Pressed Send." *Institutional Investor,* May 10, 2018.

Will, George. 2017. "The Republicans Take Aim at Academic Excellence." *Washington Post,* November 3, 2017.

Wilson, R. 1987. "Two Banking Industry Representatives Play Key Lobbying Role on Student Loans." *Chronicle of Higher Education.* April 15, 1987, 26.

Wilson, William Julius, and Robert Aponte. 2009. "Urban Poverty." *Annual Review of Sociology* 11 (1985): 231–58.

Yan, Sophia. 2009. "The 10 Best College Presidents." *Time,* November 1, 2009. https://web.archive.org/web/20091115063732/http://www.time.com/time/specials/packages/article/0,28804,1937938_1937933_1937940,00.html.

Young, Cristobal. 2017. *The Myth of Millionaire Tax Flight: How Place Still Matters for the Rich.* Stanford, CA: Stanford University Press.

Zaloom, Caitlin. 2019. *Indebted: How Families Make College Work at Any Cost.* Princeton, NJ: Princeton University Press.

Zelizer, Viviana A. 2009. *The Purchase of Intimacy.* Princeton, NJ: Princeton University Press.

———. 2013. *Economic Lives: How Culture Shapes the Economy.* Princeton, NJ: Princeton University Press.

Zhu, Jane M., Lynn M. Hua, and Daniel Polsky. 2020. "Private Equity Acquisitions of Physician Medical Groups across Specialties, 2013–2016." *Journal of the American Medical Association* 323 (7): 663–65.

INDEX

Abel, Andrea, 12, 146
accumulation by dispossession, 74–75
Action Center on Race and Economy, 131–32
Addo, Fenaba, 94
admissions policies: barriers to qualified students at elite universities and, 56–57; at California public universities, 101–2; earnings and education levels of families of students and, 156n48; elite universities endowment wealth and selectivity and, 55–56, 163n55; legacy admissions at elite universities and, 29; selectivity linked to financier support of, 34–35; stasis in, 1–2, 71–73, 102
advertising campaigns of for-profit colleges, 88–89
affirmative action, ban at California public universities, 101–2, 129
affordability, ideology of, public university funding and, 99–101
Affordable Care Act, elimination of student loan guarantee subsidy in, 52–53
African American students. *See* Black students
AFSCME, 135; education coalitions with, 129–31
alumni networks: bargaining with bankers strategy and, 125–27; college governing board representation and, 32–34; financiers' recruitment and hiring strategies and, 30–31; privatization of student loan program and, 49, 80–84; at public universities, 32, 99–102, 118–21; social ties of investors and, 80–84, 87; tax increase mobilization and, 126–27
American Bankers Association, 21–22
American Council on Capital formation, 42, 58–59
American Council on Education (ACE), 40–42; student loan program expansion and, 47–49
American Federation of Teachers, 135
American Military University, 89
American Public University, 89
Anderson, Perry, 124
Apollo Global Management, 62
Appel, Hannah, 12, 133–34, 146
Arizona State University, 120–21
asset management services: college endowments and, 24–25; market share of, 25
Association of Californians for Community Empowerment (ACCE), 122, 128, 131, 135
attendance rates for college, decline in US college attainment relative to OECD countries, 5–8
Atwell, Bob, 44
automation, endowments and, 57–60

Bain Capital, 103
ballot initiative campaigns, tax increases and use of, 126–32
banking industry: college and legislators' ties to, 46–49; financial crisis of 2008 and, 52–53; influence on tax cut policies of, 42–43; money monopoly and, 17; student debt and power of, 49–51; student loan program expansion and, 2–4, 14, 45–46, 141; subsidies for student loan programs and, 38; transformation of higher education and, 22–28
Bank of America, 24–25
bargaining with bankers strategy: borderland actors and, 125–26; financing equity for higher education and, 123; future uses for, 143; higher education funding and, 15;

bargaining with bankers strategy (*continued*)
millionaire tax initiative coalition and, 130–32; national expansion of, 131–32; private nonprofit colleges and universities, 132–38; public universities' use of, 104, 126–32
Baruch, Jordan, 60
Bass, Robert, 70
Baupost Group, 54, 60
Berman, Elizabeth Popp, 45, 47, 149
Best, Victor, 80
Biden, Joe, 137–38, 141–42
Binder, Amy, 12, 146
Birgeneau, Robert, 109–11, 120, 148
Black, Fischer, 58
Black, Leon, 62
Black Lives Matter, 138
BlackRock, 24
Black students: education gospel and, 79–80; enrollment and marketing by for-profit colleges targeted to, 87–88, 93–94; enrollment at elite, selective, and public universities, 156n48; enrollment at for-profit universities of, 77–78, 93–94; enrollment at public universities of, 73; student debt burden of, 6, 93–94, 112–14, 138, 139; underrepresentation at elite schools, 29
Blakely, William, 49
Bloom, Nick, 12, 146
blue-collar jobs, college enrollment demand increase and loss of, 43–44, 101–2
Blum, Richard, 15, 98–101, 106–11, 121–23, 129–30, 149
board interlock, bankers and corporations and, 42
bond market borrowing: enrollment growth and, 111–12; financial services underwriting of, 24–25; limitations of, 120–21; public university funding and, 15, 99–101, 107–10; student debt increase linked to, 114–17
borderland actors: financial elites and, 21–22; higher education equity reforms and, 125–26
borrowing caps, elimination of, 45–46, 51–52
Brady, Henry, 151
Brandeis, Louis, 17, 20, 157n1
Brandeis University Institute on Assets and Social Policy, 138
British universities, elite financial social ties and, 62
Brock, Alyssa, 85–86, 88–94, 97
Brostrom, Nathan, 107, 109
Brown, Jerry, 127–28, 130–31
Brown University, 76, 95
Buchanan, Bill, 87–90
Buffet, Warren, 20, 76
Bundy, McGeorge, 57–58
Bureau of Economic Analysis, 154
Bush, George W., 30
Business-financier-conservative coalition: deregulation promotion by, 58–59; higher education funding and, 41–43; tax cuts and deregulation policies, role in, 21–22, 36–37
Business Roundtable, 42

Cal Grants: to for-profit colleges, 105; for low-income UC students, 112; state funding of, 119, 129
California Calls, 126–28
California Federation of Labor, 130–31
California Federation of Teachers, 126, 128
California Legislative Analyst Office, 154
California State University System: admissions stasis at, 101–2; diversion of low-income students to, 110–12; funding squeeze at, 12; Master Plan for higher education and, 101–2; mobilization for higher education equity on campuses of, 127; Proposition 30 endorsement by, 130–31; tax avoidance and subsidy capture impact on, 101–5; underfunding and over enrollment at, 100–101
California Teachers Association, 130
CalSERVE student political party, 128
campaign contributions, financial sector spending on, 42–43
cancellation of student debt: political pressure for, 135–38; proposals for, 15, 53, 85, 93, 97, 123–24; prospects for, 139–43
capital: bond market borrowing and revenue from, 108–10; college endowments as source of, 22–24, 28–34, 60; elite social ties and resources of, 30; for federal student loans, 78–80; institutional investment as source of, 59; investment returns linked to, 66; reserves, corporate decline in, 21; shareholder value and, 95–97
capital gains taxes: cuts and caps on, 21–22; endowments and, 73–74; investment strategies and, 59

Cardoso, Fernando Enrique, 124
Career Education Corporation, 165n40
Carleton Group, 42
Carnegie, Andrew, 20
carried interest loopholes, private equity and hedge fund growth and, 101–5
Cerberus Partners, 61
Charlson, Joe, 88
Chetty, Raj, 73
Chicago Board of Trade, 58–59
Chronicle of Philanthropy, 70–71
Citigroup, 24–25
City University of New York, 12
civic leaders, coalition building for university equity and, 125–26
civil rights, higher education funding and, 10
class politics: student loan programs and, 36–39; unequal access to public universities and, 110–12
Clinton, Bill, 38–39, 48
Clotfelter, Charles, 55–56
Clyburn, James, 137
Cohen, Milton, 58
collaboration, among financiers and elites, 2–3, 17, 37, 82–87
college attainment, decline of US relative to OECD countries, 5–8
college endowments: consolidated financial service corporations and, 24–25; institutional investments by, 31, 57–60; investment strategies for, 22; private equity and hedge funds and, 27–28; social ties and, 28–34; as wealth source, 21
College Scorecard, 154
Columbia University, endowment investment at, 95
Commercial Bankers Associations, 45–46
commercialization of public universities, 117–21
community colleges: debt-free funding of, 142; diversion of low-income students to, 110–12; earnings and graduation rates for, 91–92; enrollment growth at, 10; underfunding of, 44, 51, 93–94, 100–101
compensation: consolidated financial service corporation CEOs, 25; of hedge fund and private equity managers, 25–28; of investment bankers, 25
computational methods, investment management and, 58
Congress: cancellation of student debt legislation and, 138; debt cancellation proposals in, 136–38; higher education funding and, 39–41, 104–5; student loan subsidies and regulations and, 78–80
consolidated financial service corporations: activities of, 24–25; alumni networks as recruiting tool for, 30–31; formation of, 22; as higher education financial intermediary, 22–24
Consumer Bankers Association, 38–39, 48–49, 52–53; student debt and power of, 49–51
consumers: finance and expropriation of, 75, 77–79, 107; market concentration costs for, 25; nonprofit alternatives for, 79–80
Copeland, Charles, 20
Corinthian Colleges, 87–90, 93–94, 97, 134–36
Cornell University, 95
corporate debt instruments, growth of finance and, 21
corporations. *See* publicly traded corporations: financial governance of, 87–90
Cottom, Tressie McMillan, 7, 12, 43–44, 77, 79–80, 94, 146
county tax assessment, property tax avoidance and, 103–5
Courage Campaign, 126, 128
COVID–19 pandemic, equity in higher education and, 139–43
Creamer, Glenn, 83
credit access, student debt as barrier to, 91
crowd out process: for-profit college enrollment growth and, 96–97; public university enrollment stasis and, 111–12
cultural organizations, philanthropic homophily and, 69–73

Davis, Daniel, 12, 146
Davis, Gray, 98, 106
Dean, John, 38–39, 45–52
Debt Collective, 124–26, 133–36
debt-free financial aid proposals, 131–32, 137, 142–43
debt leveraging: deregulation and, 81–82; endowments and, 58–60; private equity and hedge funds, 26–28; risks of, 61

debt strikes, 135–38
Debt Resistor's Operations Manual, The, 133
defaults on student debt, 6, 51, 90–94; Black students' share of, 94; of for-profit *vs.* public and nonprofit institutions, 91–93; at public universities, 114
Delgado, Manuel, 101–2
Democratic Party, millionaire tax coalition and, 129; support for debt cancellation and free college of, 136–142
Demos think tank, 137
deregulation: banking's power concerning, 49–51; business, financial elites and conservative coalition push for, 21–22; commercialization of public universities and, 118–21; demise of blue-collar jobs and, 43–44; as economic stimulus, 36–37; endowments and, 57–60; financial crisis of 2008 and, 52–53; financial sector influence on, 3–4, 42–43; higher education inequality and, 4–8; private equity and hedge fund groups and, 26–28; social circuitry of finance and, 19; student loan expansion as, 77–80
derivatives: deregulation and, 22; endowments and, 58–59
DeVos, Betsy, 136, 138
DeVry corporation, 103
digital technology, students' private information extraction using, 88
Dimon, Jamie, 25
direct loans: at public universities, 46–47, 51; US Department of Education management of, 46–49
disclosure requirements, public university investments and, 62, 66
distributional conflicts, 36–39; 41, 44, 46, 49, 123, 132; endowment wealth and, 55–56; student loan expansion failure to alleviate, 51
Donin, Robert B., 61–62, 65
Du Bois, W. E. B., 12, 79
Duncan, Arnie, 135–36
Du Pont, Luisa D'Anbelot, 20
Dupont Corporation, 20

earnings from college: of for-profit college students, 85, 91–94; student debt burden and, 51
economic activity, education spending in US as share of, 7–8
educational mobility: enrollment growth at public universities, 71–73; financialization and commercialization of public universities and, 117–21; mythology of, 79–80; public universities and, 100–101; US relative decline in, 5
educational organizations, philanthropic homophily and, 69–73
education gospel: demise of blue-collar jobs and, 43–44; enrollment demand at public universities and, 101–2; middle-class borrowing decisions and, 79–80
education labor unions, 131–32
Education Management Corporation (EDMC), 76, 83–91, 95, 97, 103, 135, 166n63
education spending, by elite colleges, 1, 56, 71–73; by for-profits, 94; on higher education as share of US economic activity, 7–8; on higher education by federal government and states, 40; by public universities, 99–101, 119
elite college graduates: income share owned by, 21; information asymmetries and social ties of, 29–32; public universities and, 101–2; social ties of, 26–28
elite college sports: admission stasis and support for, 73; public university support for, 108–10; social ties of financiers and, 49
elite universities: comparative qualitative and quantitative study of, 145–55; debt-free funding at, 142; donations to, 68–73, 164n76; endowment wealth at, 11–12, 54–57; federally funded access to, 9–10; financiers and, 4–8; financier tax avoidance and endowments of, 103–5; hedge funds and, 14, 73–75; hoarding of endowments at, 51–52, 56, 73; investment in for-profit universities by, 95–97; legislators from, 49; nonstudent engagement in, 32–34; per student spending at, 156n50; philanthropic homophily and, 70–73; power of financiers at, 2–4; quantitative data on, 150–55; social circuitry of finance and, 19; social ties at, 28–34; spending on students at, 1; student debt at, 1–2, 6–8, 155n6; student loan revenue at, 11–12; wealthy social ties in, 20–21
embeddedness, of social and economic ties, 28–29

Employment Retirement Income Security Acts (1974 & 1978), 59–60
"Endowment Funds: The Law and the Lore" (Bundy), 57–58, 149
endowments of universities: capital investment and, 66; data on, 162n7; deregulation, automation and institutional investment, 57–60; donations to, 68–73, 164n76; financial crisis of 2008 impact on, 66–68; financier tax avoidance and, 103–5; high-finance advantage and, 57, 65–68; hoarding of, 51–52, 56, 73; investment in for-profit universities and, 95–97; social ties and investments by, 60–65, 163n54; tax breaks for, 98–101; taxing proposals for, 142–43; tax on, 74; total wealth statistics for, 54–57
enrollment in higher education: African American and Latinx share of, 10, 146n49; bond market borrowing and student debt tradeoff and demand for, 114–17; at for-profit universities, 10, 77–78, 84–85, 90; government funding of higher education and, 39–40; growth in, 10, 37–38, 51–52; increased demand for, 43–44; in-state enrollment stasis at public universities, 108–12, 131–32; older and financially needy students and, 43–44; out-of-state enrollment, 109–10; public university underfunding and over enrollment and, 99–102; stasis in elite universities of, 1–2, 71–73; stratification in, 29; student loans and expansion of, 51–52
entitlement grants, federal programs and, 9–10
Espinoza, Max, 128–30, 148
ethnic minorities, inequality in educational funding for, 10
extractive connections, elite investment and, 75

facilities construction at public universities, bond financing of, 108–10
faculty compensation: at elite universities, 73; endowment wealth and disparities in, 56–57; inequality in, 158n50
Faletto, Enzo, 124
Fannie Mae corporation, 24, 50
Farallon Capital, 31, 61
farmworker movement, 125
Faust, Drew Gilpin, 54
Federal Credit Reform Act of 1990, 46
federal education funding, 39–41, 104–5; nonprofit colleges and universities and, 132–38
federalist politics, social welfare and, 9–10
federal student loans. *See* student loan programs
Feinstein, Dianne, 106, 129
Fidelity, 24
financial aid administrators, commercial lenders' ties to, 48–49
financial big bang strategy: borderland actors and, 125–26; coalitions, borderland actors and strategic innovation in, 124–26; equity for higher education and, 123; future uses for, 143; nonprofit colleges and universities and, 132–38
financial crisis of 2008: banking industry and, 52–53; high-finance advantage and impact of, 65; impact on for-profit college students of, 84–85; public universities and impact of, 110; weakening of social ties following, 66–68
financial oligarchy: lack of market competition and, 25; new generation of, 18–19; private equity, hedge funds, and, 25–34, 54–55; rise early in US of, 17; transformation of higher education by, 22–28
financial sector, share of income and profits, 20–21
financiers: college governing board membership of, 34–35; elite ties of, 13–14, 29–34; financial dependence and control by, 11–12; future in higher education of, 139–43; influence on tax cut policies of, 42–43; philanthropic homily and, 68–73; power elite and, 19–22; public university financialization and commercialization and, 117–21; public university funding and role of, 99–101; revolving door between government and, 42; social circuitry of finance and, 17–19; sponsorship of campus buildings and public events, 32–34; state funding declines for higher education and role of, 101–5; student exploitation by, 77–78; subsidies for student loan programs and, 38; tax increases for, 126–32; unidirectional intimacy and obfuscation by, 87–90; university ties and power of, 2–4

Florida and Midwest Career Colleges, 90, 95
food stamps, 9–10, 132
Forbes 400: college governing board members from, 33–34; financiers and elite university alumni as members of, 31–32; public university alumni in, 32; social ties of elite institutions and membership in, 29
for-profit universities: cancellation of student debt and, 136–38; closure of, 97; community college competition with, 93; educational and income mobility myth and, 5; enrollment growth at, 10, 77–78, 84–85; graduation rate decline at, 84–85; hedge funds and, 66–68; information asymmetries at, 87–90; intimate ties in predation by, 85–90; investment in, 11–12, 75, 76–78; nonprofit and public university investment in, 95–97; Pell Grants as subsidies for, 77–78, 96–97, 105; poor student outcomes at, 91–94; predatory behavior of, 76–78, 85–86, 91–94; private equity transformation of, 2–8, 66–68, 82–85; private information of students extracted by, 88; privatization of higher education and, 118–20; profit margins of investors in, 95–96; property tax avoidance by, 103–5; recruitment tactics of, 85–90; state subsidies for, 105; student debt at, 11–12, 157n52; student loan expansion and, 14–15, 38–39, 51–52, 78–80; tuition revenue at, 4–8, 80, 84–85; unidirectional intimacy and obfuscation in investor ownership at, 87–90; vocational emphasis at, 79–80
fraud-related law enforcement actions, for-profit colleges and, 85, 93
free-market mythology: invocation in privatization of student loan program, 48; public university finances and, 98–101; social ties and, 82–85

Gamble, Joelle, 137
Ganz, Marshall, 125
Gates, Bill, 76
Generation Progress, 135
Gibadullina, Albina, 13, 28, 32–34, 151–52
GI Bill programs, 9–10, 45–46
Giving Pledge, 76
Gladwell, Malcolm, 56
Golden, Daniel, 70
Goldman Sachs, 76, 84
Goldstein, Alexis, 136, 151
Goodkin, Michael, 58
governing boards of colleges and universities: academic and extracurricular structures, financier members' influence on, 34–35; competition among elites for membership on, 34–35; financial elite representation on, 59–60; financier representation on, 14, 19, 22, 32–34, 105–10; financiers influence on investment by, 61–65, 163n54; philanthropic homophily and, 71–73; public university boards, financiers on, 105–10; ties to banking and lawmakers of, 46–49
government, revolving door between finance and, 42
government funding: diversion from public and less elite colleges, 4–8, 98–99; financier role in tax avoidance and reduction of, 101–5; of higher education, 39–43; of for-profit colleges, 97; of subsidies for private federal student loan originators, 36–39
graduate students: loan expansion for, 51; mobilization for millionaire tax initiative among, 127–32
graduation rates: decline in US college attainment relative to OECD, 5–8, 51; for-profit colleges and drop in, 84–85, 91–94; in online programs, 120–21; for public university low-income students, 99–101, 112
Granholm, Jennifer, 62
grant programs: government spending on, 39–40; for low-income students, 99–101, 108–10, 119; at public universities, 46–47, 51, 109–10; tax cuts and impact on, 8–10, 37–42, 157n52
Great Society programs, 132; higher education access and, 9–10, 39
Green, Kenneth, 150
Greenpoint Mortgage, 87
gross domestic product (GDP), tax avoidance and, 103–4
guaranteed student loan (GSL) program, 45–46, 48–49; demise of, 52–53

Hacker, Jacob, 37, 41, 42
Hamilton, Darrick, 137

Hamilton, Laura, 12, 79, 146, 151
Hansmann, Henry, 79
Harvard Business School (HBS), 69; fund-raising campaign of, 54
Harvard Corporation Committee, 54
Harvard University: debt-free undergraduate education at, 1, 142; endowment investment at, 54; endowment losses, 68; development of hedge funds and, 60–61
Head Start, 9–10, 132
Heald College chain, 103
health care, private equity entry into, 82
hedge funds: alumni from elite universities in, 28–34, 54–57; capital gains tax cuts and growth of, 101–5; earnings of employees in, 27–28; elite endowments as, 55–57; elite university ties of, 3–4, 14, 19, 60–65, 73–75, 163n54; fees paid to, 68; formation of, 22; for-profit colleges and, 89, 94–95; growth in earnings of, 54–57; as higher education financial intermediary, 22–24; high-finance advantage of, 65–68; income of managers in, 25–28; information asymmetries in social ties of, 29–32; investment strategies of, 27–28; philanthropic homophily and, 71–73; predatory financial extraction and unequal intimacies of, 94–97; recruiting from elite institutions by, 30–31, 34–35, 54–57; shareholder value and, 80–82; social ties of, 26–28, 82–85; university endowment investments and, 2–8, 54, 95; university investments and, 60–65
Heiney, Mallory, 135
higher education: bottom-up reimagining of, 122–43; coalitions, borderland actors and strategic innovation for equity in, 124–26; consolidated financial service corporations and, 24–25; endowment wealth and, 55–57; equity and empowerment activism and, 97, 123–24; financial dependence and control of, 11–12; of financial elites, 13–14; financial elite transformation of, 22–28; financial restructuring of, 38–39; future of financiers in, 139–43; government funding of, 8–10, 39–43; inclusive and equitable funding proposals for, 15; increased demand for, 43–44; market ideology and equity in, 106–10; organization of financial intermediaries in, 22–24, 32–34, 156n33; private equity and hedge fund groups ties to, 26–28; public universities role in, 101–2; shareholder value and exploitation of, 82; social benefits of, 8; stratification of resources and status within, 10, 51–52; subsidies, decline in US of, 7–8; tax-funded government support for, 9–10; wealth redistribution in, 77–78
Higher Education Act of 1965, 9–10, 39; borrower defense provision in, 135–37; reauthorization in 1992 of, 45–46
Higher Education DataHub, 151
Higher Education Not Debt (HEND) coalition, 135–38, 150
high-finance advantage: endowments of elite universities and, 57; public university funding and, 98–101; social circuitry of finance and, 55–57; university ties and, 65–68
historically Black colleges and universities (HBCUs), guarantee subsidies supported by, 49
Ho, Karen, 12, 146
home mortgages, securitization of, 24
hostile takeovers, publicly traded corporations, 26, 81
Hough, Larry, 14, 38–39, 45–52
Houle, Jason, 94
Howell, Sabrina, 93, 154
Hultin, Jerry, 49
Hutchins, Robert M., 9

Icahn, Carl, 20, 26
income: debt-free status of students linked to, 6; market concentration and inequality of, 25, 158n31; in private equity and hedge funds, 27–28; student debt tied to, 1–2, 112–14, 155n6
income contingent repayment (ICR), 53
income-driven loan repayment, 53, 90–91, 139, 141–142
in-depth interviews, higher education research and, 147–49
index funds, college endowments and, 24–25

inequality in higher education: bond market borrowing and student debt tradeoff and, 114–17; bottom-up reimagining of, 122–43; coalitions, borderland actors and strategic innovation for eradication of, 124–26; comparative qualitative and quantitative study of, 145–55; COVID–19 pandemic and, 139–43; elite endowments and, 55–57; equity and empowerment activism and, 97; financial deregulation and, 4–8; for-profit colleges and growth of, 77–78, 93–94; nonprofit colleges and universities and, 132–38; per-student spending, student-faculty ratios and faculty compensation disparities, 156n50; public universities and, 99–101; quantitative data on, 150–55; social circuitry of finance and, 19; social ties of elites and, 26–28, 82–85; student debt *vs.* endowment wealth and, 1–2; unequal access to public universities, 110–12

information asymmetries: elite social ties and, 30–32; public university investing and, 62–67; unidirectional intimacy, for-profit colleges and, 87–90

in-state enrollment: bond market borrowing and student debt tradeoff and, 114–17; stasis at public universities of, 108–12, 131–32; tuition revenue and, 119–21

institutional investment, endowments and, 57–60

Integrated Postsecondary Education Data System (US Department of Education), 151–54, 155n1

interest rates: caps on, 22; reduction on student loans, 53; university bond borrowing and student debt tradeoff, impact of, 116–17

intergenerational equity, endowments and, 57

Internal Revenue Service, lax enforcement by, 103, 143

intimacy: economic exchange relationships and, 19, 56; and elite universities, 28–29; for-profit colleges' exploitation of, 85–86; millionaire tax coalition use of, 129; of private equity and hedge fund relationships, 28–33, 56, 60–62; in public universities, 123–24; of public university ties, 101–2; unidirectional intimacy, 77–78, 87–97

investment banking: capital resources and, 66; earnings of employees in, 25; elite universities and, 11–12, 19; private information access and social ties in, 30–32; recruiting from elite institutions by, 34–35; social ties in, 30; university bonds and, 2–4; university endowments and, 4–8

ITT Tech, 97, 135

Jayapal, Pramila, 137

Jenkins, Gary, 19, 33

Jensen, Michael, 58

job applicants, audit studies of for-profit colleges *vs.* non-degree applicants, 91–92

Johnson, Lyndon B., 9–10, 39

Johnson, Simon, 42

JPMorgan Chase: consolidated financial services corporation, 24–25, hedge fund division of, 19

junk bonds, private equity and, 23, 26, 59, 163n40

Kaplan Corporation, 89–90, 120–21

Kerr, Clark, 101–2

KKR, 76, 81, 84, 103

Klarman, Seth, 54, 56–57, 60

Kolb, Charles, 148

Krippner, Greta, 20, 49

Kwak, James, 42

Lansing, Sherry, 128

Latinx students: enrollment at for-profit universities of, 77–78, 93–94; marketing by for-profit colleges targeted to, 87–88, 93–94; student debt burden of, 6, 93–94, 112–14, 139; underrepresentation at elite schools, 29

Leeds Equity Partners, 84, 87

legacy admissions: philanthropic homophily and, 70; social ties of elite and, 29

legislators: from elite universities, 49; ties to colleges and banking industry of, 46–49

Lehman Brothers, 30–31, 59, 107–108

leveraged buyouts, elite ties and, 14, 23, 26–31; for-profit colleges and, 61, 84–90, 95

Lewis, Michael, 12, 30, 35, 146

Livingston, Christina, 122, 131

lobbying: financial sector spending on, 42–43; social ties as tool in, 48–49

local governments, social goods delivery by, 9–10
Loftin, Tiffany, 138
Long Term Capital Management, 61
low-income students: enrollment at for-profit universities of, 77–78, 93–94; for-profit universities exploitation of, 14–15, 93–94; grants at public universities for, 108–10; loan repayment for, 85; marketing by for-profit colleges targeted to, 87–88, 93–94; public university enrollment of, 15, 71–73, 99–101; student loan risk for, 110, 112–14; unequal access to public universities for, 110–12
Lozano, Monica, 122–23, 128, 131
LTV Steel, 30
Lundberg, Erik, 62, 65
Lybarger, Kathryn, 122, 130, 131

Magaña, Claudia, 122, 127–28, 130
Malkiel, Burton, 58
Mallaby, Sebastian, 12, 146
marketing. *See also* free-market mythology: by for-profit colleges, 87–88, 93–94
Markowitz, Harry, 58
Marshall, T. H., 8, 156n34
Mason Murray, George, 101–2
McCullough, Gary, 165n40
McDowell, Robert, 90
Medicaid, 9–10; state and federal funding of, 41–42
Medicare, 9–10
meritocracy myth, higher education inequality and, 5
Merton, Robert C., 58, 61
Mervyns, 61
middle-income students: borrowing decisions in families of, 79–80; decline in higher education spending on, 44; elimination of grant support for, 47–49; at public universities, 99–101, 108–10; student loan debt risk for, 112–14, 139; student loan programs for, 9–10, 45–46, 51–52; tuition increases for, 119–21
middlemen, financiers as, 2–4
millionaire tax initiative, coalition building for, 126–32
Mills, C. Wright, 18, 19–20, 29, 157n11
Mizruchi, Mark, 42
money monopoly, formation in US of, 17
Moody's credit rating agency, 108
Morgan, J. P., 17, 20
Morgan, Julie Margetta, 137
mortgage-backed securities: financial crisis of 2008 and, 52–53; information asymmetries concerning, 30; private lenders and subsidies for, 51
Movimiento Estudiantil Chicanx de Aztlán, 128–29
multibrand strategy, for-profit colleges' adoption of, 88–90
multiracial coalitions, millionaire tax initiative and, 128
municipal bonds: consolidate financial service corporations underwriting of, 24–25; endowments indirect tax arbitrage of, 103; public university borrowing from, 15; market concentration and, 25; public universities and, 107–108, 111; and public university student debt, 114–117
mutual funds: college endowments and, 24–25; as wealth source, 21

Nathan, Scott, 54, 61
National Association for the Advancement of Colored People (NAACP), 138
National Association of College and University Business Officers Endowment Survey, 59, 153–54
National Association of Independent Colleges and Universities (NAICU), 47–49
National Consumer Law Center (NCLC), 135
National Council of Higher Education Loan Programs (NCHELP), 45–46, 49–51
National Student Loan Data System, 151, 154
Neely, Megan, 12, 30, 61, 146
Nelson, Jonathan, 14–15, 76–77, 80–84, 87, 89–91, 95
Nelson, Todd, 88
New Deal reforms, 132; banking powers and, 17
New England Institute of Art (NEIA), 14–15, 76, 80, 84–87, 90, 97
Nielsen, 12
Nielsen, Kelly, 146

noncollege training, barriers to mobility and, 7–8
non-elite public and private colleges. *See also* private nonprofit colleges and universities; public universities: diversion of government funding from, 4–8, 97–98; earnings and graduation rates at, 91–92; enrollment growth at, 10; financiers and, 4–8; public university funding and, 99–101; social ties and, 101–2, 125; student loan expansion supported by, 46–49, 79–80; student loan financing of, 11–12, 112–117
nonprofit colleges and universities. *See* private nonprofit colleges and universities
nonprofit institutions, consumers' reliance on, 79–80
Northeast Broadcasting School, 80, 82, 84

Obama, Barack, 65, 97, 135–36
Oberlin College, 95
obfuscation strategies of for-profit colleges, 87–90
Occupy Alternative Banking Working Group, 134
Occupy Wall Street, 124, 132–33
O'Connor, Edmund, 58
offshore investment corporations, endowment tax avoidance and, 103
oligarchic structure, consolidated financial service corporations and, 25
Omar, Ilhan, 137
online program managers (OPMs), 120–21, 132
Organisation for Economic Co-operation and Development (OECD): college attainment statistics, 5; education spending in US as share of economic activity, 7–8
organizational ecology, university-financial ties and, 22–24, 32–34, 156n33
Ostrower, Francie, 69–70
Other People's Money and How the Bankers Use It (Brandeis), 17
out-of-state enrollment at public universities, tuition revenue from, 109–10, 119–21

Paradise Papers leak, 103
Parent Loan for Undergraduate Students (PLUS), 46–47, 51
Paulson, John, 30, 54
Pearson OPM, 120–21
Pechthalt, Josh, 122
Pell, Claiborne, 39, 44
Pell Grants: establishment of, 9–10, 157n52; expansion of, 40; to for-profit university students, 77–78, 96–97, 105; increased funding for, 52–53, 142; per student spending declines and, 41–42, 46–47, 52; at public universities, 99–101
pension funds: as capital source, 59; information asymmetries and management of, 30–32; investment strategies for, 22, 58; redistributive policy change and, 132–33; as wealth source, 21
PepsiCo, 88
Pérez, John A., 128–31, 148
Perlman, Liz, 131
Perry, Andre M., 140
per-student spending: admission stasis linked to, 71–72; at California public universities, 101–2; declines in, 41–42; endowment wealth and, 56–57; inequality in elite *vs.* non-elite schools of, 156n50; older financially students and, 43–44; at public universities, 99–101; reductions in, 51; by state and federal government, 39–40
philanthropic homophily: elite endowments and, 56–67; endowments of elite universities and, 68–73
Philanthropy, 50, 70–71
philanthropy, elite social status and, 34–35
Pierson, Paul, 37, 41, 42
Piketty, Thomas, 66, 73–74
politics: business, financial elites and conservative coalition and, 21–22; public university funding and, 106–10; social ties in, 42–43; state taxes and, 106–10; of student loan programs, 52–53
Poorvu, Bill, 54, 60
popcorn challenge recruitment strategy, 88
power elite, financiers and, 19–22
Power Elite, The (Mills), 18, 19–20
predatory financial extraction: by for-profit colleges, 76–78, 85–86, 90–94; intimate ties at for-profit colleges and, 85–86; reforms for slowing of, 97; social goods and, 79; unidirectional intimacy and, 94–97

prestige, 13, 19, 34–35, 54, 119, 157
Princeton Resource Committee, 96
Princeton University: endowment growth and admission stasis at, 71–72; investments in endowment of, 95–96
private equity partnerships: alumni from elite universities in, 28–34; capital gains tax cuts and growth of, 101–5; earnings of employees in, 27–28; elite university ties of, 3–4, 19, 60–65, 163n54; fees paid to, 68; formation of, 22; for-profit universities and, 2–8; growth in earnings of, 54–57; as higher education financial intermediary, 22–24; high-finance advantage of, 65–68; hostile takeovers by, 26, 81; income of managers in, 25–28; information asymmetries in social ties of, 29–32; online program managers and, 120–21; philanthropic homophily and, 71–73; predatory financial extraction and unequal intimacies of, 94–97; property tax avoidance by, 103–5; regulation of, 74–75; shareholder value and, 80–82; social ties of, 26–28, 82–85; university endowments and, 4–8, 60–65, 95
private information: financier trade in, 18, 19, 26–28, 48, 57; millionaire tax coalition exchange of, 129; social ties and transferal of, 2–4, 56–57, 87; unidirectional intimacy and filtering of, 87–90
privately held ownership, 80
private nonprofit colleges and universities: earnings and graduation rates for students at, 51, 91–92; for-profit colleges competition for subsidies with, 96–97; investment in for-profit universities by, 95–97, 166n63; nonprofit status of, 118–20
private universities: donations to, 69–73; endowment boom of, 14; investment strategies of, 62–63; per student spending at, 156n50; power elite and role of, 20–22; student loan expansion supported by, 79–80
privatization: of higher education, 118–20; public-private partnerships as catalyst for, 120–21
property tax loopholes: financiers' exploitation of, 103–5; public university funding and, 98–101; revenue loss from, 126
Proposition 30 (California), 104, 121, 128–32
Providence Equity Partners, 76, 83–85, 87, 166n63
Providian, 87
publicly traded corporations: consolidated financial service corporations as, 25; executive autonomy in, 26, 80–81; for-profit colleges as part of, 82–85; private equity owners and, 26–28; shareholder value and, 81–82
public policy, universities' role in, 159n78
public-private partnerships, at public universities, 120–21
public universities: bargaining with bankers strategy and social ties of, 126–32; bond market borrowing and student debt tradeoff at, 114–17; coalition building at, 125–26, 131–32; direct federal student loans supported by, 47–48; donations to, 69–73; earnings and graduation rates for students at, 91–92; elite sports support at, 108–10; enrollment growth at, 10, 11–12, 71–73; family earnings and education levels of students at, 156n48; financialization and commercialization of, 117–21; financiers on governing boards of, 33–34, 98–101; financiers role in funding declines for, 101–5; funding squeeze in, 15, 97–121; graduation rates at, 51, 91–92, 99–101, 112; in-state enrollment stasis at, 108–10; intimate ties at, 101–2, 123–24; investment in for-profit universities by, 95–97; investment strategies of, 62–65, 97; loan-financed tuition revenue at, 51–52; middle-income students at, 108–10; nonelite social ties at, 105–10; non-loan government funding at, 40; out-of-state enrollment at, 109–10; per student spending at, 156n50; public-private partnerships at, 120–21; shareholder value and private ties at, 105–10; social ties of alumni from, 32; state reduction in support for, 9–10, 51, 97, 101–5; student debt at, 6–8, 108–10, 112–14; student loan expansion at, 11–12, 79–80; tax avoidance and subsidy capture impact on, 101–5; tax funding increases for, 123–24; tuition revenue at, 7–8, 99–101, 107–10, 119–21; unequal access to, 110–12

qualitative data, sources for, 13, 146–150
quality of education, difficulties in assessment of, 79–80
Quan, Jean, 101–2
Quandt, Richard, 58
quantitative data, 13; elite universities, 150–55
Quijada, Don, 86, 88–94, 97, 148
Quinn, Sarah, 12, 50, 146

race: enrollment growth at public universities and, 73; inequality in educational funding for, 10; student debt burden and, 6, 93–94, 112–14, 138; unequal access to public universities and, 110–12
reciprocity: elite social ties and, 83–84; high-finance advantage and, 56–57; philanthropic homophily and, 56–57, 70–73; public university funding and, 106–10
recruitment of students, for-profit universities' tactics for, 85–90
Renaissance Technologies, 95
risk, bargaining with bankers and big bang strategies and, 123–124, 129–130; of debt for students, 110; private equity and hedge funds and, 25–28, 59–61; of debt for students, 110; university investment and role of, 61–65
Rivera, Lauren, 12, 30, 49, 146
RJR Nabisco, 81
Rolling Jubilee program, 134–35
Romer, Carl, 140
Ross, Wilbur, 30
Rosser, Richard, 47

Saban, Haim, 83–84, 87
Salem, Paul, 83–84
Salomon Brothers, 59
Sanders, Bernie, 137
Schatz, Brian, 137
Scholes, Myron, 58
Schumer, Charles, 137
Schumpeter, Joseph, 20
scientific research, marketization of, 47
Securities and Exchange Commission, 58–59
securitization, 24–25, 35
Service Employees International Union (SEIU), 127, 130, 135
Shaffer, Jono, 127
shareholder value: consolidated financial service corporations and, 25; endowments and, 58, 95–97; for-profit college expansion and, 77; hedge funds and, 80–82; impersonal profits and, 94–97; information asymmetries and, 87–90; private equity owners and, 26–28, 80–82; public university funding and, 98–101, 105–10; rise of, 43–44
Shireman, Bob, 129
short-term profit culture, shareholder value and, 82
Simon, Daniel, 94
Skocpol, Theda, 12, 146
Smith, Sabrina, 127
social circuitry of finance: evolution of, 17–19; high-finance advantage and, 55–57; impersonal profits, for-profit colleges, and, 94–97; ivory tower social ties, 28–34; philanthropic homophily and, 69–73; private equity and hedge fund groups, 26–28, 82–85; public universities and, 97; student loan expansion and, 38–39
social goods: market predation and, 79; universities as, 8–10; US expenditures on, 156n38
social homophily, elite universities and, 29, 56–57
social organizations and institutions: social circuitry of finance and, 17–19; universities' role in, 159n78
social programs, government funding commitments and, 41–42
Social Security, 9–10; creation of, 132–33
social ties: between bankers, colleges and lawmakers, 46–49; bargaining with bankers strategy and public university use of, 126–32; coalition building and role of, 125–26; economic exchange relationships and, 85–86; endowment investment and, 59–60; financial markets and, 82–85; high-finance advantage and philanthropic homophily, 56–57; millionaire tax initiative coalition and, 128–32; non-economic activities of economic actors and, 28–29; politics and, 42–43; power of financiers and, 2–4; privatization of student loan programs and role, 48–49; of public universities, 32, 100–102, 105–10, 123–24; public university funding

and role of, 99–101; reform consensus building and use of, 143; shareholder value and public university funding and, 105–10; support for subsidized student loan programs and, 38–39; university investment and, 60–65
social welfare: funding for, 36–37; higher education as tool for, 7–8; public university funding declines and prioritization of, 104–5; universities as providers of, 8–10
socioeconomic inequality, financial transformation of higher education and, 5, 39–42
Solomon Brothers, 30–31
sports at colleges and universities: admissions advantages and, 73; public university support for, 108–10; social ties of financiers and, 49
Stafford loans, 45–46, 51–52
state governments: debt-free funding of community colleges by, 142; for-profit college funding by, 105; higher education funding by, 9–10, 39–43, 160n16; millionaire tax initiative lobbying of, 128–32; public university funding reductions by, 9–10, 51, 97–101; social goods delivery by, 9–10; social ties of public universities in, 101–2; tax reforms and, 74
status: donor attraction to, 73; elite university ties to other organizations and, 32–34; middle-class borrowing decisions based on, 79–80; payoffs of prestige, 34–35; perpetuation in elite institutions of, 29; philanthropic homophily and, 69–73; power of financiers linked to, 35; stratification in higher education of, 10
Stevens, Mitchell, 151
Stevenson, Howard, 60
Steyer, Tom, 3, 14, 31, 60–61, 82
Stivers, Abby, 45, 47, 149
stock markets, growth of finance and, 21
Stop Wall Street Looting Act, 74–75
stratification of resources and status: commercialization of public universities and, 117–21; endowment wealth and admissions selectivity, 55–56; non-elite higher education and, 10; university social ties and, 29
Strike Debt, 133–34
student-faculty ratios: at elite universities, 73; endowment wealth and disparities in, 56–57; inequality in, 158n50
student loan debt: bond borrowing by public universities and, 114–17; cancellation proposals for, 15, 53, 85, 93, 97, 123–24, 135–38; class and race inequalities in, 99–101; college endowments and, 1–2; commercial banking power and, 49–51; default rate for student loans, 6, 51, 90–94; earning gains *vs.*, 51; economic and social cost of, 90–94; financial service corporation collection of payments on, 25; forgiveness of, 15, 53, 85; at for-profit universities, 11–12, 75, 77–78, 91–94; growth of, 1–2, 36–39, 108–10; for nontuition needs, 113–14; for online programs, 120–21; obfuscation of college price and, 80; politics of, 52–53; at public universities, 108–10, 112–14; public university funding from, 15; reforms for reduction of, 97; student protests over, 119, 122–24; unequal explosion of, 5–6
Student Loan Marketing Association (Sallie Mae): capitalization of, 78–80; creation of, 45–46; financial crisis of 2008 and, 52–53; founding of, 24; politics of, 52–53; private lenders and, 19; student debt cancellation and, 53
student loan programs: banking and, 2–4, 14, 24–25; capitalization of, 78–80; commercial banks and, 14, 141; Congressional changes to, 37; consolidated financial service corporations and, 24–25; deregulation and, 78–80; elite university revenue from, 11–12; expansion as deregulation of, 77–80; financiers policy influence on, 4–8, 38–39, 44–46; for-profit colleges and expansion of, 11–12, 76–80, 96–97; future of, 139–43; growth of, 36–39, 44–46; politics of, 52–53; private-sector financing of, 25; public university funding and, 99–101; redistributive policy change and, 133–38; reform proposals for, 141–43
subsidies for federal student loan private lenders: elimination of, 52–53; financiers' influence on, 38–39; mortgage-backed securities, 51; public university funding and, 98; student loan program expansion and, 44–46

Sun Capital, 61
Swarthmore, 95
Swensen, David, 3, 30–31, 57, 59–61, 74–75
Swenson, Craig, 88

TA Associates, 95
targeted primary methodology, 12, 146
tax cuts and tax avoidance: California public universities and impact of, 101–5; commercialization of public universities and, 118–21; demise of loan-free higher education and, 39–43; as economic stimulus, 36–37; endowments and, 58–60; excise tax elimination, 59; financiers' advocacy for, 42–43; higher education funding and, 8–10, 157n52; legislation for reversal of, 123–24; private equity and hedge fund growth and, 101–5; public university funding and, 98–101
taxpayer-funded support for higher education, 8–10, 39
tax rates: cuts and caps on, 21–22; endowment exemptions and, 157n52; on financiers, 104–5; income gap reduction and, 20; millionaire tax initiative for increase in, 126–32; politics and, 106–10; progressive tax policies and, 140–41; student protests for increases in, 122–24
Taylor, Peter, 107
technology billionaires: college governing board membership and, 33–34; university ties of, 3
technology sector entrepreneurs, elite university alumni as, 31–32
telecom markets: private equity investment in, 83–84; shareholder value and, 81
television revenue, elite college sports and, 108–10
The Institute for College Access and Success, 128–29
Thigpen, Anthony, 126–27
Third World Liberation strikes, 101–2
Thompson, Maggie, 137
Tiger Management hedge fund, 83–85, 95
Times Higher Education (THE) rankings, 55–56, 62–63, 152–53; and student debt, 6–8
Timmons, Becky, 42
Townsend Clubs, 133
Toys R Us, 103
Tran, Kim, 14–15, 76–77, 79–80, 84–86, 88–94, 97, 148
Trans World Airlines, 26
triangulation in data analysis, 12, 146
Trump, Donald, 53, 74–75, 136, 138
trust: elite social ties and, 30–32, 83–85; for-profit college predation and, 85–86; high-finance advantage and philanthropic homophily and, 56–57
tuition revenue: coalition for tuition freezes and, 128–32; deregulation of, 107; endowment wealth and, 56–57; at for-profit colleges, 4–8, 80, 84–85; increases in, 119–21; online programs and, 120–21; from out-of-state enrollment, 109–10; at public universities, 15, 99–101, 107–10; student loans as source of, 36–39, 99–101, 108–10, 112–14; student protests over increases in, 122–24

UC Board of Regents, 98–101, 106; financiers on, 15, 107–10; gubernatorial appointments to, 118–20; student protests of, 122–24, 126–32; student representation on, 129
UC Capital Markets Finance Department, 107
UC Student Association, 126–32
unequal access to higher education. *See* inequality in higher education
unidirectional intimacy: beneficiaries of, 94–97; economic and social price of, 90–94; between financiers and nonelites, 77–78; obfuscation in investor ownership and, 87–90
unions: barriers to mobility and decline of, 7–8; demise of, 43–44, 74–75; education labor unions, 131–32; mobilization for higher education equity in, 127–29; redistributive policy change and, 132–33
United Farm Workers, 125
United Negro College Fund, 49
United States, federalist politics in, 9–10
universality, ideology of, public university funding and, 99–101
universities, as stratified welfare providers, 8–10
university endowment: investment bankers influence on, 4–8; student debt and, 1–2
University of California: admissions stasis at, 101–2; default rates on student debt at, 114;

enrollment growth at, 99–101; financialization and commercialization of, 117–21; funding crisis for, 15; grants for low-income students at, 108–10; increases in in-state enrollment at, 131–32; in-state enrollment stasis at, 108–10, 111–12; Master Plan for higher education and, 101–2; out-of-state enrollment at, 109–10, 119–21; Proposition 30 endorsement by, 130–31; reduction in state funding for, 98–101; shareholder value and private ties at, 105–10; student debt at, 108–10, 112–14; student protests of management at, 122–24; tax avoidance and subsidy capture impact on, 101–5; tuition revenue growth at, 107–10; unequal access to, 110–12
University of California, Berkeley, 71–72
University of Michigan, investment strategies at, 62–64
University of New Hampshire, 95
University of Phoenix, 83–85, 95; marketing tactics of, 88
University of Texas, 12
University of Virginia, tuition revenue at, 119–20
university trustees. *See* college governing boards
Untz, Ron, 56
US corporations, capital reserves decline in, 21
US Department of Education: cancellation of student debt proposals and, 15, 53, 85, 93, 97, 123–24, 141; direct lending by, 46–49; financial service contracts with, 25; financiers' criticism of, 48–49; fraudulent student claims filed with, 85; guaranteed student loan program and, 45–46; interest rate reduction and loan forgiveness programs, 52, 135; resumption of direct student loans, 52–53; student debt holdings of, 36–39
US Department of Justice, suit against EDMC, 85
US Higher Education Act of 1992, 37; student loan amendments to, 151
US News & World Report college rankings, 1
US Student Association, 135, 138

venture capital: college endowment investment in, 59–60; as higher education financial intermediary, 22–24; shareholder stakes in, 26–27
vocational education, enrollment growth at, 10
Vogel, Dean, 130
Voluntary Support of Education survey, 68–69, 162n7

Waldman, Steven, 12, 48, 146
Walker, Charls, 21–22, 42, 58–59
Waller, Peter, 88
Warren, Elizabeth, 74–75, 135, 137, 143
Waters, Maxine, 136
wealth and income disparities: education inequality and, 5–8; historical growth of, 20–21; private equity and hedge fund employees and, 28; stratification of higher education and, 51–52
wealthy students, debt-free status of, 6
We Are AI Facebook group, 97
Weeks, Maurice, 131–32
Weingarten, Randi, 137
welfare state: barriers to mobility and decline of, 7–8; education and, 8, 156n34; government funding of entitlement programs and, 41–43; policy big bangs and, 15, 53, 85, 93, 97, 123–24
Wellman, Jane, 148
Wells Fargo, 24–25, 78
Wherry, Frederick, 3–4, 151
white students, racial wealth gap and student debt for, 6
Williams, Hoke, 43–44
women's movement, 125
women students: for-profit university enrollment of, 77–78, 93–94; higher education funding and, 10
work-study programs, government spending on, 39–40

Yale University: endowment at, 31; financier alumni from, 14
Yannelis, Constantine, 93, 154
Yudof, Mark, 98–101, 107–10, 121, 127–28, 131

Zaloom, Caitlin, 12, 79, 146
Zelizer, Viviana, 2–4, 56, 77, 85–86
Zovio, 120–21
Zywicki, Todd J., 62